The Real Story of the French Revolution

The Real Story of the French Revolution

Separating Myth from Reality

Mike Wells

AN IMPRINT OF PEN & SWORD BOOKS LTD
YORKSHIRE – PHILADELPHIA

First published in Great Britain in 2024 by
PEN & SWORD HISTORY
an imprint of Pen & Sword Books Ltd
Yorkshire – Philadelphia

Copyright © Mike Wells, 2024

ISBN 978-1-39908-452-9

The right of Mike Wells to be identified as the author of this work has been asserted by him in accordance with the Copyright, Designs and Patents Act 1988.

A CIP catalogue record for this book is available from the British Library.

All rights reserved. No part of this book may be reproduced or transmitted in any form or by any means, electronic or mechanical including photocopying, recording or by any information storage and retrieval system, without permission from the Publisher in writing.

Typeset by Concept, Huddersfield, West Yorkshire, HD4 5JL.
Printed and bound in England by CPI Group (UK) Ltd, Croydon, CR0 4YY.

Pen & Sword Books Ltd incorporates the imprints of Aviation, Atlas, Family History, Fiction, Maritime, Military, Discovery, Politics, History, Archaeology, Select, Wharncliffe Local History, Wharncliffe True Crime, Military Classics, Wharncliffe Transport, Leo Cooper, The Praetorian Press, Remember When, White Owl, Seaforth Publishing and Frontline Books.

For a complete list of Pen & Sword titles please contact
PEN & SWORD BOOKS LTD
47 Church Street, Barnsley, South Yorkshire, S70 2AS, England
E-mail: enquiries@pen-and-sword.co.uk
Website: www.pen-and-sword.co.uk
or
PEN & SWORD BOOKS
1950 Lawrence Rd, Havertown, PA 19083, USA
E-mail: uspen-and-sword@casematepublishers.com
Website: www.penandswordbooks.com

Contents

Introduction	vii
1. France in 1789	1
2. The Crisis of the *Ancien Régime*	21
3. The Events of the Year 1789	43
4. The Constitutional Monarchy	71
5. The Terror	91
6. The Role of Women in the Revolution	109
7. Slavery, Racism and Empire	135
8. The End of the Revolution? The Legacy	155
Bibliography	181

Introduction

Given the vast number of books which have been written in an attempt to describe, explain, praise, decry, analyse or generally understand and interpret the French Revolution, it might seem that yet another is superfluous. This short book is not an attempt to re-tell a well-known story but rather to stand back and take a critical look at how the Revolution has been perceived and portrayed, and to challenge some assumptions. It is not a definitive history of the complete and highly complex story, but rather it aims to offer a sort of 'reality check'. It is also intended as a corrective to history which is half-remembered from school history and old films. A good example is comedian Tony Hancock's brilliant portrayal of an obstreperous juror who gave him the immortal line 'Magna Carta – did she die in vain?' A good joke, but how many people, even if they know that Magna was not a heroine, are clear on what Magna Carta actually was and whether it was a key document about liberty and democracy or a complex list of obscure issues about thirteenth-century feudal rights?

The French Revolution gripped the attention of contemporaries and has subsequently fascinated commentators, historians, political theorists and the reading and viewing public worldwide. The French king Louis XVI, who was executed in 1793, was not the first or the last monarch to be killed by his subjects. However, the image of the guillotine is so strong that it has burnt itself into the world's imagination Perhaps the mental picture of a tall, dark, looming guillotine with a grotesque old woman knitting, as heads dropped into the basket, is one of the most pervasive symbols of political upheaval ever. Though, in fact, both images are false – guillotines were not that tall and nobody knitted in their shadow. Few countries, too, have a national annual holiday to celebrate a revolution which brought mass executions, years of costly war and a dictatorship. But Bastille Day passes over the brutalities of 14 July 1789. Happy dances and picnics do not evoke the prison's governor being beheaded by an angry crowd. Celebrations do not commemorate the fact that very few prisoners were there to be liberated, and the 'storming of the Bastille' is seen as a wholesome and uplifting tradition.

The Real Story of the French Revolution

Anyone actually reading the words of the Marseillaise might be surprised that this bloodthirsty revolutionary song has achieved such respectability, with conservative heads of state standing solemnly while it is played or sung. The very idea of Mrs Thatcher on a visit to Paris in best formal dress standing respectfully during the playing of a red revolutionary anthem seems faintly absurd. The Terror itself became a source of adventure stories and even humour. Audiences still enjoy TV reruns of *Carry On, Don't Lose Your Head*, but it is doubtful whether a comedy film about the murder of the Russian Tsar and his family in a cellar and their dismemberment in a mine shaft, featuring Sid James as Lenin or Barbara Windsor as the Princess Anastasia would have been popular.

There are, however, limits. Napoleon, who brought about death to hundreds of thousands through a series of wars, whose object was little more than conquest and personal glory, is honoured by a magnificent tomb and remembered in street names and souvenirs. Robespierre, the most famous of the Revolutionaries, has no public recognition and even in his hometown of Arras has his bust hidden from view. The vitriolic revolutionary Jean-Paul Marat is remembered mostly for the masterpiece which the painter David created on his dead body in the bath following his murder by Charlotte Corday. The painting has become more famous than its subject. Napoleon's image is everywhere, but the revolutionaries who made his rise to power possible have few public memorials. The concept of 'The French Revolution' and some of the violent revolutionary events themselves seem more acceptable than the people who created them.

The changes that the Revolution brought have been seen as so profound that there has been a perpetual struggle to explain them and understand them. In the short term, the events of 1789 led to civil war in France and years of European war between 1792 and 1815. The whole political geography of Europe was changed, and the way paved for massive changes in Europe. From the Revolution came, supposedly, a united Italy and Germany; the rise of both Liberalism and Nationalism; and ultimately two world wars, the rise of Fascism and Communism. The Revolution gave the world new political concepts, and bitterly divided opinions. It is said to have had an effect on science, the arts, politics, economics, race, and relations between men and women. Almost every historical explanation of any major development since 1789 comes back at some point to the French Revolution. It is not surprising when Zhou Enlai, the foreign minister of China under Mao Zedong, was asked about its significance, he is supposed to have said that it was too early after nearly 200 years to tell. Sadly, this is just another myth. Kissinger, the US

Introduction

statesman who was on a visit to China with President Nixon was asking him about the French unrest of 1968 not 1789! However, as the Italian saying goes, *'si non è vero, è ben trovato'*, but it typifies how so much accepted knowledge about the French Revolution needs to be looked at carefully.

Unsurprisingly, it is a popular study in schools and higher education, and there are a massive number of books of varying degrees of complexity for the specialist, the student and the general reader. To even attempt to outline different explanations would be a huge task, and this is not the intention of this book. Instead, the aim is to look at what has become 'common knowledge' and what has emerged through necessary simplifications of complex events and situations and to apply some 'reality checks'. Working back from the events of the Revolution, historians and writers have found 'causes' which might make it seem that the Revolution was almost inevitable. Some of these 'causes' will be looked at critically. Also, in order to create a pathway through highly complex events, there have been narratives of the Revolution which though helpful and indeed necessary have sometimes been misleading. Because the political positions taken in the Revolution reflect, if not actually cause, present divisions, it has become difficult to write about events without the choice of words or the selection of events leading to some colouring of 'the story'. One man's revolutionary 'mob' is another man's 'crowd' and another's 'popular gathering'. For some, the Revolution brought power to 'fanatics'; to others these were 'leaders'. Some, like the nineteenth-century statemen Adolphe Thiers, found 'blood and imbecility'; others have found political discourse which formed the modern world. Finally, the accepted narrative and the way that the Revolutionary events have been taught and generally assimilated means that there are inevitably some omissions, with key developments being relegated to specialist studies, rather than being central to the Revolutionary experience and significance. This is particularly true of the role of women and the impact of the revolution on France's colonial empire.

So, this book is not intended to give a comprehensive narrative or a final explanation of the 'truth' about the Revolution, but rather to offer some food for thought about what have become received ideas. French Revolutionary governments organised the state for the first time to fight a 'total war' and set a precedent for the world wars of the twentieth century and for the extreme control of civilian life. My father had never heard of Lazare Carnot, the Revolutionary minister of war. However. Carnot in 1793 set the pattern for total war, the power of the state in wartime to conscript citizens and resources that led ultimately to my father getting a brown envelope in 1943 telling him

The Real Story of the French Revolution

to report for military service preparatory to being told that it was his duty to be prepared to sacrifice is life for 'Democracy' and 'Freedom', key Revolutionary concepts. Thus, in one way of looking at history, I would not be the person I am if it had not been for the French Revolution, and, indeed, though we might not, as individuals be interested in the past, the past is always interested in us!

The following chapters are offered in a spirit of humility and taking due account of this famous, if unfairly derided, quotation from the US Secretary of State Donald Rumsfeld in 1992 regarding the invasion of Iraq:

> as we know there are known knowns; there are things we know we know. We also know there are known unknowns; that is to say, we know that there are some things we do not know. But there are also unknown unknowns – the ones we don't know we don't know. And if one looks throughout the history of our country and other free countries, it is the latter category that tends to be the difficult ones.

Chapter One

France in 1789

The active participants in the French Revolution were a minority of France's 28 million people, and 'France' was not always a strong concept for the people of 1789. They probably did not think of their nation in the way that modern post-industrial, post-railway populations think of their country.

The development of national identity came more slowly to Europe than many older studies suggest. There were relatively few German and Italian nationalists. People were in the process of seeing themselves as 'Britons' in this period and it would not have been a given that those who lived in the kingdom ruled by Louis XVI had a meaningful French identity in a modern sense.

It would possibly be more helpful to see 'France' as an accumulation of territories owing allegiance to the French king. The French Nation – a term used in the period – had strong local and regional identities because different provinces had been added to the French kingdom at different times. These regions retained laws, currencies, weights and measures, institutions and languages or dialects. An interesting illustration is the lack of an accepted national currency with a fixed value. Thus, when historians or contemporaries speak about something in eighteenth-century France having a value in *livres*, there were actually no *livre* coins available to buy it. This degree of division was not uncommon in eighteenth-century Europe before modern communications, common education systems and legal and administrative streamlining gave birth to more recognisable modern nations. Much of this was seen to have been the product of the French Revolution and its aftermath the empire of Napoleon, but, even then, the degree of unity can be overstated.

For much of France in the eighteenth century, the state was an alien intruder into local liberty, not a source of shared enterprise or the subject of loyalty. The crown, unlike in contemporary Germany and Italy with their multiplicity of local authorities, was the major unifying factor. The personality and strength of the rulers were therefore of the utmost importance.

Kings presided over a kingdom which famously had three distinct orders – the Roman Catholic Church was the 'First Estate'; the nobility the second and the rest were the so-called 'Third Estate'. The more common contemporary term was 'order' rather than 'estate' until 1788, when a special body representing the 'estates' was summoned. The nobles consisted of between 100,000 and 320,000 people (estimates vary) and included hereditary nobles with long-standing titles, and a sort of 'service nobility' called the 'Noblesse de Robe' who had gained noble status not from birth but by service or purchase of office. Nobles ranged from the ultra-rich to those who were barely different from their peasant neighbours.

There were fewer in the first estate, the clergy, and a surprisingly small number of parish priests – around 71,000. They did not own vast lands at about 5–6 per cent. (In England before Henry VIII seized it in the 1530s the church had owned about a third of the country.) The number of 'regular clergy' in monasteries and nunneries was falling and stood at approximately 60,000. Again, generalisation about wealth and status is impossible, as the gap in wealth and lifestyle between the richer noble bishops, archbishops and abbots, and the poorest of the parish priests was considerable. The Prince Bishop of Strasbourg, for example, had a revenue of 80,000 livres at a time when the total national debt stood at 1.3 million livres. Some parish priests could hardly afford to live. But, as with noble wealth, much church wealth was tied up in land or committed to fixed expenditure like pensions or debts for building. To pay the 'free gift' to the crown, which was due in place of direct tax from which the clergy were exempt, the church often had to take out loans.

The 'Third Estate' was everyone not a noble or a member of the church. As well as the great mass of country dwellers it included the urban masses, the professionals – lawyers, brokers, bankers – the intellectuals, the skilled craftsmen, the owners of shops and workshops, the apprentices, the casual workers, the urban poor. They could be wealthy merchants who benefited from France's trade expansion in the eighteenth century; they could be successful tradesmen or manufacturers, scientists, chemists, writers, painters, and musicians. They were lumped together with urban beggars, casual workers, crossing sweepers, prostitutes, professional criminals, and independent craftsmen scraping a living in the poorer parts of Paris. What characterised this Third Estate was that they did not enjoy the privileges of the First and Second Estates and that many of the avenues of advancement were closed to them. Their taxes and loans often supported a state which denied them equality of opportunity and political influence.

* * *

Rather than look at the 'estates' or 'orders' in any more detail, it would be helpful to look at the king, the countryside and urban life in this brief survey.

France in 1789

When the Revolution led to internal divisions and civil war, the conflict was less between classes but between whole areas of largely rural France resenting the demands and intrusion from Paris and other urban centres. The peasants and nobles of areas like Brittany had more in common because of regional and religious bonds while the revolutionaries saw the backward rural communities as objects of hatred and possible genocide.

The King

Louis XVI ascended the French throne in 1774 and like other monarchs who have been killed by their subjects – for example, Nicholas II of Russia, Richard II, Edward II and Charles I of England, has had a bad press. Personal failings loom large in accounts of slaughtered royals by notoriously unsympathetic historians. Unimpressive physically and by temperament indecisive, Louis seemed happier pursuing an odd collection of interests which included hunting, a virtual obsession, ships, and tinkering with locks and watches. He was the grandson of a more powerful figure, Louis XV (1715–74) but did not share his energy and sexual passions. Inexperience and possibly a tight foreskin meant that he shocked his Austrian in-laws by not properly consummating his marriage with the Austrian princess Marie Antoinette. His brother-in-law gave him some robust advice and seems to have solved the problem, but his reputation suffered from the lack of an heir and rumours about sexual ineptitude. Not all impressions of this rather portly and apparently uninspiring monarch were, however, unfavourable. It is worth considering whether the king was not quite so bad as his detractors have made out.

The British ambassador Lord Stormont wrote that 'the strongest feature of the king's character is a love of justice in general, a general desire for doing well, a passion for economy and an abhorrence of the excesses of the previous reign'.[1] The ambassador found him sharp, and noted with approval that he did not consult with his Queen over matters of state and took the 'sensible' course of not allowing women to have influenced. He also showed a sense of humour not always credited to him when it was rumoured that, tired of the endless adulation for the American savant Benjamin Franklin, he had a chamber pot made with the famous man's face painted on the inside. Louis had few hereditary nobles in high positions – only three in all and removed high-ranking nobles from his council when he came to the throne. He also encouraged the promotion of provincial nobles if they had ability in the armed forces. It is sometimes forgotten that the wars fought against England by his predecessors ended in failure but his war, the War of American Independence, which France joined in 1778 ended in success. in 1783, England ceded independence to France's American ally, but there was a high financial cost to France.

Louis came under criticism from many hereditary nobles for his lack of respect for their privileged status and was generous in grants of nobility for special services to promote talent. Contrary to beliefs at the time and subsequently, royal spending did not dominate the national debt and made up around 6 per cent. Louis was not afraid of innovating or making unorthodox appointments to high office, for example, the self-styled financial expert Necker who was not only not noble but not a Frenchman and not a Catholic. The future extremist Robespierre won a legal case by quoting the example of a wise and enlightened king in fixing lightning conductors to royal buildings. The expressions of grievances drawn up in 1789 (see Chapter Two) show affection. The Queen was less popular as a foreigner, a supposed spendthrift and because of scurrilous publications about her supposed sexual infidelities with both sexes. This was certainly made worse by an absurd scandal over a diamond necklace bought from fraudsters by a Cardinal in the hope of influencing the queen – but all this was without her knowledge, and she was unfairly criticised.

Louis inherited an absolute and 'sacramental' monarchy in which the ruler was responsible only to God, and whose coronation involved divine approval. The king did have some arbitrary powers and appointed and dismissed ministers, could order arrest and imprisonment without trial through a device called the *lettre de cachet* and could override provincial assemblies and the higher courts known as *parlements*.

There was no parliament in the British sense of elected representatives who passed laws. No royal minister needed a majority in an elected assembly. The thirteen *parlements* were self-electing bodies of high-ranking magistrates whose traditional role was to register and make formally legal royal decrees. The most senior and eminent body was the *Parlement de Paris* which sat in the capital. They spoke of the ancient 'constitution' of France. But this was misleading in modern terms, which define a 'Constitution' as a body of rules, usually written, as in the case of the USA. When the members of the *parlements* spoke of the Constitution. it was more in terms of the traditional and accepted way of doing things. But in terms of actual political power, they had no agreed authority, and if they rejected a royal edict this could be overridden by the king appearing in a special ceremony in a '*lit de justice*' or the magistrates could simply be exiled, as had happened at the end of the reign of Louis XV. This had not led to a serious political crisis, and the authority of the king had not been challenged.

However, the kings were nor despots, though this term was used about ministers who imposed measures unpopular with the *parlements*, usually undermining their 'liberties', a term used in the sense of special privileges. Louis XVI recognised his duty to rule in the interests of his people and was bound by existing laws. His powers of patronage in terms of pensions and appointments within the church and state were considerable, but there were severe limitations to his actual powers. In practice, for example, collecting taxes was a problematic task and the French crown had large debts. There was the expectation that actions would be governed by precedent. So, when faced with financial problems, there was no question of convening a new body but rather of reviving older assemblies – the Assembly of Notables in 1787 and more importantly the Estates General which had last met in 1614. The king was bound by precedent if not in an enforceable way, but simply as part of the expectations of the role. Given this somewhat dead hand of the past, what was remarkable was the openness of the king to change. He took a genuine interest in the modern developments of his time, especially ships and ship building which held the key to military power and colonial wealth. He was prepared to appoint men of talent and to accept reforms. He also was not the tool of his nobility, and not by temperament nor by any actions, was he an authoritarian or tyrannical ruler.

The Countryside

There are many things that 'we know we know' about eighteenth-century France because they are in textbooks and are generally portrayed in films, television and novels. Ignorant and poverty-stricken peasants endured terrible hardships, were oppressed by lords of the manor, suffered discrimination in the forms of taxes and dues and had low life expectancy. This seemed to be proved by the shocked accounts of foreign visitors, especially the British agricultural expert and travel writer Arthur Young, who travelled widely in France and whose best-selling personal accounts of his journeys revealed the inferiority of the French countryside compared to that of his home country. Extracts from his work are commonly used in historical surveys of the causes of the Revolution. His shock at finding young peasant girls so worn down by hardship and poverty that they had the look of aged women finds its way into many textbooks. Readers of the brilliant novel by Hilary Mantel, *A Place of Greater Safety* about three prominent French revolutionaries may be brought up with a shock by the sudden insertion by the author that the average life expectancy in France in 1789 was twenty-six. Lovers of Mozart's opera *The Marriage of Figaro* might well assume that aristocrats like the Count aimed to enjoy personal sexual rights over their servants, and the list of feudal dues in most books shows the ongoing personal dependence of peasants on their lords. They worked on the roads, they brought their corn to the lords' mill, they were subject to feudal courts, they paid to inherit lands, and they worked on the private lands of their lords. All this seemed redolent of what was studied in school about the mediaeval English serfs. On top of that, the church took its toll. There were payments to the church and the church was also a landlord. Opportunities to rise in a very stratified society were limited. Thought was controlled by church and state. Taxes and dues, because of privilege, fell on the ordinary country people.

One historian of French society in the Revolution makes the point that a 'mediaeval man, granted divine dispensation to pay a fleeting visit to France in the 1780s would have been far less astonished to witness the changes'[2] than a post-Revolutionary man sixty or seventy years in the future. France was stuck in many ways in a mediaeval past with rigid class barriers, a feudal society, an absolute monarchy, limited industry and a backward peasantry.

The peasants were at the bottom of the heap, lacking freedom, opportunity, education. They were by far the largest of the section of society known as 'The Third Estate'.

* * *

As most French people lived and worked in the countryside – well over 80 per cent, and because urban populations were, outside Paris and a few larger cities, relatively small, it seems to make sense to start by looking at the 'peasants'. It is often the starting point for a critique of French society because of emotive use of contemporary evidence and a list of burdens and dues which affected the countryside which appear in most texts. Few textbooks can do without using the writings of the British agronomist and writer Arthur Young.

In practice, there was considerable variation in rural life from region to region. In some areas there were heavy payments made to noble landowners and most peasant farmers were tightly controlled. In one area at least, the local lord of the manor had symbolic gallows erected on the lawn of his chateau to emphasize his power as judge over his tenants. Though most Frenchmen were free, there were still a million serfs who were the virtual private property of landowners. However, in many areas, this was far from the case, with peasant life being far less controlled. Much more typical than the lone starving peasant and his family were powerful peasant communities, supporting one another, making communal decisions about farming, organising rural activities and settling disputes. Where the main activity was animal husbandry, the social set up was very different from areas where there was more commercial farming for close-by urban markets or arable farming. In many areas the nobles were not remote exploiters eager to exercise sexual 'rights 'and oppress tenants, but part of an established local community. Not all nobles were rich courtiers, and many worked on their lands alongside the local farmers and were part of the life of the neighbourhood.

An interesting account of the dues and the relations between local people and 'feudal lords' was given in the memoirs of the Baroness de Bode, an Englishwoman who had married into the German aristocracy and inherited the rights to an estate in Alsace in 1788 comprising of six villages. She writes on first going to Soulltyz, her estate, 'We are entirely masters' and appointed a range of local officials. Twenty-four Jewish families paid a special tax to the Bodes for the right to live in their villages. She wrote:

> The tenths, [a payment of a tenth of the produce of the lands of tenants] both great and small, belong to us. Our subjects are obliged to furnish us with a quantity of hens, chickens and capons and more hay and potatoes than we can consume. 'It is impossible to tell you what rights we have. We hardly know them ourselves yet. Every wife is obliged to spin one or two pounds of flax or hemp and every male and female is obliged to work ten days every year for us. Every innkeeper is obliged to pay us a certain sum for the right to put up a sign for his inn and every gallon of wine that enters our manor to pay us a certain sum.'[3]

The land was good and the family also had a coal mine that they planned to exploit. The arrival of the Baron and Baroness was the occasion for a grand party and procession, bouquets, speeches, a mass in a crowded church, a formal meal, music, and a ball which went on until 3.00 am. If there was resentment or discontent, then the Baroness was not aware of it. Local customs and traditions involved a warm welcome for this German milord and his English wife. The family suffered financially from having to buy an expensive commission in the army for a relative and the purchase of salt mines. They also had to build a house in their new mini-kingdom. They relied on local labour – some 400 men to bring materials as part of their obligations but had to pay builders and – noblesse oblige – provide a feast when 130 bottles of wine had to be provided for the workers. However, for all the revelry, the locals voted with their feet and did not complete the job. By August 1789 the end of feudal rights had changed the situation and also the happy tone of the Baroness's letters to her English relations. By 1790 work is not being done. However, there was no sign of the widespread peasant disturbances known as the *Grand Peur* (Great Fear) which affected much of France in the summer of 1789. In the end, however, the Baroness fled France, ending up in Russia.

What is also not explained in many generalised accounts of peasant hardship is that there was a great deal of physical movement in the French countryside, particularly in mountainous regions where the phenomenon known to geographers as transhumance was common. But generally, it was common for younger members of the rural communities to be sent off to seek work, and, as in most European countries, there were considerable numbers of migrants.

* * *

Much of the perception of the French countryside derived from travellers' accounts and particularly those of the English agronomist Arthur Young whose bestselling *Travels in France* was published in 1792 just when British concerns about the French Revolution were growing. The accounts relate to travels in 1789 and are frequently used in school texts and examinations. Here he is in Montauban.

> To Montauban. The poor people seem poor indeed; the children terribly ragged, if possible, worse clad than if with no clothes at all; as to shoes and stockings, they are luxuries. A beautiful girl of six or seven years playing with a stick, and smiling under such a bundle of rags as made my heart ache to see her. One third of what I have seen of this province seems uncultivated, and nearly all of it in misery.

But more famous is this. The meeting took place in the Marne valley in July 1789 in a region about 20 miles from Paris.

> I was joined by a poor woman, who complained of the times, and that it was a sad country. Demanding her reasons, she said her husband had but a morsel of land, one cow, and a poor little horse, yet they had a franchar [42 lbs] of wheat and three chickens to pay as a quitrent to one seigneur; and four franchar of oats, one chicken, and one franc, to pay to another, besides very heavy tailles and other taxes. She had seven children, and the cow's milk helped to make the soup It was said, at present, that something was to be done by some great folks for such poor ones, but she did not know who nor how, but God send us better, '*car les tailles et les droits nous écrasent* [for the taxes and dues are wiping us out].'

> This woman, at no great distance, might have been taken for sixty or seventy, her figure was so bent and her face so furrowed and hardened by labour, but she said she was only twenty-eight. An Englishman who has not travelled cannot imagine the figure made by infinitely the greater part of the country women in France; it speaks, at the first sight, hard and severe labour. I am inclined to think that they work harder than the men, and this, united with the more miserable labour of bringing a new race of slaves into the world, destroys absolutely all symmetry of person and every feminine appearance. To what are we to attribute this difference, in the manners of the lower people in the two kingdoms?

So vivid is the writing that Young's evidence has achieved considerable prominence. However, the parts of the book which paint a different picture are less used. In Pau, in the South, for instance:

> A succession of many well-built, tight, and comfortable farming cottages, built of stone and covered with tiles; each having its little garden, enclosed by clipped thorn hedges, with plenty of peach and other fruit trees, some fine oaks scattered in the hedges, and young trees nursed up with so much care that nothing but the fostering attention of the owner could effect anything like it. To every house belongs a farm, perfectly well enclosed, with grass borders mown and neatly kept around the cornfields, with gates to pass from one enclosure to another.

Like travel writers subsequently, Young had a tendency to see what he wanted to see, and a common theme in his writing was to contrast the French countryside with that of England. Though he saw himself as an expert, Young's own farming efforts had ended in failure. The English had ended feudalism, but it is very doubtful whether poverty such as Young describes did not exist at home, and life expectancy in rural areas in Britain was low. Had Young toured other parts of Europe he would not have found better conditions, and most of Eastern Europe retained personal serfdom which was less common in France. The problem lay in Young's shift from the immediate reaction to poverty and suffering to generalisation. There is no evidence that 'the greater part of the country women in France' were prematurely aged or that 'slaves' is an accurate term. His experience of regional variation is consistent with statistical evidence. The burdens from the payment to lords of the manor in Brittany and Burgundy, for instance, were far higher than in the South of France – the whole Midi where it amounted to 3–4 per cent of the total produce. In some areas like the Auvergne, the dominant form of land tenue was the so-called *alleu* or freehold which was independent of any payment to lords. Where there were feudal payments there was little personal serfdom. Around 95 per cent of the rural population had personal freedom. The arrangements for landholding were bewilderingly complex, with very varied differences between the amount of land owned by peasants and the land which was held by nobles. In Béarn, for instance, in the Southwest, the overwhelming pattern was of peasant ownership. In the west of Brittany, that ownership was very much less and, in some regions there was none. One estimate for the kingdom as a whole is that the nobility owned 20–25 per cent of the land, the Catholic Church 6–10 per cent the middle classes 30 per cent and the peasants 40–43 per cent. The Revolution increased peasant ownership but did not introduce it.

Though it is convenient to speak of 'peasants', the rural community was much more complex. Confusingly for English speakers, the richer independent farmers were known as *'labourers'*. This included people who owned all their land. But they were a minority. Far more typical were people who owned some of their land but leased other lands and so were subject to dues and rents. Less wealthy cultivators on the same basis were called *personniers* or *haricotiers* or *menagers*. Those who leased a small amount of land and supplemented this by hiring themselves out as workers were known as *manouvriers*. Those with no land and just laboured were *journaliers*. There were also sharecroppers – *colons*, people who cultivated land and paid over an agreed share of the crop to richer owners called *fermiers*. Those who were barely able to scrape a living by this were called *bordagers*. Casual labourers close to the bottom of rural society were *brassiers*. The degree of social stratification varied. In mountain areas smallholders dominated and there were few larger-scale *fermiers* or aristocratic *seigneur*s. In the areas where Young found his poor women there was much less equality and greater aristocratic control. What was evident though was that the sort of agricultural improvements that had been made in Britain and have been called 'the agricultural revolution' had not been made extensively in France. Also, in areas where there was a strong aristocratic presence, the tendency was to try and raise rents and feudal payments so that pressure was being put on those who paid them. However, rural France was too complex for generalisations to be made about 'the peasantry' and the common idea of a ground-down Baldrick-type of toothless and prematurely aged peasant at the mercy of grasping nobles is more apt for novels than history books. The situation is further complicated by rural communities exaggerating poverty and grievances in tax returns and in the lists of grievances submitted at the time of the calling of the Estates General in 1789.

France in 1789

Nevertheless, there were widespread attacks on noble country houses and on the records of taxes and dues in July and August 1789. But that is usually something of a footnote in the Paris-based narrative of the Revolution. The complexity of landowning and also the very deep localism of rural France make it very difficult to identify peasant grievances as a driving force. The unrest of 1789 was brought about by rumours of attacks on rural communities rather than all being spontaneous protest about hardship.

Rural dwellers – or as a shorthand term 'peasants' – encompassed a huge variety of cultivators and workers. They made up perhaps 85 per cent of France's 28 million inhabitants by 1789. 'The French Revolution' really means an upheaval to which the majority of French inhabitants made relatively little contribution. Peasants were not at the forefront of the major revolutionary events and were in many cases not very aware of them. Key to understanding this are the issues of language, superstition, isolation.

The Revolutionary authorities were concerned about the huge differences in language which made standard French uncommon outside Paris and divided the provinces. As late as the 1860s a quarter of recruits to the French army could speak nothing but their local languages. The Abbé Gregoire, a noted scholar and researcher, produced a report in 1794 on the necessity of exterminating *patois* (dialects and other languages) and universalising the use of French. The linguistic variations were seen not as cultural enrichment but a bar to progress. In the 10 miles from Menton on the Italian border to Grasse in the south of France there were five different words for 'father'. Whole areas in Brittany and Languedoc had their own language. Over fifty major dialects have been identified and, within that, hundreds of sub-dialects. This encouraged isolation at village as well as regional level. This was reinforced by superstitions and remnants of paganism and in many areas the lack of a cash economy where local bartering agreements rather than the use of coin were common. In 1789 probably only 20 per cent of transactions were in cash. This perpetuated localism. The lack of reliable maps made it difficult to even find some local communities and when during the Revolution there was a national map-making survey, those brave enough to venture into remote areas were often attacked and even, in some cases, killed.

All this supports the view that peasant unrest was not really revolutionary. Most stemmed from local communal life. It was motivated by struggles by factions or families, and much was directed into excluding outsiders – tax collectors, recruitment officers for the army, absentee landlords and any officials bringing change. There was no instance of peasant unrest attempted on a national scale or attempts by peasants to insert themselves on a regular basis into national or regional political life. The large number of migrants, nomads, tramps and bandits meant that the roads of France well into the nineteenth century were full of travellers outside fixed communities who might have organised revolutionary activity.

In short, rural France – that is the great majority of the countryside – represented a very different world to that of what is usually seen as the French Revolution.

Poverty, isolation, and low life expectancy were not peculiar to the peasantry of France and could be seen in Europe and probably the world in the eighteenth century. If Young found suffering peasant women close to the French capital, what would he have made of the sale of wives described by Thomas Hardy or the heart-breaking hardships of the Irish famine of the 1840s? Most French people lived hard lives and if affected by infirmity could only hope for a speedy death so as not to burden the family and the community. To read back into this can be dangerous. Life expectancy in Britain after a century of economic and social progress was by 1900 equivalent to that of last-century Guatemala. Poverty and suffering as such were a fact of life in the period and not in themselves necessarily a cause of revolution. It is also necessary to point out that in all the great events of the French Revolution, the peasants played a limited direct part and were often to be found in opposition to revolutionary change. It is the urban background that has most relevance to the origins of the Revolution.

The Urban Environment

There was marked population growth in the eighteenth century which put pressure on those on the margin in both countryside and towns. There is evidence that it brought about a fall in real wages as more people struggled to find work in a static job market. People married later as they could not find housing or did not have enough income to start families, as both partners needed to work. They struggled with rising taxation, higher rents and higher feudal impositions. There was also a greater influx into urban areas, but this was often transitory with people coming in for temporary work rather than settling, as it was often hard to get permanent employment and rents were high. Guild restrictions made it hard for migrants to Paris and other cities to establish businesses or get work. The rise in local disturbances for a variety of reasons – food riots, protests against taxation and clashes with the state over such things as actions against smuggling or resistance to customs payments – increased.

When the Revolution came, though, it came as an urban phenomenon and was centred on Paris. So it is important to look at the urban world of the later eighteenth century. But first, a simple fact – most French people did not live in towns, but in rural areas. Town dwellers made up at most 20 per cent of France's 28 or 29 million inhabitants. And of those, only 600,000 or so lived in the capital. Paris was the third largest city in Europe with Constantinople the second, and London with perhaps a million people the largest. It is often thought that Paris must have grown significantly in the eighteenth century, but actually it did not. It already had 500,000 inhabitants in 1700. Larger rates of growth were seen in London which nearly doubled from 550,000 people in 1700 and Naples which also doubled in size from 215,000. The total population of France grew from 19 million to approximately 29 million in the eighteenth century, so Paris did not grow proportionately. By 1789 only a few towns in France were more than 100,000 and most were 50,000 or less. The urban population, however, had a disproportionate significance in terms of the Revolution.

Though the bulk of urban dwellers were members of the 'Third Estate', they were a very disparate section. The most prosperous city dwellers were the 'haut bourgeoisie' but only a minority of very rich merchants and financiers lived palatially. The greatest profits came from the Atlantic trade and sugar from France's West Indian colonies. But there were other sources of wealth from financial dealings and from manufactures. The overwhelming characteristic of industrial production was that it was on a small scale. Great industrial concerns were unusual, and much more common was the family firm with under fifty employees or the much smaller concerns with master and men living together in a semi-family unit. Aside from those who lived from making and trading, there was a considerable number of professionals – lawyers, doctors, surveyors, and officials. The trend was for these 'bourgeois' families to live and dress simply and to have households with relatively few servants. What was common was an interest in reading. There was an expansion of the book trade and an exceptionally large interest in what were 'forbidden' books. In fact, censorship was quite limited, and access to pornography and critical social and political opinions might be considered more akin to today's internet than in many other societies in Europe which had a much more effective 'firewall' of state censorship. There were remarkable numbers of these 'forbidden best-sellers'. Plain packages delivered to a great many seemingly respectable middle-class people contained not only a huge variety of pornography, but books of political theory and attacks on the establishment. Sometimes there was no distinction, as satires on the church often involved detailed accounts of sexual activity by priests. The growth in literacy coincided with a growing taste for subversive literature and an interest in political discussion. However, there was also a growth in interest in science, the natural world and the arts. Paris became the cultural centre of Europe, attracting a range of talents, collectors, connoisseurs, and travellers.

However, visitors, like the philosopher Jean-Jacques Rousseau who came with high expectations, were often appalled by the squalor. Alongside the fine mansions of the aristocracy and the richer bourgeoisie were the overcrowded areas inhabited by artisans, their journeymen or indentured workers, their apprentices and casual labourers. Different trades were concentrated in different districts. The Faubourg Saint Antoine, for instance, to the southeast of the centre of Paris, was a mass of small furniture workshops; the area called the *Quinze Vents* saw an accumulation of metal workers and cutlery makers. The fish sellers gathered in the market area of Les Halles. Much of the city was given over to teeming tenements of artisans and those that supported them – including itinerant workers and large numbers of prostitutes. The presence of wealth in the better districts gave rise to luxury trades and services. Food services were often the best rewarded. The rising population increased the need for bakers, cafes and eating places. Around the city were larger concerns like the Gobelins textile factory and at Sèvres, the porcelain manufacturing centre. The city had become segregated. The aristocracy had moved away into districts like the more salubrious Faubourg St Germain and poorer areas had become separate and distinct from rich and official Paris. Paris itself, because of its sheer size and reputation, had become distinct from provincial cities and from the bulk of rural France, a country within a country.

* * *

It is not hard to see the revolutionary potential of a rising population, falling wages, rising prices, a better-educated, widely-read middle class, a segregated class system and a capital with a life of its own. And above all, the much-discussed privilege and inequality. Not only was there a gap between rich and poor, but there was a system which emphasised the social inferiority of middle classes who were often richer than the aristocrats who lorded it over them.

Histories of the Revolution have often made their starting point the complaint of the Abbé Sieyès in 1789 in a famous pamphlet asked '*What is the Third Estate?*' He answered that it was everything, the backbone of the country, yet nothing because of unfair discrimination.

> By Third Estate is meant all the citizens who belong to the common order. Anybody who holds a legal privilege of any kind, does not belong

to the Third Estate; whoever is totally unprivileged must submit to every form of contempt, insult and humiliation.

This *cri de coeur* is rarely challenged, but its claims are somewhat odd. Sieyès was not a poor country priest ministering to starving peasants, but the son of a financial official who had made a generally successful career in the church as vicar general in the diocese of Chartres. His love of liberty did not prevent him from launching a coup which brought Napoleon to power in 1799 as a dictator. He himself was part of a privileged church order even if most of its members took precious little advantage from it, often administering poor parishes. But the central idea of privilege being something which discriminated against the Third Estate which was 'totally unprivileged' as Sieyès claimed ran in the face of the reality of French life in which privilege was all-pervasive. The exemption of the nobles from some taxes was no doubt irksome. (However, it is not true that this exemption was total, as some textbooks state. Nobles paid a tax called the Capitation and another called the Twentieth, as well as not being able to avoid indirect taxes.) But the middle-class trade guilds had privileges, too. There were associations of master craftsmen designed to protect privileges and restrict trade. There were brotherhoods of journeymen, skilled workers, to try and exclude interlopers and maintain their rights. Individual groups had a variety of privileges like the fish workers of Les Halles. On individual estates, there were traditional privileges for certain officials. Financial and legal officers had privileges. Offices of state were bought so that purchasers should enjoy such privileges.

Sieyès does not say much about the richer middle classes who invested in the purchase of official roles which carried with them, after a period of time, usually twenty years, noble status and privilege. In the years 1773–89, there were quite a few of these: a remarkable total of 3000 men were ennobled or entered into offices in the state which carried noble status. If families are added in, then the numbers acquiring noble status increases even more. Some 270 were rewarded for outstanding services by Louis XVI in what was known as a *lettre de noblesse*. This elevation to noble status as a reward for service would have been rare in the supposedly freer and more open society of eighteenth-century Britain. Most purchased, at a going rate of 120,000 livres, fictitious but grand-sounding posts such as Royal Secretary or Member of the Grand Chancellery. In the reign of Louis XVI, 800 people obtained the so-called ennobling offices, mostly in Paris, but over 200 in the provinces. Some 568 entered potential or actual noble status via posts in the *Bureau des Finances* and another hundred through municipal offices, such as mayors of larger towns. In addition, a thousand offices in sixteen different courts carried noble status. This meant that some of the provincial *parlements* had members of middle-class origins. This influx of the bourgeoisie into nobility and into elite offices worried the noble-led army so much that they persuaded the king to make the notorious *Loi Ségur* in 1781, a regulation that only nobles whose titles went back four generations could be army officers. This is often seen as a low point in the *ancien régime* and proof of nobles gaining greater influence, but it was probably a reaction to greater numbers of middle-class families entering the nobility and fears that army posts would be bought and sold. In Britain, the purchase of commissions went on until 1870. This confirmed the virtual monopoly of nobles in army commands. Nobles also dominated the higher posts in the church and all 135 Bishops and Archbishops were noble as well as richer abbots. But the influx of richer non-nobles into the ranks of the nobility – known as the *noblesse de robe* as opposed to the traditional *noblesse d'épée* – was a sign not of abhorrence of the principle of privilege, but a desire to acquire it.

There is the perception that there was widespread hostility to privilege. Did large numbers of the merchants, manufacturers, financiers, administrators, professionals, master craftsmen, tradesmen and workers who made up France's urban population really desire to become high-ranking army officers or bishops? Or was there a disconnect between what they thought of as a just ideal of equal opportunity and a fair society and how life was in reality. However, in practice, there was no bar to making money and, contrary to belief, the French aristocracy did not scorn trade, finance and manufacturing. Successful entrepreneurs and businessmen could rise socially quite quickly, but of course, numbers who did so were small simply because as in all societies, highly successful businessmen were likely to be quite rare. Few twenty-first-century societies with much more developed education and no official class barriers see enormously high rates of social mobility and brilliant business careers culminating in honours and universal respect. The number of British prime ministers from public school and Oxford might support this, and it would be wrong to think of France as having some rigid caste system where social mobility, both upwards and downwards, was not possible and did not happen. There were plenty of examples of noble families who were forced by economic failure to live and dress as peasants, even if they saw themselves as socially far above the country folk who were often richer. Nor were the middle classes excluded from political and administrative authority. Compared with England, which the middle-class reformers were so keen to praise, the aristocracy, while keeping status and privilege, had not been dominant in

France in 1789

royal government since the previous century. Then Louis XIV (1643–1715) effectively robbed them of their power while boosting their social status. Their role in the military was in keeping with the practice in most European countries. The aristocratic dominance in Britain was still visible in the Crimean War 1854–6 where high-born incompetents like Lord Raglan and the Earl of Cardigan held sway. A list of British prime ministers from the eighteenth century to the 1960s has a remarkable number of aristocrats. Unlike some of their dimmer British counterparts, the aristocratic leaders of the French army in the eighteenth century led the way in professional development; and much of the success of French forces in the Revolutionary and Napoleonic wars was owed to their development of organisation, tactics and weaponry. Their desire was to keep out recently ennobled middle-class social climbers, who had used wealth, not ability, to enter the ranks of the nobility – a reality not consistent with a general view that the middle classes were strong believers in equality and meritocracy. This was less true in practice as distinct from theory. The bourgeois complaints drawn up in 1789 prior to the Revolution contain a lot about how the middle classes suffered from discrimination, but much less about feudal dues. Once in power, the middle-class National Assembly, which contained virtually no peasants, was slow actually to implement the end of feudal rights, as there was a reluctance actually to interfere with property. In addition, there was no freeing of the slaves in French colonies which generated so much colonial wealth. Property and privilege were often more important than genuine equality.

Sieyès offered an elegant paradox – the middle classes were 'everything' but also 'nothing', finding only contempt and humiliation. However, it is difficult to see the enormously wealthy colonial merchants who made the ports Bordeaux and Le Havre economic powerhouses being humiliated, considering the lavish lifestyles they enjoyed in their great mansions. The forty financiers who controlled the collection of taxes – the infamous *Fermiers Généreux* (General Tax Farmers) were renowned for their cultivated, respectable and respected lifestyles. Many noble families were happy to marry into financial wealth generated by French foreign trade which quadrupled in the eighteenth century. French scientific and cultural life, dominated by the middle classes, flourished so much that Paris was widely seen by Europe's educated classes as the hub of civilisation, and French was the major international language. The hours spent learning it by generations of British schoolchildren is a reminder of this cultural supremacy. There was more fluidity between the classes than often assumed with the purchase of land by successful members of the middle class. However, at a much humbler level, there was the chance for talented people in cities to do well in life. One life story does challenge the view of humiliation and lack of opportunity – that of the future radical and architect of Revolutionary Terror, Maximilien Robespierre.

Born in the northern French town of Arras in 1758, in an area where clerical influence and aristocratic dominance of the countryside were strong, Maximilien had a troubled home life. His father, possibly the descendant of an Irish emigrant called Robert Speer, hence the unusual name, was a lawyer but was personally and financially unstable and left his wife, the daughter of a well-to-do brewer, to live abroad. When she died, Maximilian was brought up by grandparents and got the support of the local aristocratic bishop to go to a prestigious school in Paris. This was entirely due to academic ability. The boy was fussy and rather affected in dress and manner, despite having little money. He devoted himself to study, won prizes and a substantial bursary and studied law. He caught the contemporary bug for all things classical and wrote and spoke admiringly about the Roman Republic – quite freely. Back in Arras, he built up a successful legal practice and a high local reputation. Despite owing his education to the local Bishop, he showed independence by defending the churchman's tenants in a legal suit. There were no repercussions for this ingratitude. He also won a case which gained national attention by defending a local landowner who had erected a new lightning conductor on his house, something opposed by the clergy of the district and some suspicious and superstitious neighbours who feared divine wrath. Robespierre successfully used the argument that Louis XVI, a wise and forward-looking monarch, had also erected a lightning conductor. The young lawyer was seen as a progressive and wrote to Benjamin Franklin, the inventor of the lightning conductor, sending him the legal argument he had drawn up and made into a pamphlet. Robespierre was an avid reader of progressive literature, especially of the Enlightenment philosopher Rousseau. This admiration for a theorist who was seen as hostile to monarchy by such statements as *'Man is born free but is everywhere in chains'* being perfectly acceptable. Maximilien was active in local society and was part of a literary and debating club to whom he read his own poems. When it came to choosing representatives for the Estates General in 1789, he was a natural choice. This was part of a process in which 5 million taxpayers voted to send representatives to an assembly in 1789 which would solve France's financial problems and meet the grievances of the people. Few European countries offered any opportunity for elections; the electorate in Britain was pitifully small and dominated by the nobles, and even in the American Republic there was no true democracy, with voting restricted by property qualifications. This unusual opportunity gave Robespierre and hundreds like him the chance to achieve national prominence. Robespierre was an example of a man rising through his own merits and aided, not restricted, by the power of the church. Perfectly free to read the latest progressive literature and able to build a good life for himself in Arras with every prospect of rising as a lawyer, it is difficult to see quite why he was humiliated or held in contempt. However, he went on to become one of the most violent and radical Revolutionary leaders speaking against the tyranny of king and nobles – presumably in the abstract, as he did not seem to have experienced any of it first-hand.

Like Sieyès, Robespierre together with so many other middle-class urbanites were gripped more by ideas of inequality and injustice than by actual experience. This is not to say that there was not hardship, social slights, disappointments and suffering in both town and countryside, but that this was not particular to France or particular to the period 1773–89. If graphs of unrest in France in the eighteenth century are plotted, the peak was not the end of the century but the beginning. The prolonged rioting against Catholics in London in 1780, called the Gordon Riots, was seen as showing superior discipline and order in Paris. For violent and impoverished urban masses, Naples, not Paris, was the place for middle-class Europeans to look and shudder. What was more characteristic of French urban centres by 1789 was the politicisation of the urban middle class rather than the discontent of the lower orders.

Looking back, the Marquise de Bouillé in another oft-quoted source in his memoirs of 1797[3]:

> In Paris and in the other large cities, the bourgeoisie was superior to the nobility in wealth, ability and personal merit. In the provincial cities it was similarly superior to the rural nobility. The bourgeois. were conscious of this superiority, but they were everywhere humiliated, and they were excluded by military regulations from positions in the army. They were also excluded from the high clergy. Most of the sovereign courts admitted only nobles.

Bouillé was a successful general in the wars against England and belies any view of noble incompetence. He was a determined opponent of the French Revolution and even gets a mention as a hated enemy in the *Marseillaise*. He attempted to rescue the king in 1791, but the incompetence of others meant that the flight ended in failure and Bouillé left France. His memoirs are a forerunner of many later aristocratic recollections which seek to explain what went wrong and regret lack of reform, given the disasters which had overtaken the nobility. But even if is true that vital reforms were not well enough supported, the key issue is not necessarily the privilege and class exclusion as such, but why this situation, which was not new and was common in most European monarchies, was so much more discussed and had come to seem so much more irksome. France did not have the poorest countryside in Europe; its cities were not the most troubled by urban discontent; its nobles were not the most privileged; its middle classes were not the most oppressed and humiliated and its monarchy was not the most authoritarian. So why, then, did France experience the greatest political upheaval of Europe in the eighteenth century?

Notes

1. Alison Johnson, *Louis XVI and the French Revolution* (McFarland, 2013), p. 19.
2. Gwynn Lewis, *Life in Revolutionary France* (Batsford, 1972), p. 11.
3. William Childe-Pemberton, *The Baroness de Bode 1775–1803* (Longmans, 1903).
4. Francois Claud-Amour Bouillé, *Mémoires de la Revolution francais* (1797).

Chapter Two

The Crisis of the *Ancien Régime*

There was a widespread belief in the years before 1789 that France and its monarchy were in crisis and this belief has passed into history and into standard accounts of the causes of the Revolution. After the restoration of the French monarchy in 1814, books of memoirs and reminiscences of court life in the *ancien régime* became popular. '*The Private Life of Marie Antoinette*' by Jeanne Louise Campan was a best seller in the 1830s and is quite revealing. She was the daughter of a foreign office official who rose in court circles as a reader first to the princesses at Louis XV's court and then as a companion to Marie Antoinette. She wrote of the time when eminent men visited her father who was a highly respected official:

> Twenty years before the Revolution I often heard it remarked that the institution of monarchy was sinking; and that the people were crushed beneath the weight of taxes and miserable, though silent; but they were listening to the bold speeches of the philosophers. It was said that the age would not pass away without some grand shock that would unsettle France. My father respected the intentions of these persons. And he agreed that there were many abuses. He told them that even if they took over the government, they would be speedily checked in their schemes of reform by the immeasurable difference between the most brilliant theories and the administration needed to put them into practice.

There it was in a nutshell. There was a widespread perception among the educated classes that there were abuses and problems, and that there was every chance of an upheaval. There was a considerable and growing amount of knowledge about the problems. There was also a great variety of solutions and reforms offered and discussed. There was an unprecedented awareness of economic, social and financial issues, but there was also this 'immeasurable distance' between knowing there were changes needed and actually making the changes.

Louis XVI has taken a large amount of blame for not doing more to deal with this perceived crisis, but not everybody saw a passive and incompetent ruler sleepwalking into disaster. Even Madame Caplan did not think him too stupid to understand that reform was needed. She made a perceptive distinction between his character as a man of knowledge and a man of will – he was well-informed about a whole variety of matters of state and not just his obsessions of lock-making and hunting.

> The king was master of the details of any matter and if he saw injustice he would be obeyed instantly. But in important affairs of state, the man of will was not to be found.

At his trial on 26 December 1792 which would lead to his condemnation, Louis was defended by a retired lawyer called Raymond de Sèze. The defender argued that 'he had no corrupting passions, was economical and just and proved himself the friends of his people. The people asked for reforms, and he gave them reforms'. Ignored by his enemies who condemned him to death, this view is nevertheless worth considering.

In the period between 1773 and 1789, there were considerable efforts made to improve and change the government of France. There was a sort of 'Glasnost' after the much more secretive and enclosed government of Louis XIV and Louis XV. The most remarkable element was the publication of the royal accounts for scrutiny by all. The *Parlement de Paris*, exiled by Louis XV for opposition to royal edicts was recalled. Enlightened reforms were made. Under reforming ministers, considerable changes were put into practice. Consultation was introduced on a scale unknown in contemporary Europe. Older books talk about 'tyranny', but this was not a tyrannous regime. Its government was not dominated by reactionary aristocrats, but rather by highly intelligent and enlightened public officials. However, like Gorbachev's Glasnost, the consequences were not those foreseen by the reformers.

It was the French writer Alexis de Tocqueville who first suggested in a classic work of 1856 called '*The Old Regime and the Revolution*' that revolutions often happen as a result of improvements not in the depths of despair or crisis. What was notable by 1789 was the very high level, not of repression or tyranny or utter hopelessness, but rather very high expectations that a benevolent monarch would institute change. Also, when the idea of 'crisis' is introduced then a distinction should be made between real crisis and the perception of crisis. In many ways, there was no crisis in the *ancien régime*. Early modern Europe often went through eras of bad harvests and suffering, and there was widespread and endemic poverty by modern standards. But even if there was hunger, high bread prices and urban unemployment, this does not equate to a crisis of the regime. A huge amount was written about financial crisis and the deficit. But there was no direct connection between a large government debt and bad harvests and rural unrest. The recent pandemic vastly increased government debt in many countries, but the sense of crisis was apparent to most people not concerned about government spending, but in the actual pandemic with lockdowns, deaths and fear. Deficits were and are part of the life of nations and exacerbated by wars. In themselves, they do not topple regimes.

The France which Louis XVI inherited had implicit bargains between ruler and subjects. In return for stability, there had been the acceptance of royal power. The sixteenth century had seen horrific religious wars, or at least wars between noble factions that had adopted different views of Christianity that involved massacres of opponents and armed struggles for power. They had ended with compromise and the acceptance of the leading Protestant noble of the Catholic faith in return for power as the first Bourbon king Henri IV in 1598. In the mid-seventeenth century, there had been more noble unrest and popular revolt, but again stability was restored by the acceptance of a king, Louis XVI, with apparently total control who elevated the monarchy to mystical heights of ceremony and grandeur. The nobility kept status and privilege but lost power. Louis XIV claimed God-given rights of absolute power and ruled a centralised state with officials who owed their power to the king not to any noble status. The aristocracy took on the role of military leaders in a long succession of wars which characterised the reign of 'The Sun King' in his new and magnificent palace at Versailles. He sought *'La Gloire'* in conquests which aimed to push France's frontiers eastwards and to claim overseas colonies with a new naval power. These wars, principally against England, but involving coalitions of other European powers anxious about the growth of French power, continued into the reign of Louis XV.

Glory in war to advance the interests of both France and its monarch remained a key element in royal power and its acceptance. However, success was elusive, and wars proved costly. England proved a formidable opponent because of its naval dominance and the strength of its finances, supported by income from trade. Extended conflicts in various wars of succession (The War of the Spanish Succession 1701–14; the War of Austrian Succession 1740–8 and the Seven Years War 1756–63) left France with severe amounts of debt. They were, too, unfavourable in their outcome. The French lost their presence in North America which was dominated by British colonists. The British, too, were successful in ousting France from its trading posts in India. British sea power proved dominant. France still had the immensely valuable resource of its Caribbean territories, and its relatively large population and wealth, as well as its considerable armed forces and diplomatic importance, meant that it was a great European power. However, the ability of the state to access French wealth through an effective tax system was limited, and the debt took a great deal of the regular income. It was vital to increase internal wealth and to be able to tax it effectively in order to maintain the greatness of the monarchy. Much depended on the grandeur of the monarchy, as it was part of the implicit bargain of the past. In order to avoid the religious quarrels and unrest of the past, a powerful and effective monarchy would ensure internal order and control and offer glory and greatness. By 1773 this greatness was less evident. There were also growing concerns about whether France was able to be prosperous without reforms, and whether or not the centralised government established in the previous century was able to maintain stability without a major overhaul of its financial system.

The key was the concern felt about the problems which were being discussed more widely than ever before. This was an age of science and the increase of knowledge. Institutions were being questioned. Political systems were analysed. Economic ideas were debated. Philosophical tracts became best sellers. Discussion groups were common even in moderate-sized towns. Problems of state, hitherto regarded as the prerogative of royalty and royal officials, were known about and talked about by a surprisingly large number of people. The mystique of government and of the religion which had supported monarchy were undermined by scepticism about organised religion and even the existence of God. Deference towards social 'betters' was undermined by scandals, subversive literature and drama.

This is not to say that rationalism meant that love of ritual had disappeared. When Marie Antoinette entered France, as a young bride for Louis XVI, she had to be stripped naked in an elaborate ceremony and dressed in French clothes to symbolise her change of nationality. Ceremonial was important at every level. When the fishwives of Paris used their privilege of congratulating the royal family on special events such as the birth of a child, they had special ceremonial dresses of black silk to present their homage. There was elaborate court ritual but also rituals for nobles, for associations of professional men, for trade guilds, for meetings of journeymen. These ceremonies continued into the age of the Revolution and were an important part of French life. The age of rational consideration of reforms, encyclopaedias, wider reading, political, financial and economic analysis went side by side with tradition, privilege, ritual and ceremony. This was the challenge for Louis XVI and his ministers – to maintain all the rich tradition of a God-given absolute monarchy built on deference and mystic respect, there had to be modernisation, change, assaults on privilege. This is why Madame Campan was so perceptive. The king as a man with both knowledge and understanding knew this, but he could not force through the reforms or take a clear and decisive line of action partly because of the burden of tradition.

Turgot and the Best Hope for Change

One of the great 'might have beens' of history is what might have happened if the most able of Louis XVI's ministers had been allowed more time and more support for a programme of reform. While not exactly neglected, this far-sighted minister is often rather passed over in textbooks eager to get to the crisis of the monarchy. Yet his brief time in office is worth some attention.

Anne Robert Turgot (male despite his name) was born into a family of ennobled elite lawyers and royal administrators. His father was a senior figure in the administration of Louis XV, and he was given a very high-quality education with a view to his entering the church and achieving high office. But he decided to join the royal administration. He rose quickly in the law. He was well-read in the literature of the reformers and scholars known as the *philosophes*; his learning was such that he contributed erudite articles to the famous Encyclopaedia, intended by its scholarly founder Denis Diderot to be a summation of contemporary knowledge. He was particularly interested in economics and had visited many regions of France before taking on the role of Intendant or senior royal official for the province of Limoges. In theory, he had absolute authority. as the Intendants were like viceroys, taking on the authority of the king in the different regions of France. In practice, the sheer range of their duties together with the limited staff meant that their power was often quite limited and often challenged by other privileged groups like provincial assemblies, *parlements* and the ruling bodies of towns. But this energetic and scholarly figure brought important changes to a poor region. Far from being the stereotypical rural area of the textbooks, most of the *Généralité*, as it was officially known, was occupied by peasant owner occupiers mostly farming quite small areas. Noble estates made up only 15 per cent and the church owned under 5 per cent. The next biggest group were the middle classes who owned land and rented it out. Urban centres were relatively small. The region was a mass of overlapping authorities and legal jurisdictions. Faced with the reality of peasant hardship and the duty of tax collection – the land tax, the *taille* – was not farmed out as many books suggest, but gathered and paid by rural communities collectively; the Vingtième which was only levied on landowners, not all cultivators and not on tenants or labourers, and from which the nobility was not exempt, was collected directly by officials. Turgot reformed the system of collection, made assessments fairer, removed the burden of road building and maintenance (the notorious *corvée*) from individual communities and commuted the duty to a payment made by the region as a whole. Roads were considerably improved. He encouraged agricultural improvement in a particularly backward area by working with local committees and helping to improve methods and variety of cultivation. He was particularly keen to free up the closely regulated trade in grain to help increase the profitability and so the scale of wheat farming. A very serious famine which followed poor harvests and bad weather in 1768–70 resulted in effective official measures of poor relief and food imports. This sort of enlightened local rule by a well-educated professional administrator was not untypical. The Intendants were anxious to help the people in their care, but not interested in sharing political power or consultation. Turgot had a vision of a benevolent monarchy using absolute authority for the benefit of the people which was a feature of an age that has been characterised as one of 'benevolent despotism'.

When Louis XV died in 1774, Turgot was in Paris and in the jockeying for positions of high office which confronted the young Louis XVI, this high minded and efficient royal servant was made first of all Minister of Marine and then the key post of Controller General of Finance. Louis was anxious not to surrender power to a chief minister, but took the advice of the veteran minister Maurepas, who was recalled from retirement, to appoint honest and able men. It is difficult to see the equivalent of a minister like Turgot in the England of the time, and his career challenges some of the stereotypes of the *'ancien régime'* – a later term as Louis XVI saw himself as using talented men to modernise and enhance authority. The Enlightenment thinking of the time was an inspiration for good governance, not some revolutionary creed undermining it. The monarchy was receptive to change. However, beneficial reforms were seen as suspicious by established institutions such as the *parlements* and the provincial assemblies who feared the 'despotism' of ministers.

This is the element of the *ancien régime* that is so difficult for modern readers. The royal government was 'liberal' in the sense of aiming at beneficial measures and did not have the means for mass repression. But there was no appetite among men like Turgot or his royal master for power sharing, representative assemblies or governments responsible to the people via elected parliaments. This was a sort of technocratic rule with little time for participation by 'the people' or any political sensitivity. The *parlements* were less concerned with measures to alleviate suffering and modernising than maintaining the 'liberty' in the sense of traditional rights and the ability to restrict the power of the state by consenting to edicts and changes. In this sense preservation of 'liberty' meant preserving privilege.

As Controller General of Finances, the leading figure in the royal government, Turgot had to engage with the legacy of the debt from the wars of Louis XV and with a cumbersome and complex financial system that had tested his ability in Limoges. He saw that financial security was tied in with economic development. He also wanted to free up internal trade and encourage greater production and productivity. He had met the great advocate of Free Trade, the Scottish economist Adam Smith, and had a deep understanding of some of the obstacles to economic progress.

He seems a remarkably modern figure and with a suave manner, an aristocratic assurance and a love of theoretical economics might be more like a modern British Chancellor of the Exchequer or an EU finance minister than an oppressive henchman of an eighteenth-century absolute monarchy. But in one important respect, the comparison fails. He had no political skills. It was said of him that 'he did good things in a bad way'. Among the backward peasants of Limoges, he could act forcefully for the public good. In the world of the royal court, this was much less easy. Turgot's time in office was brought to an end partly by popular opposition to his ending price controls and partly by factional opposition.

However, a vigorous programme of change did not suggest a regime resistant to improvement and it was certainly more progressive than any of the faction-ridden aristocratic governments of Britain's George III at this time.

* * *

Neither was Louis's foreign minister, Charles Gravier, Compte de Vergennes, a fool or an aristocratic dullard. It is often argued that Louis and his minister made a major and disastrous mistake in joining the War of American Independence in 1778 in support of the colonists which created a crisis for the monarchy.

However, the outbreak of armed rebellion by Britain's American colonists in 1775, irked by restrictions on expansion and internal taxation imposed without their consent gave France a major opportunity. The defeats and humiliations imposed by Britain in previous wars could be revenged, but more importantly, French international leadership and influence as a great power, weakened by defeats, could be re-established. If British forces were distracted by a major revolt and other European powers could be persuaded into alliance with France, then a major turnabout in France's European and even world position could be put into effect. There were two major problems with helping the colonists and weakening France's major enemy. First, costs and second, the reluctance of the king to support rebellion against a foreign monarch. Louis XVI sensibly held back, but Vergennes, his veteran foreign minister, played a long game. Military aid was sent secretly to the colonists and helped to keep the rebellion going and Britain committed to sending more forces. Then a formal recognition of American independence was signed in 1778 – a move that was genuinely popular in France, whose literate classes saw Britain as a tyrannous colonial and the monarchy continuing to pursue enlightened and liberal policies. The new finance minister, the Swiss Protestant Necker, managed the extra spending through loans, not taxes. The naval minister, Satrine, had built up French naval power. Direct military intervention only came in 1779 after military and diplomatic preparation and France skilfully gained the support of Spain and then the Netherlands in 1780. The strategy to keep British naval forces in home waters, with the threat of invasion and a naval build-up in Brest while sending forces to keep the colonial war going and to take valuable West Indies colonies, was a sensible one and partly successful. French naval forces forced Britain to withdraw its blockade of the Southern colonies. French forces and a temporary naval supremacy helped the colonists to achieve a major victory with the British surrender at Yorktown in 1781, which effectively won the war. The whole strategy was undermined by a last-minute British naval victory at the Battle of the Saintes in the West Indies – a battle comparable in scale to the more famous Trafalgar. The coalition fell apart, Britain made its peace with the colonies whose independence it recognised. Spain gained Minorca and regained Florida. France's actual colonial gains were small; but territorial expansion had not been the central aim of the war. Britain had been humiliated. French international prestige was high. Britain lost its diplomatic supremacy. The war's outcome was welcomed in France. The war had not been brilliantly conducted, but in broad terms, it was successful in its aims and did not have the effects that, for example the First World War had on the Russian monarchy by exposing its incompetence and leading to accusations of failure and popular unrest.

However, both Turgot and Necker had had concerns about the costs and consequences that were to an extent justified. It is unlikely though that the support for American liberty led to a huge increase in criticisms of the lack of such liberty in France and was therefore a direct cause of revolution. The ideas of 'no taxation without representation' and consent by the governed were already established in France, and there was a great interest in the American Revolution and its leaders. Even if Louis XVI had remained neutral and had not acted to enter the war, this would still have been true. The soldiers and sailors who fought the war were largely professional and there is not much evidence for their returning full of new American ideas of liberty that were not already common.

Financial Problems

The more persuasive argument is that the costs of war made the national debt so great that France faced bankruptcy by 1787 and was forced to seek higher taxes which involved gaining a measure of consent. This led to the summoning of the old parliament of France, the Estates General and a great national discussion of grievances which led to even greater demands for a constitutional monarchy and a national assembly. This in turn paved the way for the end of the monarchy and the establishment of a republic. Thus, money problems deriving from war are directly linked in most accounts to an extended period of instability from 1789–99. The deficit as a result of the war, therefore, gets centre stage as the engine of revolution. The issue of the deficit seemed to sum up everything that seemed to be wrong with the rule of Louis XVI. There was an unjust tax system; hated privileges; economic discontent which made taxes hateful and resented; an educated and thrusting middle class wanting financial reform and an end to exemptions by resented social betters; a weak monarch unable to solve problems; even, in some older accounts, conspirators among the nobles and secret societies and foreign powers using financial issues to weaken the monarchy.

The famous deficit, then, has a lot to answer for. Louis XVI appointed some highly accomplished ministers to engage with it and, after the publication of the royal accounts in 1781, it was a topic about which a very unusually large number of people had knowledge and opinions. In conventional wisdom, the inability to control debt or introduce a radically more efficient tax system has condemned the king's historical reputation. Selfish privileged classes, by not seeing that change was needed, brought about their own downfall. Foolish ministers doomed the regime by trying to get consensus about financial reform.

There are some warning bells. If deficits and large national debts are so important, then why did they not have a similar revolutionary effect in other countries and at other times? In a post-Covid era when governments incurred eye-watering debt levels and relied on massive loans and also quite heavy levels of regressive indirect taxation, where were the revolutionary mobs whose passions had been aroused by deficit spending? Popular feeling is more likely to express a desire for more spending, rather than sound finance. Large debts in themselves have rarely made governments powerless, and if the French crown had wanted to rule by force rather than consent then they had more armed force available to them than most of contemporary European states. What was crucial was the decisions made about dealing with a financial problem which was common to most European states of the time; and also the unusual extent to which financial problems had become a matter of common knowledge. The 'crisis' was arguably a crisis of perception more than reality.

Recitations of figures are quite problematic as modern equivalents of eighteenth-century money are so hard to establish, but there is a general consensus of the financial situation. The war has been estimated to have cost France 1.3 million livres. This meant that the total debt was something like 3.3 million livres. At this point, generations of school and university students reading this have just thought 'a lot'. There were, in theory, 13 livres to a contemporary British pound sterling in the late eighteenth century. The annual revenue from taxes in France was 585 million livres. At the end of the war around 43 per cent of annual income went to servicing (paying interest on) the debt. The annual gap between income and expenditure – the deficit – was about 25 million livres. By comparison, Britain had spent £80 million on the war. At 13 livres to the pound, this was the equivalent of about 1 million livres; Its national debt was roughly £250 million – or 3.25 billion livres. So, the difference in debts was not that huge. In modern terms, both were weighing in with something like £35 billion of debt. Today, France has a national debt of nearly 3 trillion dollars and Britain's national debt stands at 1.6 trillion dollars. There is no widespread knowledge or discussion of these figures among the general public and relatively few know what a trillion is, anyway. The fact that Britain's debt was growing at £450 million a day in 2022 is not much publicised and even if it were, it would not be a possible cause of revolution. This is to put the French alarm about the 'great deficit' into perspective, as it was not so much the reality but rather concerns about finance that were important, especially after the figures, or a version of them, were made public.

There are some contextual points to be made. First of all, royal spending on luxuries, palaces, necklaces, dressing up, etc., did not make up much of this debt. It had been estimated at 6 million livres and much was just what was conventionally expected of an eighteenth-century monarchy. The modern British monarchy costs £102 million a year without the royals having any executive role in government. Secondly, and this is a complex point, debt was endemic in eighteenth-century France. IOUs acted as a major form of exchange, as cash had no fixed values throughout the country and was not a uniform means of payment in the way that modern currencies are. The idea of the monarchy being in debt was an extension of everyday life for many French people who often did not use actual money for transactions but relied on discounted IOUs. Thirdly, the often-repeated comparison with Britain in which the debt was managed by people investing in it through government bonds and a more developed system of public finance is not always accurate. There was quite widespread investment in the state debt of France through a system of investing a sum and then getting an annual return on it. The return on the lump sum investment was quite generous, but the investment required foregoing the capital. Investors often sold off part of their annuity, and so investors at one stage removed were common even among the lowest members of French society. Fourthly, a belief has crept in that all taxation was in the hands of greedy financiers called Tax Farmers who collected taxes and that the privileged classes paid no taxes. However, the tax farmers collected only indirect taxes like the *gabelle*, the tax on salt. The land tax, the taille, was collected directly but the first two estates were exempt. The tax on property that was actually owned – the twentieth (*Vingtième*) – was not farmed and the second estate (the nobility) was not exempt. The church paid its own tax, voted in its own assembly. It is doubtful whether a new tax unless accompanied by a radical reform of collection would have ended the national debt any more than any single tax measure today would repay even a fraction of most national debts. The vital element was the continued ability of the eighteenth-century states to be able to keep borrowing. Any danger that interest payments would be suspended would have serious consequences for the effective running of domestic and foreign policy and would lead to a loss of confidence in the state.

With the fall of Turgot, another expert was appointed who was well aware of this. The banker and economist Jacques Necker was an unusual and imaginative choice as a Protestant Swiss. It suggests an openness to innovation and a willingness to bring in the best minds. Necker aimed to economise and aimed to ensure that the regime's credit was maintained in the financial markets. He needed to finance the American war by raising loans. His most famous act to ensure confidence was the publication of the royal accounts, the so-called *Compte Rendu* in 1781 after the spiralling costs of war were putting pressure on the government's ability to raise enough money to sustain the fighting. The national budget was put before parliament in Britain, but in most regimes, it was not a matter for public knowledge. Necker was aware that British financial credit was strong and sought to establish a similar confidence about France. He reported in a detailed breakdown that there was a surplus of 10 million livres, something that brought him criticism from his rivals at the time and from later historians. It was argued that the sum was more like a 500 million livres deficit. However, Necker was talking about 'ordinary' revenue – the day-to-day income of the crown. He was not talking about the very high costs of war – what is known as 'extraordinary' revenue which cannot be planned for. He was also aware that because of the problems of collecting revenue, this was not a fixed sum but happened to be the sum in early 1781. The key to all this is that investors were concerned with the health of the ordinary revenue, not the debts incurred by war. So, this snapshot was to reassure investors in what we would call gilt-edged securities. He was well aware that for all the problems, taxation needed to rise to meet the high levels of debt and war expenditure.

There is some doubt about whether this was the first time that the accounts had been available to the public, but it was certainly the first time that they had been a bestseller. The whole issue of the deficit took a strange turn. In the mass of pamphleteering and writing and discussion, 'deficit' came to be equated with morality. To be in the red, as it were, was to lack virtue. To be in surplus was to be virtuous. This Thatcherite position was something new in public discourse and so Necker's efficiency and attempts to demonstrate the regime's creditworthiness backfired. The readers of his report became outraged not reassured. His desire to remedy the shortfall by tax raises and concerns about his accounting methods led to his fall.

It was becoming increasingly obvious that to show the required virtue of balancing the books, and to ensure that the government could go on borrowing to service its debt, some major overhaul of the financial system was necessary. It was also becoming obvious that change needed consent. Turgot's authoritarianism had led to unrest. Necker's technical expertise had not confronted the key need to tap the nation's considerable resources more effectively. If analysis of problems and attempts to solve them is seen as 'crisis', then the regime indeed was in crisis. However, all governments have to confront the need for change in the light of events. There was no sense that Louis's ministers did not understand the challenges or lacked intellectual ability. This was certainly true of the next major reforming figure, Charles Alexandre de Calonne, Compte de Hannonville.

* * *

Here was another of the intellectual ruling elite of the *ancien régime* coming up with solutions which seemed clear and rational. His portrait exudes suave self-assurance and his proposals were made with great confidence. His assessment was that, far from being in surplus, there was a significant shortfall in ordinary revenue and a big debt problem which had arisen from accumulated borrowing and the impact of a costly war. He was also aware of rising pressure. The whole public debate about finance had taken on a moral tone. Government had not only to be efficient, but good and virtuous. Virtue involved fairness. If privilege in taxation continued, then that was not merely old-fashioned but wrong. But if taxation changed there had to be a measure of consent. That was the message of the American Revolution. But theory apart, the cooperation of the ruling class was actually vital to collect revenue. Some of the privileged classes stuck to the old-fashioned view that God had set up different people to undertake different social roles. The role of the aristocracy was to serve as military chiefs, and this is why they deserved tax exemption. The king's brothers held to this medieval view, but they did not speak for all of the privileged classes. There was a widespread view that change was needed, but change imposed by intellectually arrogant ministers was seen as a form of despotism. The paradox was that the privileged *parlements* who opposed change were seen as defenders of 'liberty' while the enlightened ministers who sought to erode privilege and protect the poor taxpayers against shouldering excessive burdens were seen as 'tyrants'.

Efforts at reform were blocked by the *parlements*, and Louis was driven to restrict their power and to exile them just as his grandfather had done. They became unlikely popular heroes, and demonstrations took place in their support. In 1787 Calonne came up with an elegant way of moving forward. If the case for reforming the tax system and introducing a new universal property tax were made to key people, then there would be enough elite support for reform and creditors would see a new stability. The power of the monarchy would not be undermined, but Louis would be seen as a ruler who aimed at consent. Somewhat bizarrely, this modern financial administrator sought a solution in the history books and fell back on the precedent of inviting high-ranking nobles and officials to be a sort of royal council. These 'notables' had been summoned in 1560, 1585, 1596 and 1626 to discuss high affairs. The past lay heavily on government decisions, as Calonne did not wish to create any new institutions and wanted to be seen as acting in line with previous precedents and being 'constitutional' and not despotic

The Assembly of Notables duly met in 1787. but the discussions dragged on and no consensus emerged. In economic terms, the skies darkened as a periodic harvest failure increased prices and unrest. The problem was that the government was running out of options. Once the premise of consultation had been introduced – even if the range of those consulted was small, it was difficult then to abandon it. Some sort of arbitrary enforcement of a new taxation system without the support of the ruling elites would have been beyond the scope of Louis XVI's government. A big region like Limoges had only an Intendant (a royal official with considerable theoretical power) and thirty-two assistants. Eighteenth-century administrations, for all their aspirations to absolutism, worked under very severe constraints. The public criticism of Necker's over-optimistic financial accounts had rattled investors. As Mrs Thatcher famously said, governments cannot buck the markets, and most modern historians see the inability to guarantee interest payments as the turning point for one of history's key decisions in 1788 – the calling of the Estates General.

The Estates General

This decision gets surprisingly limited coverage in many accounts. It followed a sustained failure to get approval for financial measures which would reduce the debt and give investors confidence. The Assembly of Notables had not worked and Calonne had not succeeded in getting a consensus for a new tax which would be paid by all. His eventual successor was not a financial expert but a churchman, Cardinal Etienne-Charles de Loménie de Brienne, one of the less written about ministers. Ironically, this long-faced elegant aristocrat, a rich and influential member of the privileged first estate and not one of the enlightened middle-class technocrat ministers did so much to bring about the most revolutionary of the measures of reform. Arguably one of Louis XVI's most well-born public servants did the most to destroy the monarchy and to weaken both the church and the whole class system. It was as if a modern British government summoned the Anglo-Saxon Witan to produce solutions to post Brexit problems.

In July 1787 he presented financial measures to the *Parlement de Paris* to register. The parliament considered the Stamp Duty and the new land tax but would not register them without approval by the Estates General. Brienne exiled the body to the provincial city of Troyes for this impertinence. The members of the *parlement* became popular heroes for standing up against ministers and for consultation. So great was the support that Brienne recalled the *Parlement de Paris* in September. It was at this stage that the *Parlement* set out its demands. The Estates General would be called. It would not be an elected body along the lines of the US Congress or the English Parliament, but it would take the form it had when it last met in 1614 of an enlarged royal council drawn from the three estates. Too often the whole historical background of this body is ignored, but Brienne was all too aware of this so that he was definitely not introducing some new and potentially revolutionary body but reviving a well-established historical precedent. This proved to be a delusion but there is generally not enough consideration given to the previous history of the Estates General.

The kings of France in the early modern period were not tyrants but were bound by laws and received petitions and advice from courts and assemblies which were considered by the royal council and if necessary, measures were taken. There were different sorts of assembly – those of the whole kingdom – the Estates General; local estates of different regions; or meetings of a single estate like the clergy. The Estates General which originated in the fourteenth century was not a regular body and had met eight times between 1484 and 1614 before being convened in 1789. The idea of a meeting of the different estates went back to 1302 but the actual term dates from 1384. The representative of the three orders sent in petitions, requests and grievances. The word *cahier* was used, and the representatives were bound simply to discuss the contents of the *cahiers*, so it was not a parliament where any sort of discussion was allowed. The nobles were held to represent the countryside as a whole. The clergy were represented largely by leading churchmen with just a few ordinary priests. The rest – the third order – was represented by royal officials, members of town councils, lawyers and notaries. There were three deputies – one for each order – from each district. The orders from 1560 met separately after a plenary session with the king. The *cahiers* were bound and presented to the king. The king could then choose to make reforms on the basis of the *cahiers* – as Henri III did in a series of measures in 1579 called the Ordinance of Blois following a meeting of the Estates General there in 1577. The meeting of 1588 was the most assertive with the deputies pressuring the crown to assert the predominance of the Catholic religion. There were also demands for regular meetings of the Estates and that deputies be represented on the royal council. But the king reasserted authority by arresting leading nobles who had made these demands. The Estates General fell into disuse after 1614. But the key thing to understand is that drawing up *cahiers de doléances* or registers of grievances by the three orders for consideration by the king was not some radical idea dreamt up by Louis XVI or his ministers – it was part and parcel of the whole decision to restore this defunct institution and suited both the *Parlement de Paris* and the king. The *parlement* liked the idea of an elite body making recommendations for reform. The king liked the idea of his subjects being able to present their grievances in a traditional way for his consideration and as a basis of a rather more consensual monarchy, though with the king remaining at the centre of power and free to adopt demands as he thought fit. What was not intended was a parliament in the modern sense, but a sort of extension of the Assembly of Notables which would pave the way for acceptance of new financial measures and confidence in investors. Without an understanding of the early modern institution, the decision to call the Estates General takes on a totally different character.

However, this was historical precedent run mad. The hopes of many for more modern constitutional change were dashed and a great many hostile pamphlets saw the Estates General as a distinctly bad idea. Instead of being a chance for modernisation through a new national assembly, the aim was seen, in the words of one pamphlet 'to hurl us back into the age of feudal aristocracy'. This was because the minority of the aristocratic second estate was equal in voting rights to the vastly more numerous Third Estate. The members of the *Parlement* went from being praised to vilified. They do have defenders who argue that by insisting on this historic assembly they aimed for a new form of unity between the orders. But contemporary pamphlets talked a lot about 'the nation' needing to come together to give consent and not the old-fashioned three orders.

The government might have simply rejected the demands for greater consultation and passed new taxes through a *'lit de justice'* which could just ignore a refusal by the *Parlement de Paris* to accept new taxes. However, this would not have done much for investor confidence. Initially, Brienne thought of delaying the elections to the Estates General, but circumstances forced more immediate concession. In August 1788 following a failure to secure loans, the government suspended interest payments to its creditors. Some sort of consultative rule would reassure the markets and bring the elites represented by the *parlements* into step with the government. By taking the 1614 model, the dangers of excessive change might be avoided while there would be a move towards representation for taxation change.

In some ways, this showed a regime rooted in precedent. This body had not met since 1614 but had some validity and reassured Louis's subjects that he was not acting arbitrarily or introducing some new body which would be under the control of the royal government. In many studies, this key decision seems to come out of the blue, though. Without considering the historical background some things become unintelligible. Why ransack the history of France for this historic institution, long defunct? Why emphasize class distinctions already under some attack by a body enshrining division between the three estates? And why institute the most extraordinary measure of all, a series of meetings nationwide to draw up lists of grievances (*Cahiers des Doléances*) again in rigid class groups prior to elections which were a novelty in French life. The answers lie in the desire to make use of precedent to create a council which would authorise new members without being a threat, because such bodies had been used before and had been readily controlled. The key decision, however, was that representatives would be elected. Elections on a national scale were not part of French experience in the way that they were in Britain or the new American Republic in the same period.

Elections in contemporary Britain were quite restricted affairs. The aristocracy dominated 'rotten boroughs' with small numbers of voters happy to be bribed or too much under the sway of local bigwigs to cast their votes independently. The total electorate was small. Some rising industrial areas were not represented while decayed areas like the infamous mound outside Salisbury called Old Sarum continued to send two MPs to parliament. When there was a larger electorate as in Westminster, elections were rowdy, drink flowed, and bribery and influence were open. When MPs came to the House of Commons the government had a huge influence by giving out lucrative posts. All efforts to reform this undemocratic and corrupt system failed until 1832 and ordinary people did not vote in any significant numbers until 1867. Even in the new American Republic, voting rights were restricted to property owners; African American enslaved people had no rights and women were excluded until 1919. Most of Europe was under absolute monarchs with no democratic discussion of political issues permitted. Where there were Republics as with Venice and the Netherlands, these were dominated by rich merchants and financiers.

Yet in 1788 and 1789 France embarked on a new path with little precedent or parallel in the world of the 1780s. Indeed, it was to the world of Greece and Rome that people looked for models. Everything Greek and Roman was in fashion – even toga parties and reconstruction of the symposia of the ancient philosophers. The country was in the grip of discussion at all levels from nobles to peasants in special meetings and then voted for representatives to a body with no defined powers or responsibilities which would, they hoped, consider a massive range of grievances and solve financial problems. Was this an imaginative move forward or a recipe for disaster?

With hindsight, obviously the latter. It would have taken a ruler and a government of exceptional ability to manage this situation, mould the discussions, come up with a programme of reform that was acceptable and engage the wider political nation in working collaboratively towards a modern, prosperous state. However, contemporaries did not necessarily see themselves in the grip of a crisis in 1789.

In an interesting memoir, the deputy Eustache Hua thought 'It was not by the people that the Revolution was made in France. The voice of the nation cried out for reform, for changes in government, but all proclaimed respect for religion, loyalty to the king and desire for law and order.'[1]

Neither were the people so poor and downtrodden that they were necessarily ready for revolution when the chanced emerged. An English traveller, Dr Edward Rigby found in 1789, in contrast to the more often quoted Arthur Young, 'The general appearance of the people is different to what I expected. They are strong and well made. Few of the lower classes are in rags, idleness and misery. The differences between this country and England seems to be in favour of the former'. When he crossed into Germany, he found tyranny and oppression and a depressed population. 'How every country and every people we have seen since we left France sink in comparison to that animated country'[2]

The decision to establish forums for discussion of grievances offers a remarkable picture of attitudes on the eve of the Revolution. These equivalents to modern focus groups extended to small hamlets and villages and have been extensively analysed as historical evidence. The discussions were examined by the National Assembly, as the Estates General became in June 1789. In terms of the principles of government, the Assembly found that unanimous agreement was shown about the following:

- The French government is monarchic
- The person of the king is sacred
- The crown is hereditary

In addition, there was general agreement that:

- The king is the depository of the executive power
- The agents of authority are responsible to the king
- The royal sanction is necessary for the promulgation of the laws
- The nation-state makes the laws with the royal sanction.
- The consent of the nation is necessary for loans and taxes
- Property is sacred
- Individual liberty is sacred

Some of this has revolutionary implications, but it is not in itself evidence of revolutionary fervour. The king had already accepted, by the calling of the Assembly of Notables, by the acceptance of *parlements* need to register financial edicts and then by calling the Estates General, that France was not a state in which a tyrant-imposed taxes without any consent. Many of the aspects of France since 1773 did accept some individual liberty. There was limited censorship and control of literature, the abolition of torture, widespread political discussion and moves to free trade and reduction of guild restrictions. This is not to say that there was democracy or total liberty, but the comparison that Dr Rigby made between France and more repressive regimes, such as that of the clerical rulers of the Rhine and the Prussian monarchy should not be forgotten. The record of France with regard to liberty was not untypical of the world of the late-eighteenth century. The US maintained slavery, as did the British in their empire; few countries in Europe accepted workers' or peasants' rights; many areas in Eastern Europe maintained serfdom, which was nearly extinct in France. Class distinctions were everywhere and modern democracy virtually nowhere.

It was true that bad harvests and economic downturn were taking their toll, but the deputy Eustache Hua made the point that had there not been famine, people would have remained submissive to authority. 'They only knew present evils. And, of these, famine alone was intolerable. It is not change in the state that they demanded, it is bread. Bread was the lever by which people were moved to action, The people were not starving but were haunted by fears of starvation'.

There is a distinction between immediate problems brought about by hardships, typical of all countries in late eighteenth-century Europe, and more profound problems caused by deep underlying discontents and revolutionary ambitions.

The *Cahier* of the Third Estate at Carcassonne falls into line with the analysis of the National Assembly. The lawyers, doctors and merchants of this decayed mediaeval fortress city that was in a poor southern province, miles from Paris offered a mixture of respect for the monarchy with desire for change, which was remarkably consistent throughout France.

- The third estate of the electoral district of Carcassonne, desiring to give to a beloved monarch, and one so worthy of our affection, the most unmistakable proof of its love and respect, of its gratitude and fidelity, desiring to cooperate with the whole nation in repairing the successive misfortunes which have overwhelmed it, and with the hope of reviving once more its ancient glory, declares that the happiness of the nation must, in their opinion, depend upon that of its king.
- Persistent economy in government expenditures, and indispensable reforms in all branches of the administration, are the best and perhaps the only means of perpetuating the existence of the monarchy.
- Public worship should be confined to the Roman Catholic apostolic religion.

- The nation should be subject only to such laws and taxes as it shall itself freely ratify. The meetings of the Estates General of the kingdom should be fixed for definite periods. The Third Estate's votes in the assembly should be taken and counted by head. All taxes should be assessed on the same system throughout the nation. A law should be passed declaring members of the third estate qualified to fill all such offices for which they are judged to be personally fitted.[3]

This sums up the nature of the 'crisis' of 1789. There was no suggestion that monarchy was to be abolished. The members of the Third Estate had been asked to put forward grievances in order to improve the monarchy and loyally did so. The tone was often conservative, as with the demand for Catholicism to be the dominant religion. There were echoes of the sixteenth-century demands for regular meetings of the Estates General. There were calls for ending fiscal privileges but not all other privileges or feudal dues. There was a call for voting to be by head and not by order for obvious reasons. There were calls for equal opportunity for 'qualified' members of the Third Estate to have access to offices. The aim was to perpetuate the monarchy. The document is intended to fulfil a duty to the monarchy and is a long way from being revolutionary.

What is so fascinating about a trip through the many available *cahiers* is the way that the discussions reached even the smallest communities. We know their names and can imagine the Archers-like meetings. The village of Dampierre-sur-Boutonne in eastern France in the Generality of Poitiers submitted a summary of a meeting of nineteen of its 118 inhabitants. Of these nineteen, whose names were recorded, there was a retired army surgeon, Hugue Rene Fromy; three described as 'bourgeois' and one estate official of the lord of the manor, the Marquis de Fallifet. The chairman, René Benoist, was the 'syndic' of the village – something rather less grand than mayor and equivalent to chairman of the parish council. They dispensed with the professions of loyalty and got straight down to business by asking for an end to internal customs barriers, equal liability for taxation for all the 'orders' and pleaded that their poverty should be taken into consideration when the *taille* was assessed because of a poor grape harvest. They added their desire to be seen as patriotic. At this level, there was less concern for ideas, and the demands were mostly based on economic needs. However, that this small place had a discussion at all about matters which went beyond village level is an indication of the scale of politicisation in the widest sense that was evident in March 1789.

The Crisis of the Ancien Régime

Looking back from the execution of Louis XVI in Jan 1793 it would be possible to see the situation four years earlier when the order went out for the 60,000 meetings held to draw up the *Cahiers* prior to the elections for the Estates General as revolutionary. Who can deny there was evidence of middle-class discontent, rural poverty, urban hardship and a desire for change fuelled by political awareness and a growth in both literacy and literature? But from the perspective of January 1789, this seems less certain. The loyalty to both monarchy and church seemed evident; the government had not been one of ossified repression but was open to new ideas. Bad harvests, though harmful were a fact and if the authorities were often blamed for either not doing enough or for deliberately withholding food, this was nothing new. Contemporaries did not all paint a despairing picture. There were no organised political revolutionary parties, even if there was the potential for political agitation.

However, the international context was threatening. Successful colonial revolution in America did vindicate the principle of 'no taxation without representation'; closer to home, agitation by middle-class urban radical 'patriots' in the Netherlands is sometimes seen as a harbinger of revolution in France. On the other hand, the phenomenon known later as 'enlightened despotism' did show that monarchs could combine political control and reform. In countries such as Spain, Prussia, Austria and even Russia, authoritarian monarchs brought about significant modernisation. If Louis could have harnessed the enthusiasm to preserve monarchy through reform and managed the desire for quite moderate change then 1789 might either be remembered as a period of reform, or more likely not be remembered at all. Like most of the worthy reforms of Catherine the Great of Russia or Joseph II of Austria, the era of Louis XVI might have passed out of collective memory. But that was not to be, and 1789 turned out to be a year of developments which astonished Europe at the time and remain fixed in historical memory.

Notes

1. Memoires de Hua, *Deputé de l'Assemblée Legislative*, (1871), published by his grandson.
2. Edward Rigby, *Letters from France 1789*, reprinted (Hansebooks, 2020).
3. J.H. Robinson, ed. *Readings in European History*, (Boston: Ginn, 1906), 2: 397–400.

Chapter Three

The Events of the Year 1789

The year 1789 in public memory is the key year of the French Revolution, and the 'storming of the Bastille' on 14 July is the event which is most associated with it and continues to be celebrated in France as a public holiday. Its importance is obvious, but the events are not always as they are remembered or appear, either in history or in fiction.

With the election of the Estates General in the spring of 1789, the focus shifted to Paris and, oddly, away from the apparently burning question of the deficit. Arthur Young had found in late 1787 that the people in Paris he met were obsessing about this.

> One opinion pervaded the whole company: that they were on the eve of some great revolution in the government ... the confusion in finances is great and bankruptcy is a topic; the question is would a bankruptcy occasion a civil war, and a total overthrow of the government?

But when the Estates General finally met, after the massive discussions about the agenda and the *cahiers*, matters shifted away from debt to the whole nature of this body and its role in government. This had been anticipated in the discussions before 1789 and the key issue of whether voting was to be by order with the clergy and nobility to outvote the mass of the people or by head which would make the Estates General akin to a parliament and would allow the most numerous part of the nation to outvote the minority orders. The *cahiers* often demanded this way of voting. This issue is the one that dominated the initial meetings, paralysed progress and reform and dashed the hopes of many that consultation would solve all problems. However, it is not always asked by historians what the new body would be voting on. Traditionally, the body voted on which of the grievances in the collected *cahiers* would be passed to the royal council to consider; if that were all, then it would not have been of great importance whether the voting was by order or by head. However, this narrow view of the Estates General had been replaced by one in which it spoke for 'the nation'. This term was coming into circulation as opposed to 'the kingdom' or 'the realm' and was quite a significant development. This would mean that instead of being a sort of elected advisory body to the royal council, pointing out what needed to be addressed, it would be a regular part of government.

The shift from a medieval consultative body to being a National Assembly came remarkably quickly. The real 'French Revolution' was not really the violent and dramatic 'storming of the Bastille' of 14 July but rather the decision of the deputies of the Estates General to declare themselves a National Assembly on 17 June. It took just over a month from the first meeting of the Estates General on 4 May to get to a step which Arthur Young saw as equivalent to the English Long Parliament of 1640. It was this body which transformed the role of the English parliament, fought a long war against Charles I and paved the way for the trial and execution of the king and for an unprecedented English Republic. But the context was different in England in 1640. Calling the Long Parliament followed an unsuccessful war against the Scots, years of bitterness about unpopular domestic policies, fears about religion and a determined and organised opposition with long years of parliamentary experience. The move to a National Assembly in France in 1789 took place in peacetime, after thousands of protestations of loyalty to the crown, with very little in the way of organised resistance or real opposition to government policies. Louis XVI had been trying to reform; he shared religious convictions with the majority of his fellow Catholics; there was no revolutionary ideology to reduce the crown's authority. The Estates General met in traditional fashion at the royal palace, summoned by the king. Each Estate was dressed according to its rank – the nobles with swords and finery, the Third Estate in respectful black. The headspace of those in authority was in 1614. But within weeks this had changed radically, with elements of the clergy and nobility joining the Third Estate and against the wishes of the king declaring themselves a very different body, akin to the American Declaration of Independence, not the mediaeval grovelling expected. There was no armed rising, no storming of royal palaces; none of the colourful activity of later events, but this was the real revolution even if it is not celebrated by a national holiday. So, the first task is to understand not only why this happened, but also why it happened so very quickly and could not be reversed.

* * *

The events of 1789 could be considered as an interaction between three elements. The first was the population of the city of Paris. 1789 is perhaps better considered as 'the Paris Revolution' rather than 'the French Revolution'. The second element is the Estates General which brought deputies from all over France into Paris, though, as a body, it was not very representative of 'France', as the great majority of its people, the rural population, did not attend. The third element is the French government and state and how they reacted to the events of 1789.

In popular depictions, the people of Paris are the key element. The picture of ragged masses storming the Bastille; then enraged women leading the 'mob' to Versailles, anticipating the horrific Terror and massacres of 1792 to 1794 remains etched into historic memory.

The People of Paris and the Events of 1789

Foreign visitors in the late eighteenth century noted 'the hell' of the poorer districts, in rather a similar way that visitors to Mumbai note the slum area and even take advantage of 'Slumdog tours' offered by entrepreneurs of 'dark tourism'. However, as most eighteenth-century cities, as well as very large numbers of modern cities, have poorer districts and do not experience revolutions, poverty in itself may not explain the Parisian Revolution.

The city had grown during the eighteenth century. It had taken in internal migrants, and it has been estimated that two-thirds of the city by 1789 had come in from the provinces or the surrounding area. There was still a mass of individual districts, trades, fraternities, and congregations as in the previous century. However, there was more individualism and districts were less sealed off from one another.

Individuals could dress as they pleased, as sumptuary laws defining what different classes were entitled to wear were no longer enforced. Nobles often shared entertainments with the lower orders. Old social boundaries were breaking down. A notorious case where a noble ejected a wealthy commoner from a theatre seat which he thought was his right to occupy and ended as a court case which was decided in favour of the commoner was widely reported as unusual and not something that might have happened as a matter of course thirty years before. Riots in April 1789 against the wallpaper manufacturer Réveillon who was believed to be going to cut wages involved people from different poorer districts, unusually as previous disturbances tended to be more concentrated in particular areas. People moved around the city quicker and in and out of the city. Deference to rank was less apparent in 1789 than it had been fifty years ago. The economic links between the citizens artisans, manufacturers and wealthy or noble customers made for greater contact between the classes. More importantly, there was the growth of a 'middle sort' between the casual labourers, unskilled workers, drifters and abject poor and the richer elements; small masters, shopkeepers, tradesmen serving the bureaucracy and the well-to-do, well-born areas of the right bank of the Seine and the many churches of Paris. This more mobile, less deferential society was surprisingly literate. Paris had a daily newspaper and a great many pamphlets, especially in the wake of the discussions and elections prior to the meeting of the Estate General. The level of education was also relatively high. It has been estimated that 90 per cent of men and 80 per cent of women in Paris could read, compared with 71 per cent and 44 per cent in Northern France and far fewer in more remote provinces. Royal proclamations and decisions of *parlements* could be read by the 1780s and did not need to be shouted out by town criers, as had been usual practice in the earlier years of the century.

All these developments could be seen to have created a 'revolutionary city', but not all are especially convincing. It depends on what the public read. It also depends on explaining why hatred of the aristocracy was so much greater than in earlier years when class divisions had been more rigid.

In April 1789 an incident took place which has been seen as an indication that the city was ripe for revolution prior to the arrival of the deputies in May. It involved the destruction of the factories of the wallpaper manufacturer Réveillon, and the owner of a saltpetre works called Henriot. The repression of the riot as various groups from the Faubourg Saint-Antoine where the workshops were situated tried to cross into the wealthier area of Notre Dame have been seen as 'the first shots of the revolution'. What provoked these quite serious disturbances were rumours which spreads in the tight knot communities that Réveillon had said that workers could manage on 15 *sous* a day. This seemed to go against custom and provoked a big reaction which might have been more about the way that these manufacturers had changed traditional working practices. Both were self-made men who had brought together under one roof various elements of manufacture usually done in workshops or homes. They were hard employers, but they paid over the odds. Rumours of wage cuts may have been unacceptable to traditional tradesmen and workers at a time when bad harvests and high prices were causing concerns. Similar attacks were not uncommon on those whom the poorer communities suspected of exploitation such as bakers. This was unusual as it brought together people from different districts and got more out of hand. Some 3,000 people from the Faubourg Saint-Antoine took to the streets on 27 April and wanted to destroy Réveillon's house, but were dissuaded by some textile manufacturers from a hastily assembled body of middle-class electors and fifty *Gardes Françaises*, members of the main body of armed police in the capital. They did destroy Henriot's house. On 28 April they were joined by people from the

Saint Marcel district. The brewers, tanners, river workers, paper makers of this area, numbering perhaps 5,000, descended on Réveillon's house and factory, now guarded by the *Garde Française*. The crowd broke though, and he and his family were forced to seek shelter in the Bastille fortress. A substantial military force of the *Garde Française*, and some regular troops with cannon brought about a bloodbath, with perhaps several hundred killed and injured. In the aftermath there were some hangings, brandings and some ringleaders were sent to the galleys. The forces of law and order had remained loyal – important as the members of the *Garde Française* were not very different in social background from the rioters.

This incident which gets much less attention than other events of 1789 brought about a remarkable amount of bloodshed, but was not in itself revolutionary or political, though it obviously contributed to resentments and a sense of unrest in the communities of the Faubourgs which were later to play an influential role in the revolution. It may have also shaken the *Garde Française* and made them unwilling to repeat firing on crowds.

It was unfortunate that this incident took place at a time when there was more than usual excitement in the city with the anticipated calling of the Estates General and a rise in public meetings. There was also a forum for these in the extraordinary development of the *Palais Royale* by the Duke of Orleans. Anticipating today's development of shopping malls, this radical member of the cadet branch of the royal family developed the ancestral home in the centre of Paris into an area of shops, restaurants, a famous brothel, gaming houses, coffee houses and even an underground racetrack. In its arcades and public gardens, all classes mingled to do business and enjoy all sorts of pleasure. There was even a stock exchange for the convenience of investors and a chance for business discussions in cafes and restaurants. Conceived as a business venture, the *Palais Royale* was to take on the role of a focal point for political oratory. It attracted massive crowds of up to 10,000 and became a sort of centre to find out political news and developments. It has been described as 'a common meeting ground, a public space for those intent on debating the nation's woes'.

At the opposite moral end from an area which was a mixture of degeneracy and cultural enrichment were the many churches of Paris. Overwhelmingly Catholic and with a tradition of strong links between a privileged church and the monarchy, the religious population might have seemed a source of stability. But there was a strong vein of a religious belief called Jansenism among the capital's elite. This was close to Protestant ideas of the church being less an institution and more a gathering of true believers. This tended to weaken belief in traditional hierarchy and encourage a sense of community which some historians see as being akin to ideas of a community of the 'nation' as citizens, as opposed to a realm of subjects to 'the most catholic king'. It is, however, harder to find very specific evidence of Jansenism having this revolutionary effect. Once again, the tendency has been to search around eighteenth-century France with the benefit of hindsight, with any development in the period prior to 1789 being seen as a possible cause of revolution.

So, by May 1789 when the Estates General's deputies came from all over France to see, perhaps for the first time, they saw a massive city by eighteenth-century standards. Unlike the provincial towns they came from, they were able to see a city which in a modern term 'did not sleep' as it was lit by new oil lamps to illuminate a vibrant nightlife. Like many visitors, they might have been overwhelmed by the mixture of teeming areas of poverty, the great royal palace at Versailles where the sessions were to be held and the Palais Royale with its fabulous luxury shops, unusual social mixing, and its free discussions. They might have noticed, too, higher prices. But did they sense a capital that was ripe for revolution or the capital of a well-established and reforming monarchy? Did they see threatening lower classes or a city where the classes mixed in pursuit of pleasure and conspicuous consumption? Did they feel pressure from revolutionary ideas, or did they come confident that they would cooperate with an enlightened monarch in a national revival already partly begun by some reforming ministers? Did they fear the raging mobs of the Réveillon riots or feel secure in one of Europe's most effectively policed cities whose armed forces had suppressed popular disturbance and whose crime rate was among the lowest in Europe?

The Estates General: Who came to Paris in May 1789?

There were 604 deputies elected for the Third Estate. They were mainly well-educated, comfortably off lawyers, officials and landowners. The local areas who had chosen them wanted to be represented by substantial and articulate people who would convey the grievances discussed in the meetings and were able to meet their own travel expenses. They were, in later parlance, 'active citizens' – taxpayers with a stake in the settling of financial problems. The electors of the Third Estate even chose sixty nobles, the most famous being the highly articulate and ambitious Count Mirabeau. A good example of the choice of deputy was the father of the radical firebrand journalist and orator, Camille Desmoulins. The older Desmoulins was a royal official in the district of Guide in Picardy and an established figure in local administration.

He was able to send his son to a prestigious school in Paris where his friend was Maximilien Robespierre, who later had him executed.

A few biographies chosen at random reveal the type of people elected. Joseph-Ignace Guillotin was fifty-one when elected as one of the ten deputies for Paris. He had been a professor of literature at Bordeaux before training as a doctor. Famous for discrediting mesmerism (a form of hypnotism done with magnets, parodied in Mozart's opera *Così fan Tutte*) and for opposing capital punishment, he was well known as a physician and polemicist. It was he who suggested meeting in the Tennis Court for the famous Oath in June 1789 and the guillotine, though not his invention, bears his name.

Jean Brillat-Savarin was thirty-four when elected for Belley in Ain in Southeast France. He had studied law and medicine and became an eminent writer on gastronomy. A cheese is named after him. Antoine Barnave and his father were lawyers in Dauphiné. Antoine's mother was a minor aristocrat and he had won fame in Grenoble by supporting the exiled *Parlement de Paris* sent away for resisting royal reform plans. He helped lead the so-called 'Day of Tiles', a demonstration in favour of the exiled parlement, in which the tiles were thrown from the rooftops on 17 June 1788. He wrote political pamphlets calling for a national assembly and went on to be a leading politician.

There were only two peasant deputies, both from Brittany. This was hardly a social advance on 1614. These bulk of these well-educated talented deputies were confident, independent urban dwellers and well-thought-of local figures and would hardly behave in a deferential way, but they had no mandate for regime change or revolution. Many had taken part in local debates about the way the Estates General should vote and most expected that Louis XVI and his ministers would adopt voting by head so that their recommendations for reform would not be blocked by the votes of the other two orders.

The nobles had 278 deputies to represent the Second Estate. Many were well-known local figures, and many held military rank. It would be a mistake to think that they were there to defend privilege and block reform. A few profiles, again chosen at random, reveal people of a profile not very different from the Third Estate. The Comte de Volney, forty-two when elected, was a classical scholar, linguist and historian who had travelled in Egypt and Syria researching archaeological remains. Armand-Louis de Gontaut, forty-two when chosen as a deputy by his fellow nobles, was a professional soldier whose father was the very high-born Duc de Biron. He had fought in the War of American Independence and had liberal views, attaching himself to the radical Duke of Orleans. The Marquis de Saint-Just was a forty-four-year-old *seigneur* with estates outside Paris but was also a lawyer and had taken a leading role in the opposition of the *Parlement de Paris* in 1788 to the government. He had written advocating a constitutional monarchy. Henri-François, Marquis d'Arguesseau, was a senior lawyer called Advocate General appearing before the *Parlement de Paris*. Aged forty-seven in 1789, he was a leading intellectual and member of the *Académie Française*, the prestigious official body of French scholars and academics, and had written about money, theology and metaphysics. The idea that the Deputies of the Second Estate were boorish oppressors of the poor, anxious to defend privilege at all costs is not really true. They had already expressed willingness to sacrifice their tax privileges, but they were not as happy with the idea of voting by head rather than order. This might have opened the way to all sorts of changes, and they preferred to keep their power of veto. This should not mark them out as reactionary. The whole experience of a body representing the nation was new, and many in the Second Estate felt that voting by order was part of 'the long existing constitution' – a view supported by a declaration of the Royal Council in December 1788 on the arrangements for the Estates General. However, this does not mean that they would have opposed change, but the muddles and delays when the Estates General met meant that this was never really put to the test.

The First Estate consisted of 330 clergy, most of which – some 75 per cent – were not from the grand princes of the church and wealthy aristocratic leaders but from lower clergy. Only 46 out of France's 176 Bishops attended. The official government policy was to encourage this balance to prevent opposition from the grander and wealthier clerics to more equal tax burdens. The lower clergy were more willing, when it came to it, to ally with the Third Estate. Among the clergy who came to Paris was the Abbé Gregoire, a tailor's son from Lunéville. He became a parish priest in 1782 and devoted his spare hours to writing about history and philosophy. His fellow clerics elected him as deputy for Nancy at the age of 39, and he took a leading part in joining the Third Estate and establishing the National Assembly. Not everybody was a reformer, of course. The well-born bishop of Rouen, a member of the aristocratic de la Rochefoucauld family had little sympathy with reform and had to be ordered directly by the king to join with the Third Estate and later fled revolutionary France. However, it would be a mistake to think that the first two orders were opposed to change and that the Third Estate had revolutionary intentions.

Theoretically, there were 1,200 deputies when the Estates General met in May 1789 but only 800 had actually been elected by that time – the process of election and verification of credentials was complex, and many areas were not represented in the vital period between May and June. It is obvious that the deputies were not representative of 'France', their regions or even their class. The election of Honoré Gabriel Riqueti, Comte de Mirabeau, might seem to say a lot about this. He was chosen by the Third Estate of Aix and Marseilles even though a noble. His background was dubious – he was heavily in debt and had a chequered past, at one time sentenced to death for abduction. However, he presented himself as a well-born and well-informed radical able to express modern reformist enlightenment ideas in brilliant oratory. Mirabeau was to become a leading figure but could not be seen as representative of his class or his region. The lack of peasant deputies and the relative lack of industrialists and entrepreneurs too was unrepresentative and skewed representation of those who did not actually produce anything that France depended on economically, but were rather lawyers, officials and intellectuals. It is worth stating again that well over 20 million of France's 28 million people were rural dwellers and were hardly included. If women are taken into account, the Estates General seems even less representative. Even among nobles and clergy, the deputies who were confident, educated, opinionated and intellectually self-assured made the task of managing them formidable. The years of experience that English rulers had acquired in managing obstreperous and wealthy parliamentarians by a mixture of persuasion and bribery had no parallel in France. Ministers had to respond to problems on the hoof, as the next section shows. They lost control because they had no previous skills or experience of managing elected assemblies to fall back on. The parliamentary dark arts of eighteenth-century English statesmen like Walpole or the Duke of Newcastle, carefully handing our pensions and sinecures to MPs and managing elections in order to control parliament were unknown. The mixture of honest reforms and management of favours that kept the English prime minister Pitt in office for years after 1783 was not in the toolkit of Louis XVI's ministers.

The Royal Government

The third element is the king and his ministers. The starting point for the developments of 1789 might be the decision in 1786 to solve financial problems by going outside normal government and calling a special body which last met in 1626 – the Assembly of Notables. Louis accepted the advice of his finance minister for Comptrolleur general des finances Calonne – surely an assembly of princes, elite officials, purebred nobles and representatives from regional assemblies – the great and the good would see sweet reason and accept a new land tax which would apply to all. When they did not, without greater consultation the Assembly failed and Calonne was dismissed. Its failure might have shown the government that another such delve into the past was also likely to fail, but the lesson was not learnt.

The failure by April 1787 led to the appointment of one of the critical Assembly, the Cardinal Archbishop de Brienne. Getting nowhere with the Assembly, he had to turn to the usual method and ask the *Parlement de Paris* to register the royal will and to agree to a reform package. They were compliant with civil rights for Protestants and freeing the trade in grain, but not about reforming taxation and reducing privilege. Brienne and the king exiled them to the provincial city of Troyes. By then, the shortage of money was beginning to hit home. When Prussian forces invaded the Dutch Republic to overthrow a reforming government which Prussia feared would be revolutionary, France was unable to take action to prevent Prussian interference on its borders. This was humiliating as the new Dutch Patriot party was pro-French and Prussia, traditionally pro-British, was dominating a key area of strategic and economic interest.

With investor confidence falling, the *Parlement de Paris* was recalled on 19 November 1787, and a promise was made to call an Estates General in 1792. When criticism continued, led by the Duke of Orléans, a hard line was taken. Troops surrounded the Palais Royal to arrest two leading critics; the *Parlement* was exiled, and plans were made in May 1788 by Brienne and a minister called Lamoignon to permanently downgrade the *Parlement* by a new body to register royal edicts. These events do not show the king and his ministers as quite such passive and weak observers of decline as is sometimes implied by some textbook narratives. However, the resources of the French state did not permit totally authoritarian behaviour and a measure of consensus with the elite classes was important. Instability, too, was affecting government ability to borrow. As protests grew, the hard-line softened.

There was a wave of protests and sympathy for the magistrates and violence broke out in Grenoble in June in the so-called Day of Tiles. This affected credit and in August 1788 the ministers resigned. Necker was called as a minister likely to restore investor confidence and the *Parlement* was recalled. They demanded an Estates General, but this time very specifically based on the model of 1614 when it had last met, and Necker announced that it would meet earlier than the previously proposed date. The trouble was that problems had been kicked down the road. Once again, present difficulties were delegated to a historical body even though that had not worked with the Assembly of Notables.

The Events of the Year 1789

In the uproar and talk of a feudal reaction, with nobles and clergy likely to dominate the revived Estates General, the government compromised and announced that though voting would be by order not head, the representation of the Third Estate would be doubled to 600. But even with this concession, the whole idea of a body which had been most active in the sixteenth century having validity in an age which considered itself modern and enlightened bordered on the absurd.

While the *cahiers* were being drawn up and the whole nation was contributing its ideas on a reform agenda and electing deputies, Paris saw the most serious rioting since the 1720s in the Révelllion unrest. It was unfortunate that 1788 had seen bad harvests and rising prices and that there was obvious unrest in the capital when the 800 or so deputies met at the royal palace at Versailles on 1 May. A rambling introductory speech by Necker did not give way on the issue of voting by order. This remarkable experiment in consultation got off to a bad start. Leadership by the king and his ministers was lacking. There was no coherent plan, no discussion of grievances, no sense of forward movement. Instead, things congealed into a long process of verifying the credentials of deputies and an impasse on the issue of voting.

Because of this vacuum, the initiative passed to the Third Estate, and while Paris seethed with excitement and frustration and ministers lost valuable time, the deputies took the momentous decision on 17 June to remodel itself not as a royal advisory body based on an early modern model of class distinctions, but to represent the nation as a National Assembly. This was done without royal approval and in the name of 'the nation'. Some members of the other estates joined this assembly and when it was locked out of its meeting hall as it was shut to allow carpentry to be undertaken, they moved into a nearby Tennis Court. This was akin to a large squash court in which 'real', or 'royal' tennis was played in an enclosed space in a large high room with a gallery running around it. The representatives swore an oath on 20 June not to disband until France had a new constitution. This rather theatrical event might seem to have been quite old-fashioned and melodramatic. Oaths like this are not usually part of sophisticated modern politics any more than reviving ancient consultative bodies. It represented a major change in national politics and was the first sign that 1789 was going to be a very special year.

There now followed some bewildering U-turns from the authorities. On 23 June the king agreed on a new united assembly voting by head and ordered remaining nobles and clergy to join it. But there followed an even more dramatic change. Necker and liberal ministers were sacked, and troops ordered to concentrate around the city – potentially for a rerun of the dismissal of the *Parlement* in 1788.

Rapid developments now took place as crowds gathered in the *Palais Royale*. The loyalty of the *Garde Française* was uncertain. The April riots had unnerved some of them and they did not wish to be firing again on their fellow Parisians. A new citizens' armed force was formed to protect property and a new body created by the electors who had chosen the Estates General, the Commune, to maintain order in Paris. Rumours abounded and there were feverish searches for arms for the citizens to defend the capital against the troops. The search for arms led Parisians to the Bastille fortress and on 14 July the famous 'storming' took place with the highly significant killings of the governor and other officials. Crowds and unrest were not new, but this time there was no official suppression and members of the police force and of the citizens' militia took part.

The king and his ministers gave way. Necker was recalled to office. Unlike the Réveillon riots, there was no attempt to crush the disorders or punish the killers. The government had lost control of the capital, and in the countryside, there was mass unrest caused by rumours of attacks on local people. This so-called 'Great Fear' *(Grande Peur)* ran parallel to similar fear-driven popular unrest in the capital and unrest spread to other urban centres. The National Assembly became the National Constitutional Assembly with a view of bringing about the reforms listed in the *cahiers* and effecting a constitutional monarchy in which power would be shared between the king and an elected assembly. News of the large-scale rural unrest, with chateaux and tax offices attacked and customs barriers destroyed, led to a somewhat hysterical declaration in the newly-named Assembly on 4 August 1789 ending feudalism, and a more general and high-sounding Declaration of the Rights of Man was drawn up.

The events of 1789 had moved in a bewilderingly rapid way. On 1 May there was a meeting of a traditionally constituted historic body which had met by order of the king to advise on key changes necessary to strengthen the monarchical regime. The royal government still had control of armed forces and had the loyalty of the great majority of France. Three months later the king had failed to control urban disorder and some of his loyal officials had been slaughtered and their heads displayed on poles. The control of Paris had slipped out of his hands into a new body not ordered by him. The monopoly of the state in controlling armed forces had ended with the formation of a citizen militia the National Guard. Large areas of the countryside had got out of control and manorial and public records had been destroyed. In theory at least, the social system which supported the monarchy was destroyed and feudal rights, not very much featured in the *cahiers*, had been abolished. Even the restricted censorship that existed before 1789 had ended, and open discussion of all sorts of political theories and choices were being held with new political clubs being set up. Power had not passed totally from the king, but a rival source had been established in the National and then the Constitutional Assembly with a new political vocabulary based on talk of 'the nation' or 'the people'. Instead of 'constitution' meaning traditional monarchy supported by historic institutions, it meant a monarchy in which power was shared with a permanent elected assembly – not an *ad hoc* royal council. The principle of taxation being dependent on consent by a body elected by 'active citizens' who paid taxes had become established very quickly. The ending of the voting by order had taken away any restrictions on the possible changes and reforms to be put forward and passed as law, resulting in the theoretical overthrow of time-honoured rights and privileges in the countryside. However, by the end of August 1789, there was little suggestion of a Republic. The king himself had summoned new bodies to help resolve the financial crisis and so the new Assemblies could be seen as a continuation of that. The monarchy had espoused reform and encouraged the nation to set out its grievances and if they were being met by changes in feudalism then that too was a continuation of a process set in motion before 1789. The control of the army was still maintained by the king. Foreign policy, too, was in royal hands. The changes were not condemned by many abroad as revolutionary. England, for instance, had had a series of reforms undertaken by a conservative reformer, William Pitt, with the support of a king of no great ability, George III. Other monarchies in Europe had had to make changes. Agrarian unrest was not new, and Paris had seen unrest at various times in the eighteenth century. High prices and bad harvests, too, were nothing new either in France or in other European countries. Viewed in terms of later developments the events of the summer of 1789 were 'revolutionary' but viewed from the perspective of developments before 1789 they could be seen as less so. It is notable that many foreign observers saw France being strengthened by the changes of 1789 rather than being thrown into chaos.

* * *

This amount of change in a few weeks took everyone by surprise. It was almost impossible for contemporaries to process what was happening – 1789 was a year of political drama and understanding and memory of it are dominated by a series of operatic-type events often captured in paintings and prints.

The Storming of the Bastille became and still is seen as the defining moment when revolt became revolution, and the popular element took centre stage. The dramatic declamations that ended feudalism on 4 August 1789 following the revolution had spread to the countryside is another event where passionate speeches marked the end of the old world in France. Finally, the entry of women into the political dramas with the October days forced the king into the heart of Paris and revealed the depths to which the monarch had fallen.

Do these events really deserve the high level of importance given to them and is the image consistent with the evidence of what happened? Or did myths around them serve such a useful purpose that reality was distorted? The common idea is that the Oath of the Tennis Court was the start of the revolution. Subsequently, it was seen as so important that a large painting of the events of 20 June was commissioned from the great artist David. It was left unfinished, but that somehow adds to its heroic power. All is drama and spontaneity with images of national unity, the winds of change blowing in, attitudes being struck. An alternative version produced later is somewhat more prosaic. Both were circulated widely as prints, but David established the image for posterity of a moment of huge significance. The very fact of a solemn oath seemed redolent of an heroic classical past – like the Oath of the Horatii, the painting that was one of David's great revolutionary hits. There were 576 out of 577 deputies who took the oath. The one refuser – Martin d'Auch – is still shown in the picture to make the point that deputies acted freely and could have refused. The oath to stay together until France had a constitution did seem to be a radical step, but the sudden spontaneous demonstration of a desire for change was not quite accurate.

The deputies had already sworn an oath when they declared that they were a National Assembly on 17 June 1789. They pledged themselves to fulfil with zeal and fidelity the duties which devolved on them. But nobody painted this important expression of common responsibility and purpose. Then came the events of 20 June. The king wanted to bring all three estates together for a royal session to present a reform programme, but the hall used by the Third Estate or National Assembly in the Palace of Versailles needs to be adapted for a larger gathering. Carpenters were busy on 20 June and the self-styled Assembly could not gain access. This rather prosaic reason for exclusion was seen more as a deliberate slight and attempt to exclude and control the Third Estate. They thus went into a nearby Tennis Court and passed resolutions that the Assembly 'regarding itself as called on to establish the Constitution of the kingdom, a regeneration of the state and to maintain the true principles of monarchy' should not be prevented from continuing its deliberations. Wherever the members assembled there was the national assembly – it was not confined to a particular meeting place in the royal palace.

The vigour of David's painting might suggest a sudden reaction to a humiliation, but the idea of a constitution and the idea that the Estates General would not be a one-off, but a regular part of the state had already been discussed and partially accepted. It did not arise suddenly on 20 June. The *parlements* had referred to a constitution often in the eighteenth century and there was a well-established view that there was a constitution which marked France out from being a tyranny. Some of the *cahiers* had included demands that there should be regular meetings of the Estates General. Even the letter of summons from the king referred somewhat vaguely to establishing 'a constant and invariable order in the various parts of the government' and Necker seems to have thought that the Estates General would form a regular part of the government. The electors of Paris included a more specific requirement for their deputies to demand three yearly meetings and included in their *cahier* the principle of no taxation being granted without the approval of the nation through the Estates General.

When it came to it, the oath did make very specific what the mission of the National Assembly was going to be, but it was rooted in some long-term ideas and some shorter-term assumptions about the Estates General not being simply a unique event. Even looking back at history, the body had met on various occasions since the late Middle Ages and there had been demands for it to be a regular body in earlier times.

David's image suggests a unity that had unravelled by the time his painting was shown. It is a well-known irony that the heroic revolutionary figures of 20 June did not all survive the changes they so ardently wished for. Bailly, the mayor of Paris from July 1789, is the central figure administering the oath. His troops fired on the crowds to suppress demonstrations in 1791 and he was eventually arrested in 1792 and executed by more radical revolutionaries in 1793. The same fate befell the influential Antoine Barnave, prominent in the picture. The figure at the centre in monks' robes, Dom Christophe Geule, changed to become an opponent of change after the nationalisation of the church in 1790. The dramatically posed figure of the Comte de Mirabeau was later revealed to have been a paid agent of the queen after his death in 1791. The Revolution took a heavy toll on these statuesquely depicted lovers of liberty.

The event which more than any other, however, is associated with 1789 is the Storming of the Bastille. What more can be said about this episode? For the French left it was a triumph for the workers. Jean Jaurès, the socialist leader assassinated on the eve of the First World War in 1914, wrote about the incident in the light of his belief in Marxism. His use of 'proletariat' i.e. industrial working class in the context of 1789 where they hardly existed is particularly unhistorical.

> the proletariat was able, by the daring ladder of events, to climb for a moment to the leadership of the bourgeois revolution – or at least participate in it alongside the most daring bourgeois – was for it a title and a promise for the future. And so it is that we have without any difficulty glimpsed countless workers among the enormous mass that on 14 July first invested the Invalides and then the Bastille.[1]

For conservative historians, following the lead of Hippolyte Taine's history of the Revolution in 1876, it was a disreputable mob of *'canaille'* – the scum of the Paris slums. Out of control mobs feature in many fictional and film accounts.

It is here that problems of terminology look large. Were the people who attacked the Bastille 'proletarians', a 'mob', 'a crowd', 'patriots', 'rabble' 'lower orders' or 'the people'?

A modern consensus might be that, following fears that the king might seek to end the progress of change and disband the National Assembly by force, there was a frenzied search for arms to defend Paris. During the course of this, gatherings of people in Paris, mostly from the poorer districts, attacked possible sources of weapons. The first target was the Invalides Hospital which yielded a large stache of muskets. But in search of gunpowder, which was stored in the Bastille, the crowd also attacked a symbol of royal power, as this was a state prison and also a symbol of tyranny. There was some confusion as a new body had taken over the running of Paris and a new militia had been formed, the National Guard, to protect property after disturbances since 12 July when customs posts had been burnt. Negotiations for the surrender of the gunpowder and the Bastille fortress itself which was defended by cannon and by a relatively small force of retired soldiers and Swiss mercenaries went wrong. The garrison fired on crowds trying to break in, but the balance was turned by the arrival of members of the *Garde Française* sympathetic to the crowds. The governor, the Marquis de Launay, eventually surrendered when cannon were brought up against the fortress, but in the aftermath, revenge was taken on him and some of his men and also on the chief official of the old

Paris municipality. The Assembly members went on to meet the crowds; the king abandoned any attempt to use force; the attackers of the Bastille became especially honoured as Conquerors or *'vainquers'*; the events of the day became the subject of myth and, despite the deaths, the 'fall' of the Bastille was seen as an end of the old regime and 'tyranny'. The fortress was dismantled, and the 14 July celebrated until the present as a triumph of the forces of liberty.

Unpacking some of this is quite a complicated business. The Bastille was situated in the heart of some of the least prosperous and most restless districts, and its cannon, situated on the extensive ramparts might have been seen as a threat to the Paris people and a means of control. In the eighteenth century, best-selling accounts of being imprisoned in the mediaeval fortress had painted a picture of vile dungeons, oubliettes, tiny cells in the wall, inhuman conditions and guiltless prisoners held through *lettres de cachet*, orders obtained by enemies or hostile family members. Charles Dickens depicts such a prisoner in his novel '*A Tale of Two Cities*'. It was a state prison and so could be seen as emblematic of royal power. Because of the reputation for cruelty, there was an association between monarchy and sadistic repression. In fact, a lot of the writing about sufferings in the Bastille were fictitious. The most widely read account was by a convicted confidence trickster, unjustly seen as a hero and victim of tyranny when he was set free. The fortress had long ceased to have any meaningful function by July 1789 and held only a handful of prisoners and a small garrison. Nobody had got around to decommissioning it but there had been talk of demolishing it. The governor, the Marquis de Launay, was an ageing incompetent and most of the garrison were retired troops. There were no contingency plans to use it as a means of repression, and gunpowder had been stored there not on the orders of the king but of the Paris municipal council, fearful of it falling into the wrong hands and blowing up large areas of the city. Famously, there were seven prisoners, all housed in the towers, not the dungeons. There were two who were mentally unstable and delusional, some forgers. The famous prisoner, the Marquis de Sade, whose pornographic writings gave the world the term 'sadism', had been moved to an asylum. One 'prisoner' whom the attackers claimed to have rescued from tyrannous incarceration did not exist and was entirely invented, a creature of rumour.

However, the point is not the reality of the fortress as a symbol of tyranny but how it was seen. It had not played any part in the Réveillon disturbances and most of the writings about it by those who took part were after 14 July, proud of their assault on tyranny. The overwhelming motive for entering the

Bastille on 14 July was to gain access to the gunpowder stored there. To understand this a sequence of events needs to be explained.

The declaration of a National Assembly on 17 June and the subsequent oath produced a hostile reaction from the government with troops deployed around the meeting place of the Assembly, now unlocked. But there was some doubt about their loyalty and as some nobles and clergy joined the new Assembly, the king gave way on 27 June and accepted a future constitution.

However, there were doubts and uncertainties. There had been a mood of excitement in the capital since the meetings and elections prior to the Estates General. There was a wave of journalism which had become increasingly radical such as the paper *L'Ami du Peuple* (The People's Friend) produced by a doctor and political journalist Jean-Paul Marat. The *Palais Royale* was a no-go area for the authorities where all sorts of meetings and discussions took place. But behind all this was the fear of a royalist reaction, now stirred by the news that provincial troops had been ordered to the capital and the sight of royal forces on the Champs de Mars (now the site of the Eifel Tower). There were foreign mercenaries in the capital and the king refused a request by the Assembly to withdraw them on 8 July. The turning point was the removal of Necker as chief minister, popular as a known reformer and the appointment of the Baron de Breteuil on 11 July. This stirred up agitation in the Palais Royale. One of the orators, Camille Desmoulins, made a speech saying that the cannon at the Bastille would be turned on the Faubourg Saint Antoine, a densely populated area of small workshops and tenements notable for unrest. Fearing the arrival of troops, rumours of plots led by the king's brother and an onslaught by the commander of the royal troops, Marshal de Broglie, spread rapidly. As crowds gathered, worst fears seemed to be realised when some loyal troops fired on a crowd in the Tuileries gardens.

Because communities were close-knit, larger numbers of people from the poorer districts in the south and east of the city now took part in a communal rampage. Forty out of fifty-four customs houses were destroyed. The rich monastery of St Lazare to the Northwest of the city was ransacked. Gunsmiths were raided in a furious attempt to find arms.

This was itself a sign of panic. Eighteenth-century muskets were not like modern weapons and needed a fair amount of training and expertise to load, prime and fire. Even then they were fairly useless unless massed in the hands of experienced soldiers. But rational calculations had gone out of the window during the night of 12 July. To have a musket was to be armed against imagined menace, regardless of whether it was actually useful.

The Events of the Year 1789

Seeing the destruction which was not met by the usual deployment of *Gardes Françaises*, the middle-class electors formed an emergency committee on 13 July led by an experienced official with the title the *Prevôt des Marchands* ('Mayor' might be an equivalent translation), a businessman called Jacques de Flesselles. The electors raised a militia to protect property, which was the basis of a new National Guard. There was a huge demand for arms by those who had taken to the streets.

On 14 July a crowd assembled at the Hôtel des Invalides, a sort of military facility comparable to London's Chelsea Hospital, and its commander allowed them to seize a quantity of muskets being stored there – perhaps 28,000 or perhaps 40,000 as accounts vary, but there was no gunpowder and no shot. As the rumour spread that gunpowder had been moved to the Bastille, the fortress was the obvious next step. To prevent further agitation. the city electors (those citizens chosen to make the final choice of deputies for the Estates General) asked the governor de Launay to surrender the fortress in the same way that his colleague had allowed the crowd into the Invalides. All was quite civilised, and the representatives took lunch with the governor. But no deal was reached. Next, a local lawyer Thuriot tried. He was shown that the cannon were not loaded and had been withdrawn from the battlements, but de Launay refused to hand over the gunpowder.

All this played into the paranoia of the crowd. Had de Launay simply given up the gunpowder then the crowd would have got the largely useless arms and been ready to blow their fingers, arms and possibly faces off in trying to master not very effective weapons. The crowd pressed into the first courtyard and de Launay ordered his 'home guard' of retired soldiers and some professional troops to fire. They also got off a single cannon shot. This was around 1.30 pm. At 2.00 pm the crowds around the City Hall started to go to the Bastille. A poorly armed mass of people could not have taken a great fortress defended by professional soldiers, but they were joined by disloyal troops from the *Garde Française* led by two former officers, Hulin and Elie. Somehow, these men found some seventy soldiers and five cannon and made more effective inroads into the Bastille's defences. De Launay threatened to blow up the entire fortress with the stock of gunpowder, but his men saw sense and forced him to give up at 5.00 pm.

The Bastille was not exactly 'stormed'. The ill-armed crowd had suffered the fate of their predecessors during the Réveillon riots and a hundred were killed and seventy wounded. The arrival of some trained military personnel and cannon changed the whole situation as did the increasing reluctance of the defenders to take on what must have seemed the whole of Paris.

The seven prisoners were freed. The gunpowder seized. Then some horrifying violence took place which still makes the celebration of this event somewhat incongruous. De Launay was bayoneted in the stomach, stabbed repeatedly and shot in the head. A young man called Dénot hacked off his head with a kitchen knife. The head was paraded on a pike until later in the day it was merely thrown away. The second in command suffered a similar fate while several other officers were throttled to death. An angry crowd accused the Prevôt Flesselles of withholding arms from the people. As he came out of the Hôtel de Ville he was shot and decapitated. The veteran who had persuaded Launay from blowing up the Bastille was mistaken for someone else, had his hand cut off and hanged. Though these acts of violence were the product of the heat of the moment, they were continued a week later with the capture of the Comptroller General, an official called Foullon who had replaced Necker. Accused of comparing the rioters with horses who should eat grass he was strung up on the Place de Grève, given vinegar to drink and slashed with nettles, cut down and decapitated and his mouth stuffed with hay. His son-in-law Bethier de Sauvigny was forced to kiss the head, then lynched from a lamppost.

On 15 July after announcing the withdrawal of the troops from the capital, Louis XVI was handed the keys of the city by the new mayor, Bailly, and handed a new symbol for his hat – the red, white and blue cockade – the colours of the city of Paris were added to the white of the flag of the Bourbon royal family. The *tricolor* had become a new revolutionary symbol and of course, remains the flag of France,

The crowds had achieved this 'victory' for an Assembly which barely represented them. The principal aim was to gain arms to prevent royal forces taking control. When they were successful, as at the Invalides, they seemed not to want to do more than gain gunpowder for their muskets; but as they met resistance, the tempo upped and the Bastille itself, and later its defenders became the target. Later and in retrospect, it became a symbol of tyranny and was utterly dismantled, anticipating an action which would probably have been taken by the *ancien régime*. Crowds had swarmed round the fortress and eventually invaded it but they themselves proved powerless to do much storming. They were more adept at vengeance and murder as well as destroying unpopular customs posts and raiding for food. None of this seems to accord with the heroic view of the 'people'.

So, if it seems rather less than heroic action against tyranny, is it the terrible and depraved action of a 'mob', just a 'riot'? 'Mob' is a word that features quite a lot in histories or references to the Revolution and how it is portrayed.

The historian Taine called the *Vainquers* of the Bastille 'the lowest social scum, the dregs of society, vagabonds, beggars, criminals, armed like savages'. And so they appear as extras in films and in unguarded moments in academic histories where 'mob' is used. Was the crowd a sort of uncontrollable riff-raff? Historian Francois Furet[2] described 'the mob' gaining control of the Invalides but then having the rather un-mob-like ambition to destroy a tyrannous anachronism in the Bastille. Were they rampaging lower orders or harbingers of liberty? French socialist historian Eric Hazan[3] sees it as 'a shining point on the trajectory of the Paris insurrection' culminating in the overthrow of the monarchy and the revolutionary Terror – not 'good' action which led to 'bad' consequences. He rejects the glory of 1789 as being a contrast to the horrors of massacres and guillotining later on. And this is realistic. The violence was never disowned and came to be a characteristic of the revolution. For Hazan, however, this was all to the good. The violence of 1789 and the later terror were for him entirely justified and admirable. For many more conservative writers, it just set the period of change off to a bad start from which it never recovered. He calls the participants 'artisans' perhaps eager not to use a disparaging term.

Perhaps it is just difficult to find the right word. 'Crowd' seems rather bland for lynchers and beheaders; 'the people' seems to encompass a rather wider cross-section than those who were so active on the Paris streets. 'The poor' would not be entirely accurate as even though prices were rising, not all of the 'Vainquers' were poverty-stricken. 'The denizens of the Faubourg Saint-Antoine' is sometimes used, but not all came from this notorious district, and it would have been surprising if those who lived close to the Bastille were not involved, but it was a much wider group who took part in the tumults (or striving for freedom, if you prefer) of 12–14 July,

Unusually for this sort of event, quite detailed records were kept of who was there, and many accounts by individuals of why they joined in were produced. These records are incomplete and flawed. Women were largely excluded, for instance, though they were definitely there, and one young woman, mistaken for De Launay's daughter, was nearly burnt to death in an effort to make him surrender. As it was later rather prestigious to be a 'conqueror' there were some false claims and embellished motives. However, there is a consensus among those who have sifted through the records that the biggest group involved in the Bastille incident were cabinet makers and joiners, a speciality of the Saint-Antione district, and also locksmiths and boot and shoemakers and other independent craftsmen. Not rootless beggars but respectable tradesmen and employers of journeymen and apprentices took to the streets. And not young firebrands, but people with an average age of thirty-four. Few had criminal convictions, and most were literate. Not all of the violence and agitation took place in the districts of St Antoine and St Marcel but in the Place de Grève, around the Palais Royale and at the St Lazare monastery and around the unpopular customs wall. The area of highest poverty in the southeast of the city called the Gobelins was not the area from which most of the Bastille attackers came. Ragged, poverty-stricken, ignorant and toothless 'mobs' and 'rioters' are the myth, not the reality. Though the respectable tradesmen were capable of acting quite brutally. But even here it has been suggested that they were following traditions of retributive justice. The French state before the abolition of torture had inflicted particularly brutal punishments and executions. This same treatment was meted out to the victims of Bastille Day in a throwback to group justice. A similar phenomenon was seen in the countryside in the summer of 1789 when a 'great fear' of 'aristos' and landlords coming to massacre peasants led to attacks on chateaux and tax offices.

So why did these 'respectable' people, with certainly more to lose than criminals or tramps, risk their lives and seek to arm themselves with weapons they could probably not use safely to save rich elites trying to set up a constitutional monarchy in which only substantial taxpayers would vote?

Some left memoirs and interestingly these included a wine merchant, a grocer, craftsmen and a brewer. One of the more famous was a clockmaker's apprentice called Humbert. He had gone along with others in his district to patrol the streets to prevent a counter-revolution. Armed only with swords, they heard that weapons were being given out at the city hall. But there was no shot (ammunition) so he stopped off to buy some small nails (which surely would have exploded in his face) and then heard there was shot at the Bastille. He was among the first to try to enter the fortress but does not write of any particular political motivation or of seeing the fortress as a symbol. This is more evident in the outpourings of a clerk called Parein who wrote a play about the events. However, it is unlikely he took much of a part in the assault. Dénot, an unemployed kitchen assistant who used his kitchen knife to kill and decapitate de Launay told an enquiry that he was bored at home and saw a crowd on its way to the Bastille to see what was happening. An account by a disgraced seminarian La Reynie de la Bruyère, a sex offender, claims that he was influenced by the writings of the philosophers and wanted to overthrow tyranny. However, all these reminiscences are of dubious value especially as some describe the rescue of a victim of a *lettre de cachet* called the Count de Lorgnes who had been imprisoned. for thirty-two years. However, this was entirely fictitious, and he never was in the Bastille. That so many 'conquerors' took to print to take advantage of the excitement suggests that the view of the radical journal *L'Ami di Peuple* edited by Jean-Paul Marat, later to become a leading revolutionary figure, that 'simple poor people' stormed the Bastille is quite questionable.

However, the whole incident drifted away from the realities of confused, suspicious artisans fruitlessly trying to attack an impregnable fortress until the arrival of trained armed forces and cannon and the unwillingness of the defenders to carry on fighting ended in surrender. Instead, there were heroes, a flood of prints and pamphlets, salutes to the purity and purpose of the people on saving the nation and a host of souvenirs from the demolished fortress akin to the bits of the Berlin Wall after 1989 which were sold to politically minded tourists.

The End of Feudalism

The acceptance by the king that military force could not stop change and that the National Assembly should draw up a new Constitution meant that the Assembly took on new powers. The events in the countryside in the summer of 1789 indicated that unrest was not to be confined to Paris and other urban centres. The outbreak of rural unrest called 'the Great Fear' showed a similar paranoia and fear that infected Paris, but with far less reason. Rumours of attacks by armed men in the service of landlords spread widely and resulted in irrational attacks on chateaux and record offices over a wide area of France. More redolent of medieval peasant disturbances or food riots than revolution, the reports of this unrest galvanised the Assembly into acts which have been seen as the end of feudalism in France, and a significant acceleration of the pace of change. The dramatic repudiations of privilege and feudal dues on 4 August 1789, and the Declaration of the Rights of Man seemed to be a culmination of the first phase of revolution, and the beginnings of change which affected a much wider cross-section of France's people.

After an emotional session, the Assembly passed a sweeping measure.

> The National Assembly hereby completely abolishes the feudal system. It decrees that, among the existing rights and dues, both feudal all those originating in or representing real or personal serfdom shall be abolished without indemnification. All other dues are declared redeemable, the terms and mode of redemption to be fixed by the National Assembly. Those of the said dues which are not extinguished by this decree shall continue to be collected until indemnification shall take place.

The speakers in the debate were often aristocrats themselves and they supported apparent social change, confirming the equal liability of all to taxes and the end of all privileges. The Duc d'Aiguillon is typical: 'In this enlightened century, we must prove to all citizens that our aspirations exceed their desires and establish equality of rights between all men'.

Later in August, a Declaration of the Rights of Man set out the underlying principles of society.

> The National Assembly doth recognize and declare, in the presence of the Supreme Being, and with the hope of his blessing and favour, the following sacred rights of men and of citizens: Men are born, and always continue, free and equal in respect of their rights. Civil distinctions, therefore, can be founded only on public utility. II. The end of all political associations, is the preservation of the natural and imprescriptible rights of man; and these rights are liberty, property, security, and resistance of oppression. III. The nation is essentially the source of all sovereignty; nor can any individual, or any body of men, be entitled to any authority which is not expressly derived from it.

The 'end of feudalism' was obviously influenced by peasant unrest, but it was not presented as a concession but part of a move towards a new society and celebrated, as with the fall of the Bastille, in gushing pamphlets and inspiring prints and memorabilia.

The peasants whose plight usually exercises the writers of textbooks explaining the revolution appear centre stage in the narrative in July–August 1789 and then often disappear. Despite ongoing rural disturbances in the 1790s, the peasantry passes out of the general run of narratives of revolution. The wisdom and idealism of this phase of the revolution in meeting rural grievances and ending feudalism are implicitly approved.

There are some problems with this view. Peasant disturbances which have been estimated as over 4,000 incidents began in 1788 and continued well into 1793. The later instances however are overshadowed in narratives by events in Paris. Another wave of peasant violence from February to April 1792 was on almost as big a scale as the more publicised 'Great Fear' of 1789. Attacks and disturbance remained high after August 1789, dipping only in 1791.

The key to explaining this may be the gap between the theoretical outpourings of August 1789 and the lack of practical impact of change in the countryside. The 'small print' of the discussions and legislation was the distinction between feudal obligations which had been imposed on the peasants and those which were contractual. This complicated legal distinction prevented the wholesale abolition of 'feudal' payments as tenants had to prove that in the distant past the landowners had imposed obligations until August 1792 when the burden of proof was put on landlords. The 4 August decree made it clear that the abolition of payments had to wait for legal claims – the lawyers in the assembly did not support wholesale abolition of legal rights and payments and so peasant frustrations continued. As late as the spring of 1792 the revolutionary Georges Couthon speaking in what had become the Legislative Assembly spoke of the changes of August 1789 giving 'nothing more to the people than a beautiful dream, whose deceitful illusion left nothing but regrets'.[4]

The principles of the revolution desired by the urban elite of 1789 were based on liberty, fraternity and equality which are the words most remembered but also 'property' which tends to fall into the background. Ending feudal rights, a form of property, had not featured very strongly in the *cahiers* and was hedged around in the rhetoric of 1789. What changed the approach was the war which broke out in April 1789. If French troops were to 'liberate' areas where feudalism still existed in neighbouring states then feudal dues and obligations clearly had to go; if they still existed in France because of long drawn-out legal cases and if there was still peasant violence and unrest, then there was an obvious problem.

The October Days

The last great tableau of 1789 is the 'October Days'. Following high prices and bread shortages in Paris in the autumn of 1789 and dismay at reports of royalist officers disrespecting the revolution and the revolutionary symbol of the red, white and blue cockade in a banquet given for Louis XVI, a procession of women with some of the usual crowds and National Guard went in the rain to Versailles, invaded the palace, demanded that the king act on the issue of food supplies and forced both the royal family and the Constituent Assembly to accompany them back to Paris. Though casualties were small, the significance of this development was considerable. It added to the humiliation of the king and the disrespect shown to him; it left both king and assembly subject to popular pressure in central Paris; it was hugely symbolic that the gap between the king and his subjects shown by government being in Versailles away from the centre of the capital had closed. It alarmed foreign powers and opened the way for further popular pressure on events. It is arguably the most important of the great revolutionary dramas of 1789 and has generally been seen as a turning point. However, the nature of the events and particularly the role of women, coming unusually centre stage in the Revolution is not all that it has been portrayed to be. The event is considered in the light of how women have been seen, and forms part of Chapter Six.

The Position at the End of 1789

The events of 1789 seem so tumultuous and dramatic that any attempt to question them might seem problematic. The whole process of having elections and drawing up grievances for a body whose role had not been firmly established was itself a dangerous move. That the elections produced a body of highly educated and independent-minded deputies unlikely to accept a purely advisory role in the recreation of a late medieval assembly made matters worse. The crisis was, to a large extent, self-inflicted but a product of a belief that change was needed. This was not really forced on the monarchy but once started, developed a momentum of its own. There was a widespread belief that a monarchy with more consultation and a fixed assembly would be stronger. The Oath of the Tennis Court was not an oath to abolish monarchy. It is not really the case that the Bastille was attacked as a symbol of monarchy and the Assembly offered the king its loyalty and the keys to the city. The changes made in 1789 such as the 'abolition of feudalism' were made not by radical firebrands but by reforming landowners and they were very aware of the need to preserve legal rights. The new Constituent Assembly was not aiming to establish a Republic and was less radical than the American colonies who deposed George III as their king. Before 1789 Louis had appointed reforming ministers, had consulted an Assembly of Notables and agreed to summon a nationally elected body. A constitutional monarchy in which a monarch and a highly intelligent and talented cross-section of the social elite worked together to effect the sort of changes coming about in other countries in the period was not a ridiculous idea. In effect, with the introduction of a potentially powerful president, the American colonists had instituted a sort of elected constitutional monarch. Britain managed a limited monarchy and had achieved huge economic success and naval power; its elites maintained effective social stability. However, it was not a common form of government in contemporary Europe, and even reforming monarchs had kept a very tight grip on power.

Moreover, this enlightened vision had some very severe limitations. Louis had not shown himself capable of understanding this possibility. The Estates General was poorly managed; his policies had swung between conciliation and repression and left dangerous uncertainty. His officials were inconsistent. The governor of the Invalides made realistic concessions to the crowds and avoided bloodshed; the governor of the Bastille provoked escalation and paid with his life. The emergence of more radical ideas was dangerous and more important the power of the people of Paris who were not part of the ruling elite had been demonstrated twice in a very serious way. The disturbances in the countryside added another destabilising element.

All depended now on whether the relatively new political and social path opened up by the events of 1789 could be followed in such a way as to bring stability, or whether it would lead France into a much darker future.

Notes

1. Jean Jaurès, *Histoire Socialiste de la Révolution Française* (Paris, 1901), www.marxists.org/archive/jaures/1901/history/bastille.htm.
2. Francois Furet, *Revolutionary France* (Blackwell, 1995).
3. Eric Hazan, *A People's History of the French Revolution* (Verso, 2012).
4. John Markoff, 'Violence, Emancipation and Democracy', in *The French Revolution, Rewriting Histories*, ed Gary Kates (Routledge, 1998), p. 183.

Chapter Four

The Constitutional Monarchy

The events of 1789 saw a remarkable change. The 'great and the good' of the French urban middle class, full of enthusiasm for change and in alliance with liberal clergy and nobles, created an assembly which claimed to represent 'the nation' and had begun to push forward reformers based on modern 'enlightened' ideas. There was no suggestion of abolishing the monarchy and setting up a republic, but rather that power should be shared between 'the nation' as they saw it and the monarch. The Estates General morphed into a National Assembly, far beyond a royal advisory body which in turn became a Constituent Assembly, self-charged with the task of establishing a new formal constitution for France. This did not appear finally until 1791 but the process of change went on from the autumn of 1789. The anticipated modern constitutional monarchy was short-lived. External war, crowd violence, unrest in the provinces, the rise of extreme leaders and political terror pushed the Revolution a long way from the hopes of most of the deputies of 1789.

The failure of the Constitutional Monarchy has been seen as a tragedy. Explanations have centred on what 'went wrong'. Often blame has been put on the king and the royalists who rejected the whole idea of power-sharing and wanted to return to 'tyranny'. Many accounts blame the rise of Republican 'extremists' who resorted to the support of 'mobs' and violence to achieve a more radical revolution and ended by killing not only the king but moderate reformers and even their own fellow radicals in an unprecedented and bloodthirsty 'terror'. Then there were 'counter revolutionaries' and hostile foreign powers whose opposition to change led to the revolutionary rulers having to resort to repression and centralisation, subverting the ideals of 1789. Inherent in the narrative of 'failure' is a view of the moderate reformers as essentially 'the good guys', the hope for a peaceful and prosperous future. However, even outside their enemies within France, not all contemporaries agreed that the reformers of 1789 were on the side of the angels.

The British politician and commentator Edmund Burke wrote a scathing condemnation of the Revolution in November 1790. Burke was not a reactionary and as a Whig MP supported reform. His view, however, was that by attempting to rule by 'extravagant theory' and condemning everything in the past, France had been led into a calamity. In an interesting analysis[1] he argued that the French had rebelled against a mild and lawful monarch 'with more fury, outrage and insult' than any other people had risen against the most bloodthirsty tyrants. His analysis of those elected to the Estates General was that though there were 'shining talents', the deputies lacked practical experience in the state. He noticed the preponderance of lawyers, obscure provincial advocates, 'stewards of petty local jurisdictions', notaries and legal officials. As well as this were other professionals, such as doctors and financiers. He found these people to be inferior to the 'natural landed interest' that guided Britain. Rejecting key elements that had held society together such as religion, deference and respect for tradition and monarchy, these middle-class Enlightenment figures, unrepresentative and overly theoretical had set France on a ruinous course, politically and financially, and the likely outcome would be the overthrow of the revolution by a successful general – something that did occur in 1799, two years after Burke's death.

Burke's view was not widely shared. The developments in France in 1789 and 1790 seemed to many in England to be a move towards the constitutional monarchy which had emerged in Britain after the so-called 'Glorious Revolution' of 1688. The Catholic monarch James II (1685–8) had shown signs of wanting to be an absolute monarch and had alienated key members of the aristocratic and clerical elite. His sister Mary, a Protestant, was married to the ruler of the Netherlands, William of Orange, a bitter opponent of the powerful and absolute French monarch Louis XIV. An influential group of nobles asked for his help in ridding Britain of a potential tyrant. William, happy to get British help against Louis arrived with an armed force in 1688. James fled to Ireland where he was defeated in 1690 by Protestant forces at the Battle of the Boyne, lovingly remembered by Ulster loyalists. He then fled to France, unable to prevent William and Mary from being installed as monarchs. To avoid a repeat of a possible absolute monarch, there were guarantees of parliaments meeting every three years. Parliament would control the king by voting money. Parliament controlled the army by dint of having to pass an annual Mutiny Act making military discipline legal. The Act of Succession made being Protestant a requirement for being monarch. Thus, a form of constitutional monarchy was established.

Britain, then, because of its history and because of the strange mix of reform and conservatism would be a difficult model for any state moving from the sort of absolute monarchy that was the usual form of government in Europe in 1789 to a 'constitutional monarchy'.

The Constitutional Monarchy

The French legislators had to try and develop support for a mixed constitution of king and nation, to develop a respect for parliamentary forms with no tradition of elected assemblies. They had no aristocratic control of the countryside to rely on and they had to deal with widespread support for a Catholic Church which was linked to the throne. They also had to deal with popular feeling. This had manifested itself in a desire for retributive justice and direct action. The crowds in 1789 who had killed de Launay, had lynched bakers, had taken it into their own hands to insist that the king deal with food shortages, and had seized weapons to prevent a royal reaction. They were not going to be too interested in abstract debates about constitutional forms. There was also no desire on the part of the middle-class, educated, elites to hand power to the masses. In the countryside resentment against dues and exploitation continued during the period of political change and reform in 1790. The so-called counter-revolution was a traditional resentment against those in authority – now the revolutionary reforms and a reaction to interference with local matters, especially Catholicism.

Few now share Burke's idealisation of the 'organic' constitution of the eighteenth century or his belief in deference and the benevolence of the landed interest. However, in some ways his analysis was perceptive. The Third Estate, who made up the majority of the Estates General which developed into the National Assembly, then the Constituent Assembly and then the Legislative Assembly of the 1791 Constitution, was indeed from a narrow class and did ignore traditions. The middle class reformers were trying to create new political forms rapidly and relied on abstract ideas in a voyage of discovery towards a new type of state. They were also trying to manage an increasingly difficult series of national and international problems that had defeated people of a similar background who had been ministers under the old monarchy.

The eventual failure of the Constitutional monarchy has often been blamed not on the enlightened middle classes but on unreasonable radicalism from below, and a stubborn and unintelligent monarch. The 'blame game' is a strong feature of revolutionary history, whether directly or by implication. The narrative runs rather like this; an incompetent monarch presiding over an oppressive regime was forced by bankruptcy to share power but could not adjust to the realities of a new order. He failed to work to develop a constitutional regime. His old-fashioned views on religion and his own divine right, as being appointed by God to rule led to rifts. He never accepted loss of influence and he dreamed of restoring royal power. To that end, he first tried to flee France in July 1791, and then unwisely supported a war that would bring disruption and foreign invasion. Instead, the war brought a rise in radicalism and brought down the monarchy in 1792. He paid for his lack of understanding of what should have happened to ensure stability by his execution in January 1793.

On the other hand, the enlightened progress to rational reform and modernity was also undermined by the development of 'extreme' political ideas and radical groups who manipulated popular discontent. These dangerous radicals sought an end to traditional monarchy, religion and a new revolution by an idealised 'people'. A moderate balance between tradition and reform was not acceptable to these groups who formed a barrier to peaceful development and eventually plunged France into terror and violence on an unprecedented scale. The high ideals of the enlightened reforming middle class were undermined from both above and below.

* * *

The problem with the 'what went wrong?' approach is in the presumption that there was a time when something was unquestionably 'right'. There is also the tendency for the period between October 1789 and the end of the monarchy in 1792 to be neglected in general surveys. The perception of a failed monarchy and of a France suffering by 1789 is very strong so that Burke's view of 'a mild and lawful monarch' seems almost surprising. But on the other hand, the bad reputation of the 'extremists' is so engrained that attempts to defend their opposition to the middle classes who dominated the revolution from 1789 and whom Burke so despised seem to be eccentric or over-conservative.

The aims of the Constituent Assembly have seemed idealistic and redolent of modern democratic values. The classic text is the Declaration of the Rights of Man. Statements of inherent human rights have been part of the modern way of thinking in the West and a way of establishing what is just, even if it has not been possible to achieve them in the face of undemocratic and tyrannous regimes. Broadly, the statement in the American Declaration of Independence that all men are created equal and endowed by their creator with inalienable rights such as life, liberty and the pursuit of happiness has indeed, as Jefferson's declaration stated, been seen as self-evident truth. In this light, the French Assembly's sweeping away of feudal privileges, or at least condemning them seems very much the right thing to have done. Establishing a constitutional which offered representation by the nation and shared power has seemed admirable. Ending privilege, taking away noble titles, restricting the arbitrary power of the monarch, establishing a general liability for taxes and modernising local government by replacing old-fashioned provinces with modern 'departments' seems forward-thinking. The steady stream of reforms carried out in the aftermath of the events of June and July 1789 puts the Enlightened and progressive idealism pretty much at the centre of the moderate changes brought about by the early Revolution. Burke's view of interfering and over-ambitious lawyers and professionals, remote from reality seemed, and may still seem, unjustified. However, he may have had a point.

The problem was that these men who claimed to represent the nation did nothing of the sort. Though more of France had a voice because of the events of 1789, the great majority of rural dwellers and those in provincial France did not. The anticlericalism of the educated urban middle-class elite came to the fore quickly with the solution to the financial crisis which had not gone away but was not the focus of attention that it had been in late 1788. The state's lack of money could be solved by taking over the lands of the church, nationalising the clergy, making them state employees and issuing paper money supported by the wealth of the confiscated property. Thus, the Civil Constitution of the Clergy of 1790 was a vindication of the Burke view that traditional sensibilities and values were attacked, and religious change was to be one of the key reasons for internal revolt and subsequent civil war.

This quick-fix solution did not take into account the inflationary effects of new currency which put large amounts of paper money into circulation. It did not take into account that a devout Catholic king could not accept the massive change in the role and status of the church. However, the main problem not fully grasped by the reformers in Paris was that large numbers of rural inhabitants in the provinces were devoted to traditional Catholic practices and bitterly resented interference from middle-class 'Godless' interference from Paris in their religion and way of life. The church successfully accommodated itself to the traditions and superstitions of rural France so that plans to nationalise it and take its property were a threat to valued and established local ways of life.

To the rational men of property and learning it was, too, obvious that the vast mass of people could not be what was called 'active citizens'. An 'active citizen' paid taxes and had an interest in seeing how they were spent. He (and definitely not she) had the education to understand political debates and ideas. He had the ability and the time to take part in local and central government. He had the independence to make the right decisions, not being bound to a master or a farmer or being poor or unemployed. Good government depended on propertied, independent, male, active citizens. Women were not included, nor were poorer wage earners or the non-white people of France's colonies. Actors, too, were excluded for some inexplicable reason redolent of a puritanical middle class attitude. Nature had marked out large sections of the population as separate from the world of political power and undertaking sound administration for the public good.

However, the 'nation' did consist of more than the active citizens and the passive citizens had the right to sound government, equality before the law, and freedom to better themselves. In America, too, it had been the educated, propertied citizens who had made a constitution to maintain just authority and prevent unruly democratic elements from causing trouble. States maintained restricted voting rights as did leading cities. Noble ideals – all men being created equal – moved the founding fathers of the United States to tears. However, they did not extend these rights to black enslaved people, a mass of indentured white labour barely distinguishable from slaves, or women. Voting was the preserve of white, male, property owners and an elite class of legislators and statesmen, often slaveowners like Washington and Jefferson ruled. Democracy as such did not come to the US until the 1830s and it did not include women, enslaved people and Native Americans.

But the urban underclasses and the mass of small masters, craftsmen and workers were more concerned with day-to-day problems of food and wanted help with rising prices and food security. They also had different ideas of a future France than the legislators. There also emerged radicals from the middle class whose vision was very different from the moderate deputies. Freedom of political debates in the different clubs that had arisen in Paris and other large cities had given rise to discussion of a range of ideas not on the agenda of most of the assembly members. A Republic of Virtue which had much greater social equality than the active citizens envisaged was a common theme. Radicals looked to the models of the ancient world where an austere patriotic republicanism offered a different sort of state. The corruption of monarchy, aristocracy, clericalism and privilege would be swept away, and mankind would make a new start.

Ideas spread from debating clubs and captured the hearts and minds of vigorous radicals, often men and some women with a propensity for emotive expression or a willingness to take ideas as far as they would go. But also, the obvious poverty, inequality and hardship of the time moved many to seek more radical solutions. Given that these radicals were urban middle-class intellectuals, they were not much more representative of the 'people' they claimed to love and to work for than the prosperous liberal middle class which made up the majority of the Assembly. However, their writings and speeches could mobilise popular support in Paris much more effectively.

* * *

The Constitutional Monarchy

By August 1789 the atmosphere in the Assembly could be described as feverish. News of the widespread peasant disturbances of the summer had led to demands for a total transformation of society and the end of Feudalism. There was a rush to relinquish privileges and then to express a belief in human rights. The Declaration of the Rights of Man and Citizen of 26 August 1789 spoke of 'the natural, inalienable and sacred rights of man'. 'Men are born free and remain equal in rights'. The rights were stated to be 'liberty, property, security and resistance to oppression'. All citizens had the right to take part personally or through their representatives in making the law which must be the same for all. There was no longer to be nobility, hereditary distinctions or any privilege which derived from birth. There were to be no corporations, guilds, professions or religious vows.

* * *

The French Revolution is mostly associated in collective memory with big public events like the storming of the Bastille, but it was the implementing of these highly revolutionary ideas in a rapid and overwhelming series of measures that was truly revolutionary. The jump from the eighteenth-century acceptance of monarchy, natural leadership by aristocracy, a powerful and privileged Catholic Church and a network of privileges and customs in a nation made up of historic provinces with their own history and individual ways to a modern 'enlightened' nation was utterly extraordinary and went far beyond the expectations of the Estates General and most of the people of France. This part of the narrative, however, seems sometimes rather neglected.

On 11 August 1789, the decree of the Assembly stated that the feudal regime was entirely destroyed. In practice, feudal payments continued where they could be collected because there was to be compensation for the loss of property by landlords. But the principle of an end to privilege was revolutionary, as it affected the whole of French society. The Assembly was not bound by the famous *cahiers*. As it spoke for the Nation it felt able to put in place any measure that accorded with the principles of enlightened change.

The first was the decision to give France a new constitution. From 7 July the official name of the National Assembly which emerged from the Estates General was the National Constituent Assembly. This had not been part of the original remit of the deputies who had come to Paris in May 1789, and the whole idea of this body grappling with the task of establishing a formal set of rules was startling. There were discussions about whether there should be two houses of parliament as in the British and US models and about what powers the king should have. Rather out of the blue, and without much debate in September 1789, it was voted by 673 votes to 352 that Louis XVI should have a 'suspensive veto' which could delay laws passed by the Assembly but not stop them permanently.

In the end, the veto was limited to delaying laws by a maximum of three years. The king appointed ministers, but they could be impeached by the Assembly. The king could not propose laws. The final constitution of 1791 was based on academic notions of separation of powers. To avoid 'tyranny' and any one person or body having too much power, the government was to be separate from the Assembly. The Legislative Assembly – so-called because it made the laws but did not run the government – was to be elected for two years and they voted the money available to the government, thereby controlling it.

It took a substantial amount of time to come up with the Constitution, but some key decisions were taken early on. In October 1789 the deputies agreed on a key distinction. Voting was to be the sole right of 4.3 million men over twenty-five who paid the equivalent of three days' wages for unskilled labour in taxes. They had the right to choose 'electors' – one for every 100 voters. The voters had to be wealthier men and pay the equivalent of fifty-four days wages. There were only 10,000 of such men. The electors then chose the actual deputies.

The voters had to be 'active citizens' – with enough income to have a stake in how taxes should be raised and spent. 40 per cent of France had to rely on their betters to represent them. As 'passive citizens', they had rights but were not to take part in elections.

The elections were more redolent of the US system than that of Britain in that not just deputies were elected but also local officials, judges, magistrates and parish priests. The entire system of courts from the *parlements* to local courts was swept away by September 1790. In addition, the entire existing structure of local government was ended. The historic provinces of France were replaced by eighty-three new Departments. The change extended to local level with new councils for towns and villages. As early as May and June 1790 there were elections for local authorities. Smaller towns elected mayors, a legal official called a procurator and a council. Larger towns and cities with more than 25,000 people were divided into new electoral districts for voting purposes called 'sections'. Paris had 48 of these sections.

To maintain order, local militias and *ad hoc* armed bodies created to maintain order were placed under a newly organised National Guard and put under the new local authorities as a police force. This ended the previous practice of relying on the army for public order. Local authorities were given the right to declare Martial Law from October 1789 and a red flag was the signal that rioters could face being fired on by the National Guard.

In June 1790 the abolition of titles, orders and coats of arms saw the end of noble status. Struggles in the countryside between feudal landowners and peasants over dues and payments continued throughout 1790 and many nobles fled the country. In a similar way to the decline in feudal dues, taxes too were changed, with old payments being abolished and replaced by three new national taxes with no exemptions on land, on moveable property and on profits. The unpopular but profitable indirect taxes such as the *gabelle* were ended.

However, the collection of taxes was difficult and sporadic, given the total upheaval of government, and the deficit increased. The immediate solution was a vote in November 1789 to put the property of the church at the disposal of the state. This allowed for one of the most fundamental changes of the Revolution as in April 1790 *Assignats* became legal currency. These were bonds in which people lent money to the government on the security of the lands – the so-called *biens nationaux*. They had a good interest rate which could be financed by sales of church land or income from it. The proceeds from the church lands were paid into a special department to make sure they were reserved to finance the Assignats which had the necessary security to be used as currency. Given the very limited amount of paper money used before 1789, this marked a major change.

Thus, in a short period of time, an Assembly which had not been voted in for that purpose, made radical changes to almost every sphere of life. Frenchmen did not live in their old provinces. They elected their local officials. They no longer accepted traditions of respect for social 'betters'. They no longer craved privileges, bought offices, paid traditional dues and taxes. Local policing changed. Participation in public life changed.

However, the greatest change for most Frenchmen who did not live in towns was the position of the church. Parish priests had lost their traditional income from titles in August 1789. Payments to Rome ended. The Catholic Church lost its monopoly as the official church as rights were given to Protestants and Jews. In February 1790 monasteries and convents were dissolved. The official treaty with the Pope making Catholicism the state religion ended. Parishes were reduced and the clergy were to be paid by the state. Strict rules were established for higher clergy to have experience of actually working in parishes. Clerics were to be elected by the laity and to swear an oath to this new Civil Constitution of the Clergy which was finally made law in August 1790.

In a short time, France experienced the changes that had convulsed and divided other nations. There was virtually a reformation along the lines of Henry VIII's control of the church and abolition of monasteries in England in the 1530s – but it went further in having elected clergy. Traditions were swept away in all areas of French life. The massive interest in political ideas saw the growth of political discussion and clubs where even more radical change was discussed. Ordinary people were politicised in a way that was highly unusual in the Europe of the eighteenth century. The monarchy and its special status and semi-divine nature were subordinated to the idea of 'the nation', and religious antagonisms of previous centuries were revived.

This amount of change was put into place not as a result of real national debates and consensus, but rather in a headlong desire for change by men who were not representative of the nation as a whole and who had not stood for election to gain approval for the scale of change which was made. There was little in the 1789 *cahiers* requesting a fundamental change in monarchy, an end to the established church, an end to many traditional and widely shared privileges. It was almost inevitable that opposition should develop and very hard to see this mass of change as being likely to lead to a lasting constitutional monarchy. The whole process of change did not throw up a leader or leaders who could communicate, moderate or achieve a consensus. Religious, social and political divisions inevitably began to emerge.

The lack of experience of the realities of government became evident when the practicalities of holding elections for local government took place in the summer of 1789. Elections could take a week or more and the electors gathered in a meeting hall to write down on a list those they wished to nominate. Not everyone wanted the expense in time and money, and some were nominated against their will and turned down. The experience of local areas such as Bayeux in Normandy shows that many of those elected refused to serve on the local council and eventually men were chosen with few votes. They refused to raise local taxes to finance their authority for fear of reprisals. Initially about half of the active citizens entitled to vote took part but this subsequently declined. Those landowners, professionals and tradesmen who had to earn a living were reluctant or unable to give their time or eventually make their way to Paris. Increasingly, local government and then the Legislative Assembly of 1791 were dominated by wealthier lawyers and merchants. The elected officials and deputies were even less representative of the population of France as a whole than the deputies of the Estates General. The rapid introduction of new systems proved more difficult in practice at local level than it had seemed in theory to lawmakers in the capital.

However, the exercise of law-making had created experience in the men of 1789, but theory overcame good practical sense and it was decided that the new Legislative Assembly of 1791 would exclude those who had been elected previously. So inexperienced and not very representative men from a narrow social range of occupations had to grapple with making the new constitution work.

The 'blame' however is most usually put on those groups who opposed the changes, not on those who pursued unrealistic goals. These are usually the 'counter revolutionaries', the king and the 'extremists'.

'The counter revolution' is the term given to those who thought the changes should be brought to a halt. The principal source of opposition was to the religious changes. There had been an exodus of nobles, principally the king's brothers who attempted to gain European support for a restoration of full monarchy. These *Émigrés* as they were called had limited success and influence, and their headquarters at Koblenz just over the border was a hotbed of intrigue rather than a powerhouse of resistance. However, the internal opposition to change was more significant. There were incidents in the south in the spring and summer of 1790. The changes in religion had revitalised dormant antagonisms between Protestants and Catholics that had been a key element in civil war in the sixteenth and seventeenth centuries. Then a substantial Protestant minority – the so-called Huguenots – had fought against a Catholic monarchy. Now the position was reversed. Power had gone into the hands of opponents of the Catholic Church. Many of the reforming elements were Protestant or were middle-class anti-clericals with a grievance against the church. Just as in the early modern period, religious hatred could be combined with social tensions. In the city Nimes, for instance, Catholic workers turned against Protestant employers in support of opposition to religious change. Far from being an exercise in democracy, the conflict became a 'brawl' and the Protestant dominated National Guard killed 300 Catholics. Opposition intensified as clergy were required to take an oath to the state and to the civil constitution. The deadline was set for January 1791 and only half of the clergy were prepared to swear. The opposition was strong in the west of France and in some regions where Catholic support was particularly strong such as Alsace and Flanders. When the Pope came out officially against the oath, opinion became even more divided, and burnings of effigies of the Pope were reminiscent of the wars of religion in previous centuries. There was open hostility to what was called 'non juror' priests and, in some cases, attacks on religious communities in areas such as Paris where anti-clericalism was strong. The ground had been prepared for a major revolt of the provinces which erupted in 1793. With this level of discontent, it would be very hard for a new constitutional monarchy to achieve stability.

On the other hand, the changes for some did not seem to go far enough. The Constitutional Monarchy faced challenges from radical opponents. Given the undermining of most elements of the state and the intensity of political discussion, it is not surprising that more radical ideas which were not evident in the discussions prior to the Estates General grew. If all institutions were seen as vulnerable to assault, the very basis of the state – the monarchy – was bound to be threatened. If the Nation was the source of all authority and legitimacy, then, for some, monarchy was redundant. This had been clear when there had been discussions about the extent of the royal veto, with some arguing that a hereditary king should not be able to block the wishes of 'the nation'. The Assembly, however, did not go that far, and also was careful to restrict the power of 'the nation' by complex electoral rules and the key concept of active citizenship. Property was a key element and so slavery on which France's lucrative colonial trade depended was not abolished, and the influence of workers was restricted by a key law which restricted the right of workers to organise. The Le Chapelier law of 1791 prevented strikes and collective bargaining. The idea of property was so important that it overrode the rhetoric on feudal rights, and these were not abolished without compensation. This led to continued unrest in the countryside. There was also increased resentment about the limited attention given to the needs of the poorer element in cities, especially Paris. The confident, educated, middle-class reformers found themselves unable to stop the momentum of change as political clubs in the 48 Paris sections or electoral districts in which 'passive citizens' debated new and more radical ideas. In the countryside peasants continued to attack châteaux, taxpayers stopped paying and the urban lower classes refused to settle down to accept the benefits of constitutional change.

Debating and literary clubs were a feature of the *ancien régime* but the turmoil of 1789 and the end of censorship led to a new phenomenon, the political club. A contemporary conservative pamphlet which called for 'No More Clubs' in 1791 explained these groups.

> What is a club? It is a society of men who regularly assemble to discuss the affairs of state in order to influence the public and pressure the National Assembly and the king. Every type of club is useless and dangerous.

The Constitutional Monarchy

Usually, the emphasis is on radical clubs, but they ranged across the political spectrum and there were monarchist clubs as well as more radical ones. The leading Paris clubs began as associations of deputies of the Estates General – initially from Brittany and then more widely. In the autumn of 1789, the Society of the Friends of the Constitution was admitting non-deputies to its meetings in a former convent of St Jacques – hence the name Jacobins. Though associated with 'extremist' ideas later in the Revolution, its initial object was to get support for reforms, thus moving beyond a debating society but nowhere near a modern political party. Initially the clubs were open only to 'active citizens', but more radical organisations such as the Society of the Friends of Liberty and Equality were more democratic. The Jacobins had affiliated clubs in provincial cities and one historian has estimated that there were 1,000 of these by the end of 1791. In Paris, the more moderate supporters of monarchy in the Jacobin club broke away in 1791 to form the Feuillants, named after the former convent of the Cistercian Feuillant religious order. The minority of Jacobins kept their original name but neither group advocated ending the monarchy. A Republican position was taken by the Cordeliers, or the Society of the Friends of the Rights of Man and the Citizen. The club had been formed in the spring of 1790 and had been moderate in its views but moved to the left after the attempted flight of the king and his family in June 1791.

What the clubs represented was a politicisation of urban France, and this extended to women, as there were fifty-six women's clubs. This growth in political awareness was unprecedented, but the dangers were considerable. The jump from a restricted scope for debate and influence to a much greater freedom of discussion was not accompanied by the sort of restraint that comes with years of parliamentary democracy. In December 1790, after a prolonged period of ill feeling between the monarchist club of the city of Aix in southern France and the Jacobin club, violence broke out. A popular crowd lynched three monarchists who led the *Club des Amis de la Paix*. The radical *Club des Anti-Politiques* had joined in opposing this club and connived in the murder of the conservative Marquis La Roquette. Interestingly this aristocrat was unpopular locally because in 1788 his carriage had run over a local mother and her two children. A similar incident was featured in Charles Dickens' French Revolution novel *'A Tale of Two Cities'*, though in the book the offending aristocrat is murdered in his chateau by a vengeful husband.

The Monarchist clubs are not featured much in standard narratives but are an indication of underlying divisions and concerns about the principle of 'the nation' rather than the monarch being the source of authority and the growing religious conflicts. More attention is given to the emergence of radical clubs and the links with popular discontent. The urban unrest seen in 1789 and the economic hardships of the poorer districts had not disappeared. Very little was done in the mass of change to actually alleviate poverty. The middle classes were more interested in promoting individualism and reducing barriers to individual enterprise by ending trade guilds, and corporations and preventing workers' organisations than in dealing with shortages and rising prices. The eruption of popular discontent in the events of 1789 had enabled the middle-class revolution to take place but the 'passive citizens' had to be kept in their place. This was made abundantly clear in the incident known as the Massacre of the Champs de Mars in July 1791.

This was a result of a poorly organised and unsuccessful attempt of the royal family to flee Paris on 21 June 1791 in the so-called Flight to Varennes. The Cordeliers and the other radical clubs organised petitions hostile to the monarchy. Around 30,000 signatures were obtained for a popular petition presented to the Assembly that liberty was not compatible with royalty. The Assembly voted on 15 July that the king was to be reinstated and that he had been 'abducted' and was not guilty of abandoning his country. This was a deliberate lie, as the king had been trying to flee to loyal forces as he was increasingly concerned about his safety. The more radical Jacobins and Cordeliers gathered more Republican petitions and meetings were held to sign them on the Champs de Mars, a large parade ground. A crowd of 20,000 gathered and there were fears or expectations that another big popular demonstration would bring about the fall of the Monarchy. This time there was no equivalent to the Bastille or the March on Versailles. When the crowds lynched two men they discovered hiding under the 'Altar of the Fatherland' on which the petitions were signed, there were obvious danger signs. The Assembly, the municipal government of Paris and the National Guard led by the Marquis de Lafayette agreed on Martial Law. The red flag was raised and the National Guard acted decisively by shooting into protesting crowds and killing between twelve and fifty and then brutally dispersing the gatherings. In keeping with the new rhetoric of 'the Nation', the demonstrators were described not as 'the people' but as vagrants and troublemakers, threatening the people's peace. A clampdown on radical clubs, and a strengthening of property qualifications for the National Guard, saw a reaction against radicalism and popular influence. The new Constitution took effect in September amid growing resentment from the radical clubs and their supporters in the cities.

The Constitutional Monarchy

The third element which reduced any great chance of this new regime being stable and successful has been seen as the king himself. Few would argue that he had great leadership qualities, but it is difficult to see what even the strongest and most dynamic monarch would have done. He had been aware of the financial problems prior to 1789 and appointed ministers not unlike the middle-class intellectuals and reformers who pushed through change after mid-1789. He had taken the risk of a national consultation prior to the calling of the Estates General and was not opposed to change. He is usually accused of mismanaging the Estates General, but there was little precedent for parliamentary management and few thought that this body would assume so much authority. The so-called 'failure' to use force in the face of popular unrest and the actions of the Third Estate in declaring a national assembly has an air of unreality. A bloodbath and the dismissal of the Assembly would have left the government with all the existing problems and no way forward except a period of arbitrary rule backed by military force which was alien to the king personally and also to the way that he ruled. It is not at all sure that the French state had the resources for widespread martial law and an authoritarian monarchy. It is also likely that the market, that is lenders and investors, would have reacted catastrophically and that credit to pay for this absolutism would have been unavailable.

The *Cahiers* had contained very little anti-monarchist feeling and there was a considerable amount of goodwill and loyalty so presiding over a period of modernisation and innovation and being guided by an eminent body of distinguished subjects and a respected former minister, Necker did not seem a radically different course from reliance on the reforms and novelties of his pre-1789 rule.

The deteriorating position of the crown developed gradually. The move to central Paris as a result of the October Days was perhaps the turning point. The debate about the veto was a distinct danger sign, even if the king was left with the power to delay legislation. The best way forward was probably by 1790 to make a constitutional monarchy work. But this would have required political skills and abilities beyond most monarchs and certainly beyond Louis XVI. The suddenness of change and the lack of precedent were barriers to establishing a unique European experiment. The king did not have outstanding advisers and ministers, and the Assembly did not have the experience in government to develop a working constitutional monarchy. Instead for the reasons outlined above, deep divisions developed. The king accepted a great deal for the good of his country but the assault on the church was a bridge too far. It was the Civil Constitution of the Clergy that ended any hope that the Louis could accept and even lead a process of change.

By June 1791 it was clear that a partnership was not going to be possible; that divisions were deep; that religion was under threat and that the time had passed for some sort of military coup to restore authority. The only alternative was flight. Quite what the aim was is uncertain. Did Louis intend to join his family and seek to rally military forces loyal to him and to enlist foreign monarchies in a future assault on the new regime, hoping to take advantage of monarchical elements and Catholic sentiment? This was not really a bad idea as the dangers of remaining in Paris were considerable. Agonisingly slow, the flight was poorly planned, and the royal party was recognised by a postmaster in the small town of Varennes. The king at Varennes and his family were returned in disgrace to Paris along streets with silent and hostile onlookers.

Now no one knew what to do. Radical petitions demanded abolition, but that was not on the agenda for the majority of the Assembly. There was no overwhelming popular demand for a Republic and the majority of France which lived in the countryside had no desire to see traditional monarchy replaced by a regime dominated by urban elites, Protestants or unbelievers.

So there was a tacit decision to pretend that nothing had happened and, as there was now no real alternative, the king accepted the 1791 Constitution in September with its restricted royal power and its inexperienced Legislative Assembly. Given the divisions in France, the suspicions of the European monarchs egged on by émigré aristocrats, the hostility of the Pope, disturbances in the countryside, problems of urban poverty and inflation brought about by the new paper money, the prospects were not good, and Louis had no real interest in seeing the new regime succeed. Failure and crisis would very possibly see a restoration of royal power. But it might also see its demise.

Because we know the ending – the suspension of the monarchy in August 1792, its abolition in September 1792 and the trial and execution of the king in January 1793 – it is tempting to see these events as inevitable and to see the Constitutional Monarchy as doomed. The problems it faced in September 1791 were not necessarily the responsibility of any one of four toxic elements – overconfident middle-class deputies, extremist radials, reactionary counter-revolutionaries or a feeble king.

A case could be made for the situation still not to have been irretrievable by September 1791. The celebrations in the capital when the new constitution was announced showed a considerable affection for the king and queen at odds with the bitter hatreds of the following year. The new Legislative

Louis XVI in 1774. The image is of a popular and well-meaning young king who welcomed change. (*www.parismuseescollections.paris.fr*)

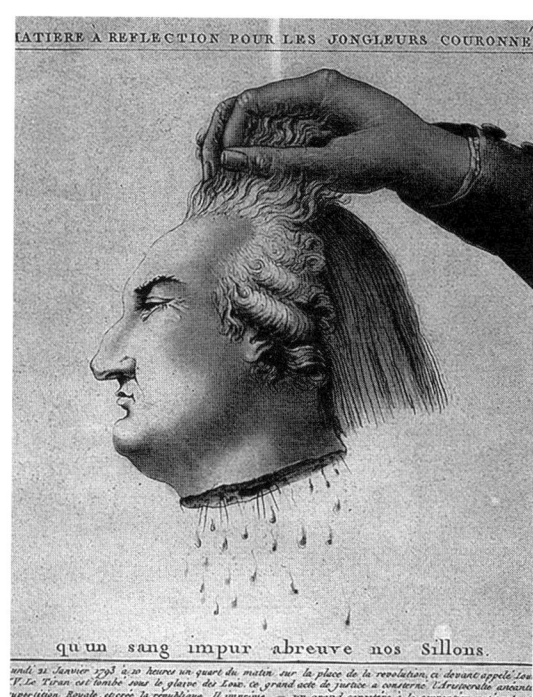

Louis XVI after execution January 1793. The reality when the king failed to manage change.

Marie-Antoinette, Queen of France, in 1787, a picture which shows the importance of a commanding wig in high society during the ancient regime. (*www.parismuseescollections.paris.fr*)

Marie Antoinette on the way to execution in 1793, drawn from life by the famous artist, David. Her hair has been cut so that the blade of the guillotine can sever her head cleanly.

The Estates General of 1560. Not enough is usually written about this assembly's history prior to 1789.

The Estates General in 1789.

A postcard of the Faubourg Saint Antoine in 1911, which suggests the busy atmosphere of this key district of small shops and businesses in the southeast of the city.

An anonymous print of the taking of the Bastille which shows the attackers as mostly uniformed Gardes.

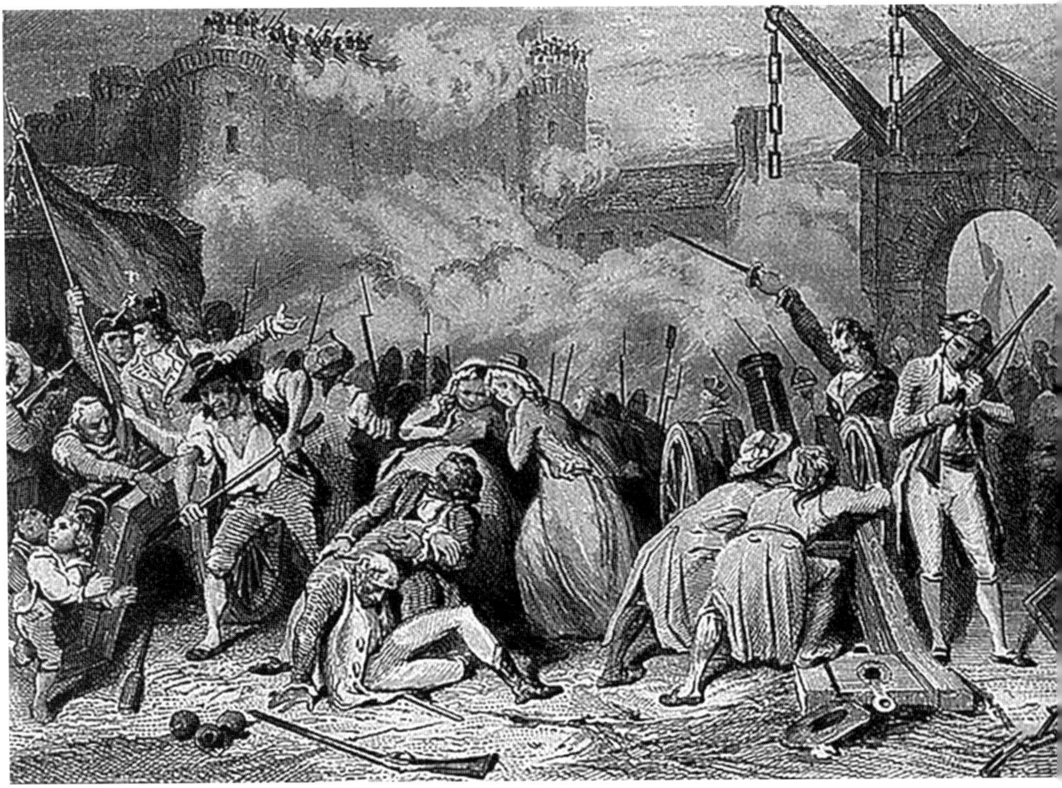

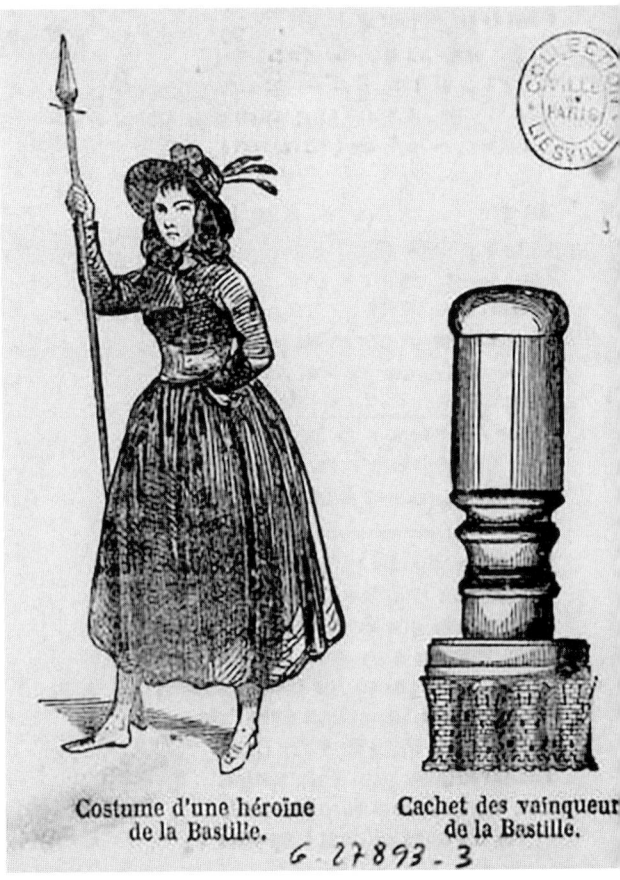

A print of later in the Revolution which puts more emphasis on the general populace including women and children.

COLLECTION VILLE DE PARIS LIESVILLE
Costume d'une héroïne de la Bastille.
Cachet des vainqueur de la Bastille.
6 27893-3

A female heroine of the Bastille. In fact, women's participation was not officially recognised when the list of 'Vainquers' (conquerors) was drawn up and special rewards given.

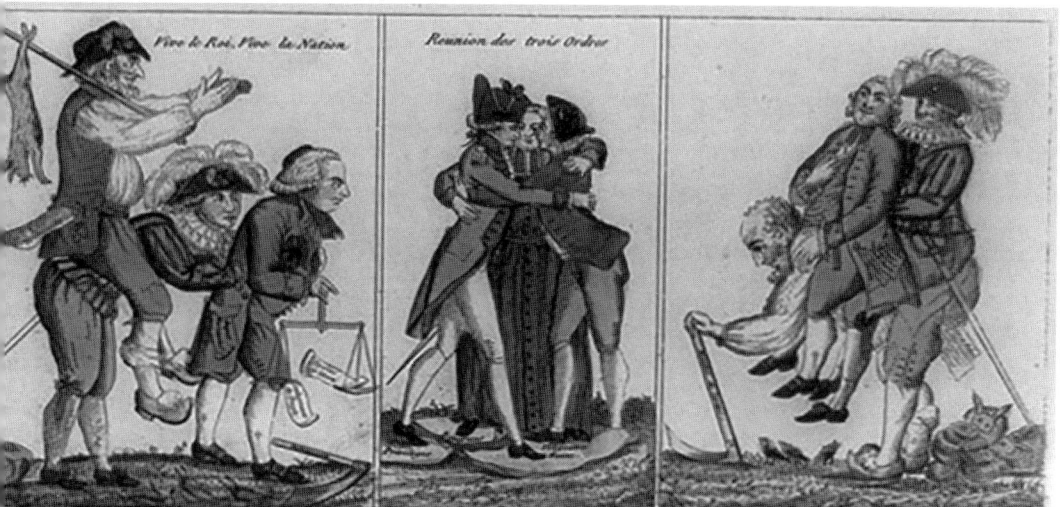

An optimistic sequence. The peasant is oppressed by the privileged estates (*right*) then the estates join together in harmony (*centre*) and the position is reversed. This version of events does not stand up to scrutiny.

A medal issued to commemorate the end of feudalism in August 1789. In fact, dues were not abolished overnight and rural unrest continued.

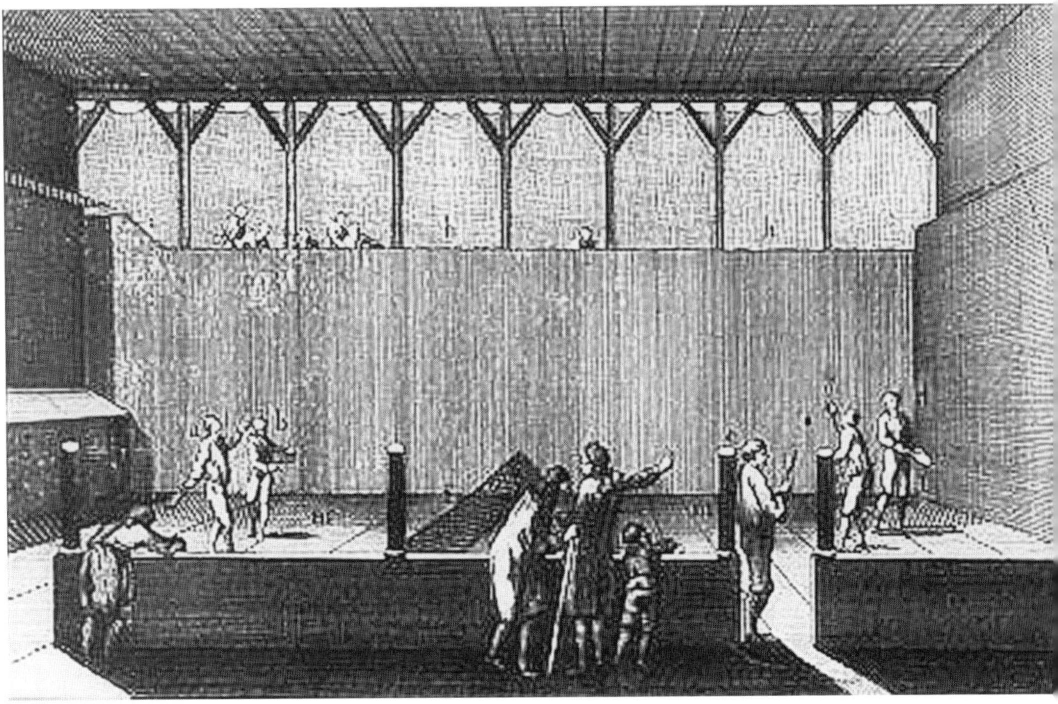

The famous 'Tennis Court' before the Revolution.

The depiction of the Oath of the Tennis Court in 1789, an engraving of the famous painting by David, part of the legend of the Revolution.

Brissot, the self-satisfied and foolish architect of the war policy in 1792 that proved so disastrous.

Typical of hostile depictions of the sans-culottes by the English artist Gillray. English prosperity under a conservative regime is contrasted with the miserable state of France.

The alternative view of a sans culotte – sturdy, heroic. Neither depiction accords with the reality

Robespierre. This is typical of depictions of this revolutionary ideologue with a neat wig.
(*www.parismuseescollections.paris.fr*)

The assassination of Marat by Charlotte Corday – a matter of fact representation.

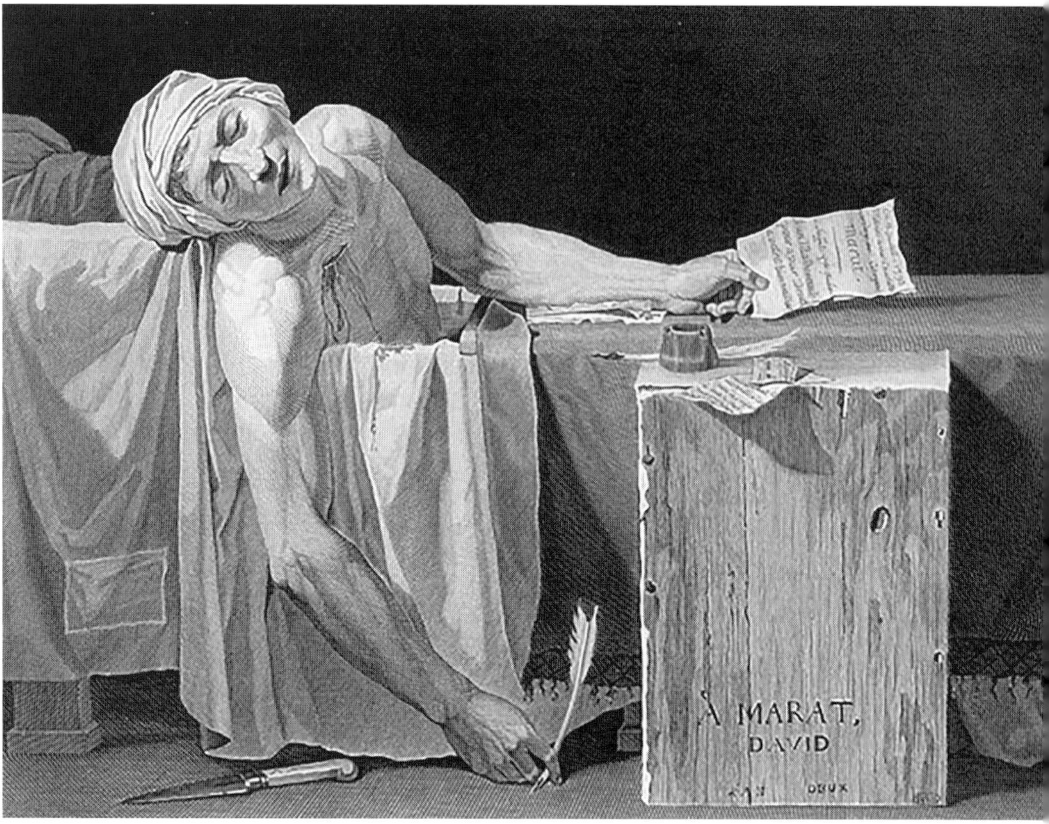

Marat as heroic revolutionary martyr in a version of David's painting which is at another emotional level.

The execution of the feminist pioneer Olympe de Gouges.

The mobile guillotine which the Convention's Representatives took into the rebellious provinces. Ideas of liberty and fraternity were harder to enforce, but the guillotine ensured that Paris and the Provinces were given equality of punishment.

The execution of Louis XVI, January 1793.

The depiction of violence by slaves in the Saint-Domingue revolt that appeared in French publications.

(*Left*) The golden couple – M. and Mme Roland. Like so many liberal minded middle-class supporters of the Revolution, they failed to see its dangers until it was too late.

(*Below, left*) Théroigne de Méricourt. Not the deranged harridan of popular imagination. (*www.parismuseescollections.paris.fr*)

(*Below, right*) An attempt to depict Toussaint Louverture. There is no reliable picture drawn or painted from life of this enigmatic leader. (*www.parismuseescollections.paris.fr*)

A woodcut illustrating the populist Pere Duchesne publication, typically hostile to priests.

The trial of Danton.

French atrocities in Saint Domingue. The level of violence during the Haitian Revolution has been overstated, but nevertheless there was a disturbing amount of killing.

Bonaparte in 1797 – the early stages of the legend. (*www.parismuseescollections.paris.fr*)

A bust of the Emperor Napoleon – the image of 'greatness'.

The Elephant which was erected on the site of the Bastille. For some, this irrelevant and poorly-constructed memorial is a symbol of the futility of the whole Revolution.

The Constitutional Monarchy

Assembly contained some distinguished figures and contemporary criticisms of the quality of the deputies have been questioned. The king, having failed to leave, had an incentive to make the system work. Relying on foreign intervention stood to weaken the monarchy. The emergence of moderate royalist deputies and clubs gave Louis the chance to appoint a sympathetic government made up of moderate royalist *Feuillant* leaders. The power of popular unrest to influence events had been weakened by the stand taken at the Champs de Mars incident. Property owners and active citizens were beneficiaries of the changes and had an incentive to establish stability.

* * *

Few people would see the period in France following the establishment of the Constitutional Monarchy as one of the crucial periods of European or even world history. Counterfactual speculation, rightly, has little place in serious history, but in this case, it might be worth considering what was at stake. If the experiment in government that had been taking place since 1789 had been as successful, as was the case with the establishment of the United States, itself seen as an experiment, and a stable regime had been established, then a lot might have followed. One of the monarchist clubs took as its title 'The Society for Peace.' If a conservative regime which nevertheless recognised the changes since 1789 had managed to end the religious conflicts and established peaceful relations with other European powers, contained popular violence and restrained the relatively limited number of radical Republicans, then an intriguing 'might have been' scenario emerges of peace and stability.

The actual story is bleaker and hinges on a crucial decision. In April 1792 the constitutional monarchy took the decision to go to war. Failure in war, the threat of invasion, the re-emergence of popular unrest and violence, civil war in France itself and an upsurge of hostility towards the monarchy all plunged France into crisis. Terror became the order of the day as the Revolution lurched leftwards and took draconian measures against real and perceived enemies.

Peace and stability would have avoided a long series of wars in Europe in which the monarchies pitted themselves against first Revolutionary France and then the military leader who took power in 1799, Napoleon Bonaparte. Millions of lives would have been saved. Napoleon would have remained an obscure Corsican officer. His conquests in Europe which destroyed the old order and led to the emergence of nationalism and eventually to new unified states in Italy and Germany would not have taken place. Britain would not have emerged as a dominant naval power and the basis for its enlarged empire would not have taken place. The powerful new Germany which brought about two world wars and the Holocaust would not have happened. The Russian Revolution which came about as a result of the First World War might not have occurred. There would have been no worldwide communism, no Cold War, no rise of the superpowers, no atomic bomb and even possibly no global warming.

Well, perhaps, or perhaps not. Counterfactual speculation is usually unprofitable, but it does help to understand how important the failure of the Constitutional Monarch was. A great deal followed from the fatal decision of the new regime in France to go to war with its neighbours and that is worth some close consideration.

The declaration of war against Austria by the Legislative Assembly on 21 April 1792 was a major turning point of the Revolution and owed much to the influence of Jacques Pierre Brissot. While not an unknown figure, this foolish and obnoxious person is not a household name and does not always receive the criticism he deserves for launching a war that was to have such tragic consequences. He was typical of the self-confident, self-styled intellectuals who gained prominence as a result of the revolution. The son of a well-to-do restaurateur of Chartres he trained as a lawyer but moved into journalism and pamphleteering. He was a devotee of all things enlightened and soaked up the ideas of the liberal philosophers such as Locke and Montesquieu. Modern reforming ideas were dished up in his pamphlets on a range of topics – legal theory, literature, political ideas, philosophy. He visited London and went off to his beloved American Republic for a visit to Philadelphia. He signed up to the progressive Franco-American society in 1789 and notwithstanding the US retention of slavery, he took up the cause of improving conditions of France's West Indian enslaved people by forming the *Amis des Noirs*. Everything modern and progressive was represented by this busy reformer. Though he showed his progressive credentials by being imprisoned in 1784 for libelling the government, there is evidence of some shady financial dealings and there were accusations that he had been a police spy, though this is uncertain. After the king's flight to Varennes in June 1791, he urged a national vote on the abolition of the monarchy. He was elected to the Legislative Assembly formed after the Constitution and became a leading figure of a group of like-minded progressive deputies known as the Girondins because many came from the Gironde region in the southwest, through Brissot himself represented a constituency in northern France. He acquired an undeserved reputation as an expert on foreign affairs and led a pressure group which urged war against Austria. Less extreme in his domestic policies

The Constitutional Monarchy

than other reformers and suspicious of too much popular action, Brissot nevertheless took a radical line on the ending of the monarchy and a war to spread revolution.

This was a highly irresponsible course of action and rooted in a number of preconceptions. The French army was larger than that of Austria and Britain, its traditional enemies. Such was Brissot's enthusiasm for the moral revival of France brought about by like-minded, middle-class reformers since 1789 that he thought that revolutionary forces would have the high morale and sense of right that would overcome corrupt monarchical forces from countries that had not experienced the benefits of the political changes in France. War would unite the famous 'nation' and help to end the unrest in provincial France about religion. It would also distract from economic and social distress and harness the energies of the 'good people' behind the enlightened middle-class revolutionaries. He and his supporters thought there would be a short war with easy victories which would weaken opposition to the Revolution developing in Austria and Prussia. It would drive the *émigré* opposition from France's border and spread 'liberty' to key neighbouring areas such as the Netherlands. The revolution had been so beneficial that it was a positive duty to give other European areas the chance to experience it. Brissot ignored warnings from more radical individuals such as Robespierre that armed missionaries are rarely welcomed and that failure would increase the danger of a return to monarchy.

This was an unnecessary war because the European monarchies largely accepted the Constitutional Monarchy. Austria had accepted a French demand to pressure the rulers of neighbouring German states to expel the émigré forces who had established themselves at Mainz and Koblenz. The idea of a war to spread revolution ran contrary to the express rejection of war as a means of conquest which was actually written into the Constitution as Article 6. It was also ridiculous to choose war as a means of spreading enlightenment when the leading Enlightenment philosophers had rejected war and saw it as immoral and wasteful. The actual justification was slight. The Austrian state had objected to the loss of the feudal rights of German landowners in Alsace. When Louis fled, the European monarchs had issued a demand called the Declaration of Pillnitz that he be restored, but no actual plans were made to help their fellow monarch, and when he accepted the status of constitutional monarch, there was some relief in Europe. Austria and Prussia were more concerned with affairs in Eastern Europe and the division of Poland and the threat from the Turks than they were about intervening in France. The émigrés had had little support.

A war would be costly and some of the aims seemed ridiculous. Brissot claimed it would test the loyalty of Louis XVI to the new state and 'cleanse liberty from the vices of despotism'. There were under 2,000 émigré forces so the threat from the exiled aristocrats was minimal given that 180,000 French troops were stationed in the east of France. In the event of failure, the war party argued that the true enemies of the revolution would stand revealed and could be eliminated. This opened the way for further violence and division as well as a real threat from foreign powers and that it could have been made as an argument in support of war was astonishing.

Brissot and his followers gained support in the Legislative Assembly and were joined in an unexpected alliance with some of the Feuillants and moderate monarchists because the king himself decided to support war and used his powers under the constitution to appoint a Girondin ministry.

The decision to support a war was one of the worst choices ever made by a ruler. Louis may have thought that a popular war would show his true patriotism and enhance his status. If the war went badly, as he hoped, his fellow monarchs would blame the Girondins and restore his power so it seemed a 'win-win' option. Neither Brissot nor the king took into account the state of France's armed forces or the dangers of defeat. The general who was appointed commander, Doumouriez, had ambitions for military dictatorship and in the end, defected to Austria so unreliable was he. Defeat would unleash the resentment dormant since the king's flight and bolster radical demands for an end to the monarchy. War was declared on 21 April 1792. The French forces and their enemies the Austrians and Prussians were both poorly prepared, but the French were defeated when they invaded Belgium and as they fell back Lille was taken by the enemy. The Prussian commander the Duke of Brunswick issued a famous manifesto – a warning that Paris would be destroyed if Louis were harmed. A wave of fear swept Paris comparable to the fear of 1789. Alliance between the Paris crowds and radical political agitators proved toxic. A popular rising on 10 August 1792 led to the king fleeing from the Tuileries palace into the Assembly and the suspension of the monarchy. It was abolished on 21 September by a new body – the Convention elected by a wide male franchise and dominated by radical Republicans. The Constitutional experiment had ended. The Republic was to be marked now by a degree of violence that took the Revolution into a new and terrifying phase, far from the hopes and dreams of the enlightened middle classes of 1789.

Note

1. Edmund Burke, *Reflections on the Revolution in France*, 1790 (Penguin Edition, 1968).

Chapter Five

The Terror

From the beginning, the Revolution had involved violence. The beheading of the governor of the Bastille was a warning sign that change might be accompanied by bloodshed, but in the euphoria of the creation of a new National Assembly, the middle-class elites chose not to dwell on this. When it was necessary, the new rulers were prepared to use it themselves, as when they ordered the shooting down of demonstrators in the so-called Massacre of the Champs de Mars in 1791. Verbal violence, however, was harder to control, and the oratory and publications became more virulent in tone as the Revolution progressed. The ultimate violence was war, and there is little doubt that the decision for revolutionary war in 1792 was the turning point for earlier trends to lead to an acceleration of terror. Faced with the possibility of defeat and foreign occupation, toleration of any dissent lessened. Elements in France who might gain from a restoration of the old order were seen to be enemies who were actually working actively for this. As the war went badly, suspicion, rumour and paranoia increased. With the end of the Monarchy in the summer of 1792, the last restraint was removed. Suspects filled the Paris prisons and there were fears that there would be revolts, that enemies would surge out of the prisons and massacre the people of Paris. This led to the most shocking incident in the violence meted out by French Revolutionary popular disturbance, the so-called September Massacres.

The September Massacres

The phenomenon known as the September Massacres horrified contemporary observers and accounts of attacks on Paris's prison inmates over four days are sickening. The murders of 1,500 prisoners were carried out in an extremely brutal way through cutting, bludgeoning and hacking – not even shooting. The killing of the Princesse de Lamballe, the Savoyard friend and confidante of Queen Marie Antoinette, involved the cutting off of limbs and the thrusting of her head and also her private parts onto pikes.

Through the summer of 1792, the prison population had been growing as fears and rumours of plots and criminality spread through Paris. There had been repeated calls to arms in the Paris sections and when the Prussians took the fortress of Verdun and Paris lay open, the sense of danger rapidly increased. Passions had been stirred by the proclamation of the Prussian commander the Duke of Brunswick, head of an invading army of professional troops. He threatened to destroy Paris if the king were harmed. The focus of fears fell on the many prisons. These were not full of suspected aristocrats and non-juror priests (who refused to take an oath of loyalty to the new regime) but ordinary criminals, prostitutes and even some members of child gangs, the Parisian equivalent of Fagin's child robbers. There had been repeated expressions of fear that plots in the prisons could result in inmates emerging and killing, raping and robbing citizens as well as welcoming foreign troops into the capital. Reports on rumours from various sources mention these and radical news sheets referred to the dangers. The radical journalist Marat called for the prisons to be burnt with the inmates inside. The Paris sections were concerned about the dangers, but this dangerous fantasy held more than the people of the poorer districts in its grip. Members of the Commune and deputies in the Assembly expressed concerns. Modern research has shown that this was not only the fervid imagining of the more radical Jacobin deputies, but also of more moderate Girondins and even some of the Feuillant royalists. As with 1789 and the fears of royal troops leading to the storming of the Bastille, the power of rumour was so overwhelming that it led to protracted murders. The bulk of those killed were not overt political enemies, but ordinary criminals held routinely in a variety of prisons. The most pointless murders were of thirty-five women prisoners in the Salpetrière prison. That children were sabred or beaten to death with iron bars is heart-rending in its gratuitous and pointless brutality. For conservative writers, this was an indication of the immorality of revolutionary leaders and the dangers of crowd hysteria. Any progress towards democratic organisation and awareness among the ordinary people of Paris was negated by this brutality. However, the actual killing was done largely by small numbers of people, mainly members of the National Guard and provincial troops on their way to the front to fight the Prussians rather than the civilian population of Paris. As far as guilt by association goes, the obvious approval of ending the supposed threat was disturbingly widespread among the elite as well as the Paris populace.

The brutal slaughter of defenceless prisoners in the Paris prisons followed the slaughter of the king's Swiss Guards on 10 August by crowds assaulting the royal palace and forcing the end of the monarchy. The threat of popular violence had been present since July 1789, but this violence of August and

September 1792 was unusual in its scale and ferocity. These irregular massacres did not reappear, but instead violence passed into official hands, with the revolutionary state undertaking killings both in Paris and in provincial France, some of which have been compared to the genocides of the twentieth century. This was only possible because of the bonds formed between the radicalised inhabitants of the poorer Paris sections – increasingly known as 'sans-culottes' and key political leaders and groups. State violence was just as brutal, but it removed from the scene the anarchic murders of crowds which was not a feature of political life after September 1792. The crowds did not rally when the leading advocate of terror, the leading Jacobin Maximilien Robespierre was overthrown in 1794 and popular disturbances did not bring about any great political effects after that and were put down by an increasingly dominant middle-class elite backed by military force.

The Establishment of Legal Terror

Once the rumours died down and it was clear that foreign troops were not going to invade the capital, then more reflection led to regret about the random brutality. Security and revolutionary justice remained important, but there had to be procedures and legal forms and a greater sense of central direction. What followed was death by cleaner means. It has been said with some justification that the key element in the subsequent official terror in Paris was the condemnation of enemies. The resulting execution was quick and clean – the fast, efficient expression of the will of the people in ridding the Revolution of its enemies by the modern instrument of execution. No protracted strangulation by hanging or botched blows by the executioner's attempt to behead, or protracted physical torture, such as the old regime's infliction of death by breaking on the wheel.

The period between the September Massacres and the beginning of the period known as the Terror saw fast-moving changes both in Paris and France as a whole. The end of the Monarchy left a void. Constitutional monarchy had not worked, but what was to replace it? The National Assembly was replaced by a Convention dominated by revolutionary groups and unusually elected by universal male suffrage, though excluding domestic servants. After the new Convention's ceremonial procession to the meeting room, the more radical deputies, often from the Jacobin club, decided to sit on the upper benches of the room, earning the name 'Mountain men' – *Montagnards*. The less radical groups took the lower benches and became 'the Plain'. The supporters of Brissot earned the name Girondins from the region where many deputies came from – the Gironde. There was bitter rivalry between the two groups.

The Real Story of the French Revolution

On a personal level, Robespierre, the Jacobin and dominant *Montagnard* clashed with Brissot, and there were two visions of a new France. The Girondins favoured a federation on the lines of the USA; the *Montagnards* favoured a centralised structure, especially as the demands of war needed tight controls and wholesale change in society needed strong overall leadership.

Divisions increased with the trial of the king in December 1792. Both groups condemned him, but it was Robespierre and his supporters who favoured the death penalty on the authority of the Convention. The Girondins favoured putting the decision about execution to a referendum. The Mountain prevailed and Louis was guillotined in January 1793, leading to an extension of the war. The execution horrified opinion in Europe and hostility to the revolutionary regime in France. So as to forestall British and Dutch action, the Convention declared war on these states.

The need for mobilising resources had led to a powerful committee, the Committee of Public Safety, being formed. This was not the suggestion of Robespierre but of his fellow radical, the lawyer and orator Georges Danton. Together with the previous, but less radical, Committee of General Security, these bodies became the *de facto* executive, responsible for the day-to-day government and for the protection of the Revolution against its domestic and foreign enemies.

Robespierre had proposed in August another body, the Revolutionary Tribunal as a means of trying and punishing threats to the Revolution. It tried and condemned only twenty-eight people up to the end of 1792 and these were mostly common criminals, not political 'traitors'. It used, however, the means of a new revolutionary justice: denunciation, a swift trial and beheading. Robespierre had opposed capital punishment earlier in his career, but somehow the new instrument of death, the guillotine seemed more acceptable.

* * *

The guillotine was not in fact developed or invented by the man who it is named after. Dr Joseph-Ignace Guillotin advocated its use and developed it. However, it was first used in Britain in the seventeenth century, notably at Halifax in Yorkshire, and reinvented by a French surgeon from Strasbourg and a German harpsichord maker.

Its first French victim was a criminal, not an aristocrat or a political opponent, but it appealed to the radicals because beheading had hitherto been the prerogative of aristocratic victims. Ordinary people suffered slow strangulation by hanging and often preliminary torture by being broken on the

The Terror

wheel. Now there was the same mode of death for all. The Revolutionary aim of equality was being delivered.

Robespierre did not believe in random slaughter such as the September Massacres. It was not he but Danton who proposed reviving and extending the Revolutionary Tribunal. But there was an agreement among the *Montagnards* that Revolutionary justice and punishment were essential elements in the survival of the Republic. Why this belief developed and became such an obsession remains one of the most perplexing developments of the Revolution.

By mid-1793 the survival of the Republic was seriously in doubt. The religious conflicts and dislike of domination by Paris and total war involving taxation and conscription had driven large areas of provincial France into open revolt. The government had been forced to send Representatives – radical deputies accompanied by substantial armed forces – into counter-revolutionary areas. Given the views of these leaders and their men and the atrocities committed by the peasant rebels, there was little restraint. As is so often the case in civil war, the barbarity of conflict was considerable. Massacres, reprisals, killings of civilians, rapes, torture and mutilation became the norm.

What is widely remembered as 'The Terror' in films and books and to a certain degree in school accounts was the least violent aspect. The guillotine in Paris took the lives of an estimated 2,585 people between April 1793 and July 1794. Not all those who were accused were actually killed and 2,306 were acquitted. However, the Terror accelerated after September 1793 with stricter repressive laws denying rights of defence. The mass murders in La Vendée, Lyons and the virtual genocide in Brittany took far more lives and not by the swift killings of revolutionary justice but by drownings, shootings, cannonades and random bayonetting. Over 8,700 people were condemned to execution in La Vendée, though the real death toll may have been more. Not only were the victims shot or guillotined but drowned in the river Loire. In Lyons, a much smaller city than Paris, the Revolutionary Commission headed by Coillot d'Herbois and Joseph Fouché were frustrated at the limited number of deaths imposed prior to November 1793, with 'only' 113 being condemned. They killed another 1,673 some of whom died by cannon firing sharp fragments of metal called grapeshot at them at close range. It is possible that as many as 200,000 died outside Paris. Ironically, the largest single group of those executed in the capital itself were the followers of Robespierre following his overthrow in July 1794.

The Real Story of the French Revolution

The Paris Terror was supported by popular feeling. Here were all sorts of forums for political discussion where radical ideas could spread and hatred of 'enemies' could fester. Paris had set up its own radical local government, the Revolutionary Commune, at the time of the popular demonstrations in August 1792. There were also the unofficial but influential clubs – the Cordeliers and the Jacobin clubs; as well as that, the 48 electoral districts had their own *de facto* local governments. The elected Convention and the committees were not the only forums for discussion. The Mountain and the Girondins (or 'the Plain') were not political parties in a modern sense and their influence was challenged by a movement called the *Enragés* led by a journalist and radical called Hébert who poured forth obscene class hatred in a newssheet called *Le Père Duchesne*. This took the way of speaking of the sans-culotte and encouraged hatred of their enemies. The term 'aristo' could mean anyone suggested of charging high prices or hoarding as well as those plotting to overthrow the republic or massacre the radicals. The paranoia which the 91 issues of this sordid publication can be seen in this extract. Hébert invents a sailor who meets a former priest on a coach journey.[1]

> Oh the fucking priests and all they fucking wanted us to believe! It's absolutely fucking necessary that I tell you this story. I found in the coach a man with a look, oh fuck me, a fucking horrible look. And this monsieur sets himself to talking to me and says terrible things to me about the National Assembly. I make pamphlets, he tells me. pamphlets that try to win over the people, to make them believe that the Assembly's decrees harm them, that their good friends the patriots take them down the wrong path, and that they themselves must help us return them to slavery. I gave him the fucking hardest slap that the fucking face of a rascal ever received.

Hébert was a well-dressed, bewigged member of the middle classes whose father had been a judge but his 'news sheet' was a mass of obscenity and paranoia – former nobles and priests conspiring against the people. In the end, he was guillotined himself and his readership did little to help him.

The September Massacres had shown the dangers of fear and rumour and with news of provincial revolt and of setbacks such as the British talking the port of Toulon, the situation in the capital became even more volatile.

In May 1793 Robespierre succeeded in having a truly frightening law passed – the so-called Law of Suspects which met public demands for protection and was in line with a policy of total war. Anyone brought before the Revolutionary Tribunal had no right of defence. The jurors were to be chosen

The Terror

not by the Convention but were to come from the populist Revolutionary Commune. An extreme radical *Montagnard*, Fouquier-Tinville was to be the prosecutor. In practice, simply being brought before the Tribunal was a death sentence. It was a forerunner of the logic of the Soviet Secret Police under Stalin the NKVD, later the KGB, who told people whom they had arrested who insisted on their innocence that such protestations only proved their guilt by claiming that the people's state could be unjust and make mistakes.

This Terror was a way to clear the jails, still thought of as sources of possible opposition. The explosion of popular discussion, extreme publications and democratic local committees had increased the pressure from below for violence.

As has been well established, most victims were not the hated aristos and priests, but ordinary citizens accused of opposition or those who were thought guilty of economic exploitation. To please the sans-culottes, there were controls on the prices of basic foods and some luxury goods like coffee and sugar. Black marketeers or shopkeepers not keeping to the fixed prices were likely to find themselves condemned. The Terror was also a political weapon. Popular demonstrations backed by the National Guard, now radicalised, forced the arrest of the Girondins. These once powerful middle-class radicals now were faced with the consequences of their decision for war and were tried and guillotined, among them the suave Madame Roland, once the friend of Robespierre. Pétion, an ex-mayor of Paris. Robespierre's former friend and the distinguished politician Roland committed suicide. The radical middle classes were finding, in the later words of China's Mao Zedong, that 'a revolution is not a dinner party' but a highly dangerous and violent phenomenon.

In-fighting continued. When Robespierre's former allies and friends Danton and the orator Camille Desmoulins expressed concern about the scale of terror they were condemned and executed. For no apparent reason except revenge and to appease popular vengeance, the Queen was tried and executed. The degree of hatred shown by the *enragés* was shown by the odious Hébert's accusation that she had had sex with her own son – to Robespierre's fury who objected not so much to the death of the queen as to obvious and scurrilous untruths which sullied the purity of the Revolution.

This austere, celibate leader, fastidious and having religious beliefs and no taste for obscenity or mob violence had had enough of the extreme radicals. Hébert went the way of his other political rivals and enemies and was quickly tried, condemned and executed.

The popular image is of a huge guillotine in the modern Place de la Concorde (then the Place de la Révolution) killing its aristocratic victims who had been taken in carts – tumbrils – from prisons. That is unless they had been rescued by daring deeds such as the Scarlet Pimpernel. In fact, the guillotines were not huge – that was an image shown in opposition engravings. Victims were not all aristocrats and included criminals, tradesmen, ordinary artisans who had made unwise remarks, political rivals and extreme sans-culottes. As well as that, the site of the executions was moved as the tempo of death quickened in the final phase of the Terror after September 1793. It took too long to get from the Conciergerie where the tribunal sat to the Place de la Révolution so the site was moved closer to the much less famous Place du Trône Renversé (now the Place de la Nation).

It is also, perhaps understandably, common to see the zenith of revolutionary activity – the Republic during 1792–4 – as characterised by Terror. However, that would be to emphasise one aspect. In a wider context, there was an attempt at regeneration which had been talked about before 1789 and was often strikingly modern. Robespierre and his close ally Louis de St Just aspired to greater welfare for the ordinary person and had plans for educational change and greater economic equality. There was artistic activity in the First Republic and the state patronised painting, music and drama. In terms of defence, the mobilisation of national resources by war minister Carnot laid the basis for a new national army and a national war effort which looked forward to the twentieth century. There was a sense of new beginning with the new Revolutionary Calendar that renamed months which got away from terms derived from old gods to a brighter and more optimistic future. Public ceremonies aimed at national unity and Robespierre wanted to institute a new sense of spirituality though the Cult of the Supreme Being – an all-encompassing respect for a creator independent of particular religious sects. The emphasis in Revolutionary rhetoric was not on violence but on 'Virtue'. Unfortunately for him, Danton responded to one of Robespierre's windier outpourings about this by saying that he showed his virtue three times a night in bed with his wife. Robespierre duly noted this un-Revolutionary sentiment. Whether these developments are seen as in any way mitigating the Terror is a matter of judgement. Robespierre's desire for social equality and moral regeneration does not appear in many films or novels such as '*The Scarlet Pimpernel*' when the Revolutionary extremists are cast as villains. The English poet Coleridge may be nearer the mark when he wrote that Robespierre was so intent on the beautiful distant vision that he did not notice the mud and blood on the road he was treading towards it.

* * *

The Terror

The September Massacres had achieved an astonishing amount of support among both sans-culottes and elites. The Terror in itself won a surprising amount of acceptance, even if there were disagreements about its scale. It did not come to an end because of popular revulsion. The evidence about attitudes among the sans-culottes suggests that it was pretty acceptable. A rather chilling example of this comes from a letter from a carpenter called Trincherd who was a paid juryman at the Revolutionary Tribunal and dates from 13 April 1794. He had had a busy week condemning people to death and among those who were sent off to die had been the widow of the orator Desmoulins, Lucille, who had once had Robespierre as a guest in her house. Also sent to the guillotine by his vote was the widow of the infamous Hébert. But the thirteenth was a special day when twenty-four former presidents of provincial *parlements* and former councillors were to be tried. These were top legal establishment figures, and the carpenter was conscious of his place in history. It was an interesting day, and he wanted his wife to see what was going on:

> If you are not alone and the journeyman is working, you can, my dear wife, come to the court to see the twenty four gentlemen, all of them former presidents of the Parlements de Paris and Toulouse being sentenced. I advise you to get something to eat as we shall not have finished until three o'clock. I embrace you[2]

This matter-of-fact note shows how death had become commonplace. The note is interesting as this is from a master craftsman and employer, and it is not in the heat of some demonstration. It has become merely interesting to see some eminent people sent to a horrific public execution – part of banal everyday life which includes making sure his wife has enough to eat. It shows how easily quite horrible aspects can become accepted.

A low point in this was the condemnation of sixteen Carmelite nuns who refused the oath of loyalty to the Republic and insisted on maintaining their religious community. They were condemned even though they could not possibly have been a threat to anyone and were simply carrying on with what they saw as their vocation. Perhaps the jurors invited family members with their snacks to see their condemnation.

Some nuns who were more fortunate than the Carmelites had already left their convent when they were arrested in October 1793. One of their number, Angelique Vitasse, left an account of her interrogation at La Force prison by a judge called Antoine Savory. Here was a forty-seven-year-old well-educated member of a middle-class elite family of lawyers who had chosen to serve as a judge on the Revolutionary Tribunal but showed little signs of rabid revolutionary fervour. He spoke kindly to Angelique urging her to take the oath of loyalty required of all churchmen and female members of religious communities. 'We are not asking you to do anything except to swear that you regard all men as brothers. You as a person can continue to live simply and continue to be celibate.' It was just a matter of 'rendering under Caesar what is Caesar's'. But he did warn here that he had a duty to judge and condemn all who are against the Republic' There was no evidence that Angelique or the six other former nuns were against the Republic, they just did not want to swear an oath or reveal any information about priests who had visited them. This reasonable and learned middle-aged man nevertheless was so much part of the system that he handed them over for trial and they were abused by the public prosecutor. No death was sufficiently cruel for such as these, they were told. Waiting their fate, they were taken to the Salpetrière prison, but delays in the process helped them as before they could be transported – a virtual death sentence – Robespierre fell, and the repression was relaxed. But like the carpenter, the judge and the prosecutor seemed to have been so involved in the system that they had lost any sense of judgement and perspective, and Angelique had lost through the law of Prairial of May/June 1793 any rights of defence and could only stand and be insulted. There is no sense in which the juryman, the judge or the prosecutor were being pressured by maddened mobs.

The fall of Robespierre in July 1794 did mark a change, but he was not brought down by moderates who were sickened by the violence. Increasingly remote and unpredictable, he was a major cause of concern for colleagues and deputies who had been active supporters of the Terror. He was not supported by the sans-culottes, not because they wanted to end the Terror but because they objected to changes in laws about price fixing that made them worse off. To ensure food supply it was not possible to hold down prices perpetually and there had to be some incentive for producers. This was unpopular and when Robespierre's enemies turned against him there was no popular uprising to support him. His fellow enthusiasts for violence feared that he was about to launch a campaign of terror against them.

The Sans-culottes

The term was not in wide use in its modern form until 20 June 1792 when a crowd burst into the Tuileries and forced Louis XVI to wear the red cap of liberty. Up to that point, and in the period before the Revolution, it had denoted writers without a patron who were satirical and anti-establishment.

'bare-arses' might be a possible translation. But the same term developed into a far more honourable description. Those who wore trousers and were 'without breeches' were hard working ordinary people who wanted a better world. After the end of the Terror, the opponents of extremism used the term as synonymous with lower class rabble.

The idea that the Terror was driven by the very poorest of the poor, a rag-clad rabble of toothless workers and 'peasants' has long gone. The besiegers of the Bastille and the people who made possible key events in the Revolution known as *journées* were artisans, small masters, craftsmen and even creative workers. In his brilliant fictional study of one such revolutionary, the novelist Anatole France[4] makes this ardent supporter of terror a working artist – producing portraits and playing cards. This self-educated and politically aware young man – Gamelin – is active in the local Section. In this case that of Pont Neuf. He is chosen as a juryman of the revolutionary tribunal – not as in the usual sense of the word but a permanent and paid official whose job it is to judge the accused in this revolutionary court presided over by a judge with a black plumed hat and led by a fanatical public prosecutor. Initially the accused had the right to defend themselves, but after the law of Prairial (September 1793) this was lost. The jurors merely confirmed the pseudo-legality of delivering a wide variety of people from all backgrounds to the guillotine. Initially keen to be impartial and saving some of the accused, Gamelin, in the novel, becomes obsessed with vengeance against 'aristos', though few prisoners are nobles. 'Aristo' becomes a general term of abuse. His creative work as an artist stops. He is a stranger to his mother and sister, utterly absorbed by his revolutionary duty. He spends nights making passionate love to his mistress who is excited by the whole idea of death and bloodshed. His erstwhile friends go to their deaths accused of speaking against the Revolution in unguarded comments. His admiration for Robespierre is his inspiration. A member of the Commune, he goes in his sash of office to defend his idol in July 1794 only to see him shot, arrested and guillotined. The artist follows him and is executed in the purge of Robespierre's followers. Gamelin has betrayed his calling, has only a loose and undeveloped political philosophy, loses any sense of natural justice, is over-reliant on the example of Robespierre and destroys all around him, losing his own life in a pointless gesture. But he is not a maniac or a monster, does not run around with a pike and has a strong sense of duty. Anatole France's meticulously researched novel work was written in 1912 but is utterly convincing in its portrayal of the erosion of a sense of proportion and humanity as the Terror developed its own momentum.

The Real Story of the French Revolution

Though like most novels of the Revolution, it is set in Paris, the main terror was, in fact, not in the capital but in the provinces. As with the killings in Paris, the main victims were not nobles but a wide cross-section of men, women and children who fell foul of troops sent under the command of representatives of the Convention. One of these fanatical leaders, Louis-Marie Turreau, not a well-known name to any but specialists, instituted 'infernal columns' of prisoners from provinces in revolt where men women and children were led on brutal marches before being bayonetted. At Nantes, the Representative Carrier loaded his victims into barges on the river Loire which were then bombarded and sank. The war between revolution and counter-revolution in La Vendée resembled a genocide. A former priest Joseph le Bon pursued his enemies in his home region of Arras with a mobile guillotine. Those selected for execution for opposition to the Revolution were paraded and then subjected to a ceremony resembling an *auto da fé*, or a religious ceremony in which heretics were burned to death in earlier times when the Inquisition killed heretics. Le Bon orated on the purity of the evolution and the crime of disloyalty. The miliary band played revolutionary songs, like the ubiquitous '*ça ira*' and then there was mass beheading. Lyons was subject to particularly harsh punishment because of the murder by frustrated citizens of the mentally disturbed Jacobin who had taken control of the city and ruined its trade. Once revolutionary troops had taken control, this individual was given a funeral on quite a lavish scale with all sorts of quasi-religious trappings and symbolism. Literary treatments of the provincial terror that far exceeded in scope and violence the terror in the capital are not common. In popular memory, Paris retains its supremacy.

The support for violence among the people of Paris has made the term 'sans-culotte' almost one of abuse, suggesting relentless supporters of mob and official killings. The term was not widely used before 1789 and remains quite difficult to define. Historians are thrown back on a very common document which is worth quoting.

> A sans-culotte you rogues? It is a being who goes about on foot, who has no millions, as you would like to have, no chateaux, no valets to serve him and who is housed simply with his wife and children, if he has them on the fourth or fifth floor. He is useful because he knows how to work a field, how to forge, saw, tile, roof, make shoes, and spill his blood to the very last drop for the good of the Republic. And because he works, one is sure not to see his face at the Café de Chartres, nor in the dives where there is conspiring and gaming, nor in the Theatre ... In the evening he goes to the Section, not powdered, perfumed and dressed up in the

hope of attracting the attention of all the citizenesses in the stands, but rather to support the good motions with all his energy and to brush those which come from the abominable faction of the statesmen. He always walks with his sabre ... to cut off the ears of the all the wrong-doers. Sometimes he walks with his pike; but at the first sound of the drum, he can be seen leaving for the Vendée ... or for the army of the North.[5]

This shows that there was a body of politically engaged skilled tradesmen, utterly devoted to the Republic, proud of simple living and engaged with local politics in the regular meetings of the Sections that were also ready for horrible violence and armed with sword and pike.

Often quoted, this description is not always attributed. It was found in fact in the papers of Jean Baptiste Vingtrinier a revolutionary who was arrested in the summer of 1793. It is a fragment and apparently an answer to a question by somebody we don't know, as its title is '*Response to an Impertinent Question. But what is a sans-culotte?*' Other sources suggest that there was a strong element of continuity with trade associations of these small masters and craftsmen overlaid by some acquired revolutionary language conveyed as much by word of mouth as by any profound reading of political theory.

The interest in political discussion shown in this source had also been seen in the growth of popular societies. This emerged in the period 1790 to 1792 and though their membership probably never exceeded 3,000 and membership rarely include the very poor, these societies did play a role in politicising the class from which the sans-culottes emerged. Societies like *the Fraternelle*, the *Indigens*, the *Nomophiles*, the *Halles*, and the *Minimes* were open to both men and women. They discussed liberal ideas and espoused the cause of more democracy urging the rights of passive citizens and an end to monarchy. In these clubs from 1790–2 in the words of one historian 'hard-working men and women had striven to arouse the political and civic aspirations of ordinary Parisians and to instil in them a degree of awareness and self-confidence, creating the preconditions for the experiment in popular democracy that was to follow'. The clubs were not wholly made up of the sans-culotte class but contained substantial elements and their work is a corrective to a view of 'mobs'. In a study of 1988[6], the historian Gwyn Williams wrote that 'In the passionate anarchy of 1793 the Sections emerged virtually as sovereign powers'. Despite illiteracy and lack of experience, he claimed that 1792 was the year that 'the people entered politics'. A study of the discussions of the committees of the Sections shows the interest and knowledge of political ideas, particularly those of Rousseau whose 'Social Contract' had made the famous statement that 'Man is born free but is everywhere in chains' and saw legitimate government only in terms of a social contract between rulers and ruled not the divine right of monarchs.

And yet this burgeoning democracy expressed itself in often violent language. The various nicknames for the guillotine suggest an acceptance of violence – 'the people's axe', 'the scythe of equality'. Expressions of hatred towards 'aristos' and a desire for even more executions suggest a way of thought that is disturbing. A police report of 1794 reports an inoffensive and moderate sans-culotte asking whether there were to be executions to be told by another 'Let's hope so, as there is always treason'. An account of the prison massacres of 2 September 1792 by a Commune official called Mehée de Latouche recalls prisoners being taken to the Abbaye prison by a guard of provincial troops. One of the prisoners put out his arm and hit a soldier on the head. The soldier drew his sabre and plunged it into the man's heart causing a flood of blood. A cry went up 'We ought to kill them all – they are scum, aristocrats' and other troopers started hacking at the prisoners, including a young sick man in a dressing gown. When the remaining prisoners were eventually delivered Mehée saw 'a crowd armed with pikes, swords, sabres, bayonets kill them'.[5] Words had turned to deeds.

The sans-culotte phenomenon which had a short life – not being well established until 1792 and then being crushed by 1795 could either be seen as an experiment in direct and popular democracy or, less favourably, it could be seen as a dire example of what happens when traditional restraints and a sense of crisis allow popular prejudices and resentments to take centre stage. The willingness and ability of extreme political leaders to promote and use popular fears and anger and the links between the sans-culottes and wayward members of the intellectual elite have often been seen as they key to this strange period of terror.

Architects of Terror

Though popular perceptions of the Revolution associate the violence and terror with 'the mob', in fact, the incidents of violent popular action were relatively limited, and the streets were not perpetually filled with angry sans-culottes. The more typical political activity was the local meetings and discussions and as has been seen the numbers involved in actual violence, as in the September Massacres were low. Though there was widespread acceptance of Terror, the principal originators of the much more widespread violence meted out by the revolutionary state were the educated middle-class political leaders and writers.

The Terror

Had the middle-class reformers of 1789 foreseen the Terror then there is little doubt that most would have been aghast, but they unwittingly laid the basis for it. Firstly, the outbursts of popular violence which made possible the changes of 1789 were accepted as somehow necessary and widely celebrated. The brilliant study of the Revolution by Simon Schama '*Citizens*' looks at the iconography of the Bastille – with its medals and models and special uniforms and status for veterans of the assault. The painstaking demolition of the fortress and the strange sculpture of an elephant which replaced it were implicit acceptance of the right of 'the people' to take direct action even if incidental violence did result. The acceptance in the summer that widespread agrarian violence and unrest should result in the end of feudalism again showed that the traditional eighteenth-century view that popular illegality should be suppressed and not rewarded was suspended. Similarly, the seeming surrender in October 1789 to the popular will with the march on Versailles with the Assembly leaving Versailles and meeting in central Paris, not from its own decision but under pressure, showed uncertainty about the source of legitimacy. If it was not hereditary royal authority anymore, was it more vaguely to do with 'the will of the people'? However, the will of the people was hard to ascertain, but middle-class enthusiasts were happy to try to do so.

Many politicians find the use of 'the people' a very useful rhetorical device. If the people want something then who has the right to stand in the way, except if what the people want is not in line with what ruling elites think is right or can realistically deliver. Hitler had a vision of 'One people (Volk), one nation (Reich) and one Führer (leader). Communist 'People's Republics' actually dominated by new elites were apparently sure that their dictatorships were representing what the people really wanted. A lot of this thinking went back to the philosopher Rousseau who was the most popular thinker among the French revolutionary elites. He had made a distinction between the immediate wishes of the people and 'the General Will' which was what they really wanted – a very useful tool for governments who decide what is really best for the governed as opposed to what their short-sighted immediate wishes are.

So when war and opposition in the provinces offered opposition to the Republic then the people had to be saved, avenged, defended and those who wanted to destroy, betray, enslave 'the people' deserved only death. Without this rhetoric and these concepts then terror on the scale exercised by the Revolution could not have taken place. Governments and repression had been bedfellows throughout history and the eighteenth century was not short of examples of killings in the course of wars and in suppressing or inciting revolts. However, an ideologically justified secular terror was something new and was a major legacy of the Revolution. Terror was not just mob violence, not just a means of restoring authority in rebellious provinces but a means of purification. It had antecedents more in religious persecutions of past ages and relied on similar ceremonials of death and an aim to regenerate the world.

This accounts for a paradox that has concerned historians and commentators. The revolutionary leaders who used the sans-culottes to gain power and destroy their enemies were also deeply interested in moral and spiritual rebirth.

Psychologists often refer to the close association of euphoria and violence and Robespierre certainly displayed this in one of his final speeches in 1794.

> If the mainspring of popular government in peacetime is virtue, amid revolution it is at the same time virtue and terror; virtue without terror is fatal; terror without virtue is impotent. Terror is simply prompt, severe, inflexible justice; therefore, it is an expression of virtue.

The progressive provincial member of the Arras debating society had lofty ideals. He had drafted a bill for universal and compulsory state education for both boys and girls which was years ahead of its time and spoke in the Convention, which rejected the proposal, movingly of needing to help the poorest in society. He saw children as 'young trees which will be transplanted into the national nursery ... where they will grow and develop under the gentle influence of the fatherland'. His fellow advocate of terror St Just shared a vision of a welfare state. The radical ex-actor Fabre d'Eglantine drew up a new calendar based on nature 'not the prejudices and falsehoods of the throne and the church'. The new months were named poetically after 'mist', 'frost', 'snow', 'fruit', and so on. The reality was very different. The most tyrannical measure robbing suspects of any legal rights was passed in Prairial, (May) the month of meadows. Robespierre was overthrown in the month of 'warmth' Thermidor (July). In disposing of the Girondins Robespierre and his allies turned to extreme violence against men and women who had shared some of their idealism. One of them, Valazé, stabbed himself in the court room with a knife he had smuggled in. His body was dragged along with the living victims in a cart to the guillotine in a remarkable act of spite. Robespierre did not find any contradiction between his belief in a Supreme Being, his love of 'virtue' and such sordid actions. In one utterance he orated that death was not an eternal sleep but rather 'Death is the beginning of immortality!' Abstract verbiage had hidden the reality of savage violence.

Oddly, the Terror still finds defenders. The Marxist historian Peter Taafe has tried to put the Terror into perspective by considering the large amount of repression of the sans-culottes in 1795 with 149 executions and 1,200 arrests, by the executions during the Paris Commune of 1871 which might have amounted to 15,000 and by the 40,000 killed in revenge for collaboration with the Nazis when France was liberated 1944–5. These atrocities he contrasts with the necessary defence of the French Republic which foreign powers and counter-revolutionaries were trying to 'drown in blood'.[3] Though even the Russian revolutionary Trotsky drew a distinction between necessary terror during a period of emergency and the political terror in the later part of Robespierre's period of dominance which he saw as 'absurdity'.

After Robespierre's fall, the Jacobin club reflected on how the Terror had been allowed to occur. The easiest thing was to blame Robespierre. Rather in the way that post-war Germans who had been active and enthusiastic supporters of the Third Reich claimed they had been blinded and deceived by one evil man, so previous supporters of terror now explained that they had been misled by 'this rogue and his vile accomplices' – of whom seventy-one had been killed a short time before. 'Who would have dared suspect this monster?' they piously asked because he had disguised his true intentions with words of virtue and 'love of public good' and belief in a Supreme Being.

The explanations that Terror was a result of deception or a necessary act to save the Republic from its enemies are unconvincing. Robespierre himself told the Convention shortly before he was overthrown that new threats were emerging. But when it was clear that not harmless nuns or atheists or political opponents who questioned his authority and repression, but his fellow supporters might be endangering the Republic, then the Terror ended with a final burst of violence directed against some, if not all of its architects.

Whatever the ultimate cause of the Terror, whether it was the impact of war or the abstract ideals of curdled Enlightenment enthusiasts, the last word should go to the victims. Farewell letters have survived from a variety of condemned people.[7] Whom to select to remember that the Terror had a variety of victims? The forger Guillaume Leonard, the geologist and former mayor of Strasbourg, Baron Dietrich, the notary (solicitor) Jean-Francois Dufouler accused of falsifying legal documents, the famous chemist Antoine-Laurent de Lavoisier accused of taxation fraud. Louis-Francois Poire who was a foreign correspondent for English newspapers, the former sea captain Nicolas-Bernard Groult de la Motte. What a sad selection there is to choose from. But the last letter of Charles-Antoine Pinard reveals the sheer futility of these executions in any attempt to 'save the Revolution'.

Pinard was a tailor who saw an opening in making tunics for the revolutionary army. In December 1793 he was denounced for substandard work.

Hardly a threat to national security. On 19 Frimaire, he wrote from prison to his girlfriend whom he loyally addressed on the envelope as 'Citizeness' in the best republican style.

> Farewell, my dear friend. When you get this, your good friend will be no more. I would have preferred to die fighting for my country, but I shall accept my fate and carry to the grave the peace of a quiet conscience. Take care of yourself for the sake of the child you bear in your womb and raise the child in the principles of the Republic. Tell our son or daughter that its father died a true republican.

His partner in the firm Philippe Rigaud who was also condemned wrote to his brother.

> Farewell. You must all love the Republic. Do not forget our family and embrace Francois my friend for me. Pay him I beg you the 50 livres I owe to madame Rhoze and do not forget to pay the wig maker. I owe him money and do the same for Clermont, the porter of the house where I lived. Farewell my brother, farewell and concern yourself only with the Fatherland.

There was no reason for either of these two unlucky tradesmen to write in defence of the Republic which was about to behead them in public. Both, as is seen in many of this type of letter, are concerned with settling everyday matters in a way that shows them valuable members of the community, anxious that their children are brought up well, loyal to the new regime and concerned with their obligation to others. In very few cases did their deaths do anything to ensure the survival of the Revolution. Little, if any, of this tragic and murderous activity had any 'virtue', revolutionary or otherwise.

Notes

1. Quoted www.marxists.org/history/france/revolution/hebert/1790/pere-duchesne.htm.
2. Quoted G. Lenotre, *The Tribunal of the Terror* (London, 1909).
3. P Taafe, *The Masses Arise* (Socialist Publications, 2009).
4. Anatole France, *The Gods Will Have Blood* (1912) (Penguin edition 2017).
5. L. Mason and T. Rizzio, *The French Revolution, a Documentary Collection* (New York, 1999), pp. 198–9.
6. G. Williams, *Artisans and Sans-culottes* (Arnold, 1968).
7. *Last Letters*, ed Olivier Blanc (Deutsch, 1987).

Chapter Six

The Role of Women in the Revolution

'Women hold up half the sky' was the famous view of Mao Zedong, but their role in the French Revolution remains neglected. The socialist historian Eric Hazan[1] summed up the neglect of women's role: 'The role of women remains vague and is dealt with in only a few lines even by the best historians'. He argued that the two who have inspired the most books, plays and films are Marie Antoinette and Charlotte Corday. After that, but a long way after that, are those who have never become well known, such as Jeanne-Marie (Manon) Roland, Olympe de Gouges and Théroigne de Méricourt. The rest, the women of the people, he wrote 'are often grouped under the term "tricoteuses"'. The writer Baroness Orczy depicted the *tricoteuses* in her novel, *The Scarlet Pimpernel* of 1908. They 'sat beneath the guillotine platform to knit whilst head after head fell beneath the knife, and they themselves got quite bespattered with the blood of those cursed aristos'. In 1856 Charles Dickens in the novel *A Tale of Two Cities* created a leader, Madame Defarge, a bloodthirsty hag who came to represent radical women who sat in the Convention and then when banished watched avidly as the guillotine did its deadly work. They appear in films and novels, as a grim parody of politically active and aware women. Hazan makes the point that many women took part in the great revolutionary events in Paris. To this could be added their role in the political agitation prior to the Estates General, and their role in both revolution and counter-revolution in the provinces. They showed a high level of political interest, remarkable for the time, and their role was far more significant than the study of a few individuals would indicate.

It would be wrong to say that there is a lack of writing about this, but there is still a limited popular perception of women's significance in the Revolution and relatively slight coverage in school and university textbooks. More specialist studies have tended to focus on individuals, which can give a distorted view of the role of women. The popular image of elements of the French Revolution is often at odds with reality, but in the case of women, it is difficult to pin down quite what is generally thought. To offer a rough summary, women are most often seen as victims, sometimes as deluded and sometimes deranged. But mostly, their role in the overall narrative of the French Revolution is simply ignored, aside from a handful of moments which have captured the attention of those writing about it or dramatizing it. In most general accounts there are glimpses of the actions of women and the impact that the Revolution had on them, or token sections; but overall. this is, as Hazan says, a neglected aspect.

In a commonly used A-level textbook, there is no index entry for 'women'. Apart from Marie Antoinette, the only individual to be given any prominence is Charlotte Corday who is said to have wanted to bring the revolution to an end by killing the radical agitator Marat in 1793, even though she was a dedicated Republican and supporter of change. Women as a whole appear in the context of the events of 5 October 1789 when 6,000–7,000 marched on the Palace of Versailles then disappear from history. Surveys for more general readership often offer little more. The historian John Roberts[2] has the women of October as 'rioters' who were 'manipulated' into marching to Versailles. As we shall see, this is questionable. When not rioting, women in the two pages devoted to them took some part in the meetings and elections prior to the Estates General, but then are seen as devout provincial Catholics 'voting with their knees' in prayer to support a threatened Catholic Church and suffering from the loss of Catholic charity. So, the reader is left with a view of women, once the Revolution gets going, either getting out of control or being passive and pious. One leading French study of the Revolution has no index entry as such for women. Their role in the events of 5 October 1789 is virtually written out. The revolutionary lower class is patronised by saying they confused the grain issue with politics. Surely having enough food is a political issue! When dealing with the 5 October and the women's march on Versailles, their role is hardly considered and they are wrongly accused of being 'armed' when they returned to Paris with the royal family, even though more than one testimony indicated that they had left weapons behind. Simon Schama in his study *Citizens*[3] has a fuller account of the events of 5 October but inserts the colourful figure of Théroigne de Méricourt into the narrative, – an 'Amazon' 'emblematic of a pathetic revolutionary career' dressed in an ostentatious plumed hat and 'blood red' riding coat. She stands apart from the 'bedraggled, angry and famished' women, relishing the revolutionary action even though she had 'a banal history'. However, she is made to pay for her swaggering as at the end of the book when she was confined to an asylum, her madness is seen as 'a logical destination for the compulsions of the revolution' and she is said to undeserving of sympathy. Individual women campaigners do get mentions in general histories but have been more often the subject of specialist biographical studies which have not always put them in the context of the overall role of women and have seen them more as trailblazers of future feminism.

Women as Victims

In terms of women as victims, the head of the list is Marie Antoinette. Brought to France from the Austrian court to marry a portly and sexually incompetent French prince for reasons of state, she became the subject of abuse, pornography, intense unpopularity and a symbol of all that was apparently so detested about the Old Regime. Mobbed by crowds, forced into virtual captivity, forced to watch as the dismembered body parts of her favourite were paraded in front of her, she was finally tried and executed. The one thing that everyone remembers – her supposed response to bread shortage 'Let them eat cake' is false. She stands as a symbol of the sufferings of an upper class, for tragic aristocratic victims of the Revolution. These are remembered as women rescued by fictional anti-revolutionary heroes like Sir Percy Blakeney, the Scarlet Pimpernel of Baroness Orczy's novel (*They seek him here, they seek him there, that damn'd elusive pimpernel!*), or the less well-known Roger Brook of the once popular works of right-wing novelist Dennis Wheatley. Better known, but rather less heroical is the rescuer of lovely young aristos played by Jim Dale in the film *Carry On Don't Lose Your Head*. Aristocratic ladies in stinking prison cells waiting for execution as part of a fervid class war stirred the imagination of writers and film makers. The image of suffering was confirmed by those who fled leaving behind memoirs of the sufferings of exile and the horrors of revolution. One of many, the memoirs, published in 1843, of Mlle des Echerolles,[4] a well-born lady of Lyons describes how her aunt, who was bringing her up, was arrested in November 1793 when the Revolutionary authorities could not find her brother, a counter-revolutionary, and thrown into a disgusting prison. Mlle de Echerolles was forced to live in squalid quarters with a woman whose main joy was to watch the guillotine at work. Though innocent, the aunt was condemned 'She knew from the first day she was to die and prepared herself for it.'

But the saddest victims were the pioneers of women's rights who found that the revolution 'devoured its own'. The political activist Madame Roland ended by being guillotined, as did the civil rights pioneer Olympe de Gouges. This fearless proponent of women's equality left a poignant final letter as she awaited execution. She had outraged the Revolutionary authorities, not only by a Declaration of the Rights of Woman, but also by offering to defend the king at his trial in January 1793.

> Following five months imprisonment, I was transferred to a lunatic asylum, but I demanded a fair trial. I was kept as if ordered to be in solitary confinement. I was taken before the Tribunal, weakened and ill. They allowed me no defence counsel and condemned me. Farewell, my dear son. When you receive this, I shall be dead.[5]

Thus, women rich and poor, queens, peasants, intellectuals, or urban beggars shared the image of victim, to be pitied, laughed at, rescued or killed.

Delusions

But women have also been seen as deluded. Did not Marie Antoinette and the noblewomen see what was coming? Did they not see that their lifestyle was unsustainable given the terrible inequalities and rising suffering of the people? From the relative austerity of the Austrian court, Marie Antoinette was catapulted into the far more elaborate and costly ceremonial of Versailles. A substantial permanent establishment supported a very high level of court rituals and entertainments. Amateur theatricals, picnics, fireworks, fabulous silks and satins abounded. The historian John Fisher[6] in his study of the Revolution '*The Elysian Fields*' might have been providing a film scenario 'in a typical fete, the young and beautiful; Duchesse de Bourbon dressed as a voluptuous water nymph sailed in a gilded gondola to the Isle of Love'. The ladies were warned in advance that they were to be 'kidnapped' and they repaired to a temple in the park where they were 'seized' by 300 Turks and carried off to an Illuminated Garden. The royals were surrounded by ceremonial troops, by courtiers honoured to see to their every need. It took four people to serve the Queen with a glass of wine. A rather less glamorous reality was the stench of urine and faecal matter that permeated Versailles and its park. Years later an elderly courtier was taken to revisit and during the visit, a waste pipe overflowed, and sewage poured out. The old man is said to have cried 'Ah that was Versailles in my day. It was like that everywhere!' That might be a symbol of delusion – surface glamour but underlying squalor.

The Queen's famous nods to the simple life – a model farm at Rambouillet or pretending to be a serving maid dispensing lemonade at the Petit Trianon at Versailles might be seen as insensitive parodies. In the overall scheme of things, court extravagance was not the main cause of financial problems, but it is easy to see why the Queen was known as 'Madame Deficit'. The flood of pornographic pamphlets in the 1780s might have given some indication of the tide of ill will that this ostentation gave rise to. As well as being a victim, Marie Antoinette has been seen as symbolic of a class that was blind to the dangers facing it.

* * *

Just as delusional were the proponents of change. The desire for enlightened change affected the famous salons of Paris where hostesses brought together persons of influence to discuss the great questions of the day. Active before the Revolution, these drawing room influencers blossomed in 1789. Of these hostesses, the daughter of the great financial expert, Necker, the future Mme de Staël was the most renowned. The US ambassador was so overwhelmed that he compared her drawing room to a temple of Apollo. Convinced that her father had the answers to all of France's political and financial problems, she used her social skills to promote his influence. Necker was dismissed by the king, but popular pressure led to his reinstatement on 20 July 1789 to his daughter's delight. The hope was for a peaceful transition to an enlightened constitutional monarchy. She was at Versailles in October when the people of Paris attacked the royal guard. She saw the bloodstains and a terrified Marie Antoinette told her that the people wanted her to go to Paris in a procession with the heads of the bodyguards on pikes. Undeterred, the salon discussions went on with much talk of liberty and progress. Mme de Staël's evenings at the Swedish embassy were not the only forums for political hostesses. The Marquise de Condorcet dabbled in radical politics. The Marquise de Fontenay, daughter of a wealthy Spanish banker, gathered leading political figures for her soirées. The ladies adopted tricolour dress, and fragments of the Bastille were fashion accessories, such as the brooch worn by the radical Duc d'Orléan's mistress. There was a sense of playing at Revolution. The Countess de Beauharnais revelled in talk of liberty at her salon but the reality was more dangerous.

If any group of people could be seen as deluded, then it was these women. The events of 1789 had been accompanied by significant violence and the radicalism that was building up in Paris was making it hard for the new Constitutional Monarchy to be an end rather than a steppingstone for greater change. Necker was increasingly side-lined and by October 1790 both he and his devoted liberal daughter were in exile. The Marquise de Condorcet suffered when her husband was forced to flee after orders for his arrest in 1793 on political charges. He died in prison. She had to make a living selling underwear. The golden liberal couple suffered from the move to the left in the Revolution. The liberal Marquise de Fontenay went on to marry a leading Republican political figure, Tallien, and was imprisoned when he fell foul of his enemies. She went on to be a mistress of Napoleon and a scandalous social figure in the Directory period appearing at the Opera bedecked in jewels but with no underwear. The idea of revolution as a social opportunity was as delusional in its way as the failure to foresee it.

The famous individuals who are most often studied as being influential in the Revolution are also usually seen as deluded and victims of the change they helped to bring about.

Madame Roland

Of the individuals who played a part in the Revolution, Jeanne-Marie (Manon) Roland was probably the most influential on the course. Born in 1754 to a Paris engraver of radical views and a pious mother, she was brought up by fond and admiring parents who delighted in her quiet, scholarly and devout ways. Her father found her a ready audience for his enlightenment views of reform and equality. Her mother admired her religious devotion, as did the nuns who supervised her education. The family had some upper-class connections and Manon, as she was known, was able to visit Versailles and move in well-connected literary circles. Through friends made at the convent, she met one of the *ancien régimes* serious-minded local administrators, the Inspector of Manufactures at Amiens, M. Roland de la Platière. This sober and bookish man of forty and the scholarly young woman, twenty years his junior, formed a bond, and Manon had second thoughts about a decision to become a nun and married Roland in 1780. As part of the ruling elite, they moved to Lyons where he was a leading official, Inspector General of Commerce, and lived in his family property. Her wide reading had led her to ideas of reform and Republicanism and a belief in the rights of the people. She did charitable work, and the couple was in some ways typical products of the Enlightenment – well educated, socially conscious, committed to reform and modernisation. They followed the events of 1789 and 1790 with huge interest, and in 1791 they returned to Paris when Roland was elected to the Assembly of the constitutional monarchy. One of her endless series of pamphlets about reform had a wide circulation and the couple were already quite well known when they set up house in Paris. Their home became a meeting place for radical deputies. These included Maximilien Robespierre who was taken with Manon's scholarship and appearance.

In September the Assembly was dissolved and they returned home, but by now both had the taste for politics and a desire for power and influence. In

December they returned, and Roland's efforts resulted in his being appointed Minister of the Interior in a Girondin ministry appointed by the king which included reformers. The king had to decide to compromise with moderate radicals, and the Girondins formed a government. Roland showed his revolutionary credentials by wearing a plain black coat and not court dress but was on good terms with the king. Manon warned him about the dangers of compromise 'Distrust the court! Your virtue is too elevated to see its snares.' In some ways, that sums up the view that the Rolands had of themselves – high-minded and virtuous. No doubt they thought they were natural leaders – sober, learned, moderate, efficient, and well-read in modern ideas. But like their Girondin friends they were caught between a king who at heart disliked sharing power and was looking to end the revolution and more radical Republicans ready to use the power of the people to bring about a quite different kind of state than the well-run constitutional monarchy that Roland aspired to. The decision to go to war transformed the situation and encouraged a much greater radicalism which increased when it was clear that the Revolution was threatened by foreign forces and royalist nobles.

However, Mme Roland was all for putting the king in his place. When an issue arose about a decree against priests who would not take an oath swearing loyalty to the state control of the church in the 1791 Civil Constitution of the Clergy, she was all fire. She drafted for Roland a famous letter to the legislators. This urged action against the priests 'Deposed priests agitate the provinces. Paris trembles as it views the dangers it faces. Surround the walls with an army of defence.' 'Love and serve the Revolution'. Louis XVI dismissed Roland and this together with the widely circulated letter made Roland a heroic figure, standing for the defence of the Revolution. Manon's radicalism led her to support the end of the monarchy. If foreign forces invaded, then she was all for a new Republic in the provinces. Her influence on the Girondins was quite considerable, but the implications of this radicalism were not all to her liking. The increase in violence and extremism in Paris did not really accord with her theoretical view of change. When Danton came to her salon, she found him dangerous and shunned him. Now she and the Girondins found themselves between the king and growing popular violence. Roland was recalled to office, and he became more and more reliant on his wife's drafting of letters, speeches and state papers. But with a deteriorating military situation, rising prices and food shortages, unrest in the provinces and political radicalism in Paris allied to crowd violence, the sort of elevated scholarly politics of the Rolands was becoming irrelevant. The overthrow of the monarchy on 10 August and the massacres of September horrified her. She wrote to a friend.

> We are under the knife of Robespierre and Marat. You know my enthusiasm for the revolution, well, I am ashamed of it. Women violated before being torn to pieces, entrails being cut out and carried like ribbons ...[7]

France moved away from enlightened reform to a dictatorship with the Law of Suspects and reliance on terror. Manon Roland could not accept lawlessness, an affront to her belief in civilised and orderly change and she supported the perpetrators of mob violence being brought to trial. The Jacobins called for Roland's resignation and ominously Danton spoke scathingly of the influence of Madame Roland who was helping with her husband's speeches and criticism of the revolutionary terror. A spy was infiltrated into the Roland circle and accusations of corresponding to restore the monarchy were made. Mme Roland was summoned to the Convention but was acquitted. However, the writing as on the wall. There was more pressure to conform to extreme actions. When the king was tried in January 1793, the Girondins were pressured to show their commitment to the Revolution and voted for his death.

This was a low point. War and political extremism had created a situation which for Madame Roland was worse than 'regal tyranny'. The fashionable political ideas for reform had not resulted in the ideal format – something like the new American Republic in which educated administrators could rule a new efficient France with old privileges and divisions swept away. Madame Roland could not be a charming and gracious hostess and adviser to Roland and his moderate reforming friends, producing pamphlets for reform and looking to improve the life of an adored and idealised people. Instead, they were forced to accept greater inroads into individual liberty than any Bourbon king could have enforced and the execution of a king who had consistently promoted and rewarded Roland. The sovereign people had gone from grateful recipients of charity from the kindly and gracious Manon to violent slayers of suspects in a welter of blood.

With news of a rising in La Vendée, the start of a murderous repression by the Republic and ever more bitter verbal attacks on the Girondins, why did the Rolands not flee? Roland resigned but the couple stayed in Paris, with Manon devoting herself more and more to writing. There was a poignancy to her reaction, when after an insurrection on 31 May, the Jacobin extremists gained control and condemned the Girondin leaders. She wrote a long letter to the Convention, offering rational and considered arguments against this.

The Role of Women in the Revolution

She was genuinely surprised when it was not delivered, let alone read. M. Roland escaped but Mme Roland remained. Even when arrested, she devoted her time, when possible, to extensive writing. It was as though the written word could prevail and that she was thinking of her place in the history of the revolution as a progressive woman intellectual. The Girondins were tried in October 1793 and after their execution, she was moved to the cell in which they were imprisoned. She wrote a futile letter to Robespierre, whom she had once sheltered from a hostile crowd and entertained in her salon. Her belief in the written word once again was misplaced. She was tried, condemned and executed on 10 November 1793. Her husband could not bear to live without her and committed suicide in a particularly gruesome way by fixing a blade to a tree and falling on it.

Madame Roland may not have actually said the famous words 'Liberty, what crimes are committed in thy name!' but she did leave written testimony of her disillusion.

> Truth! friendship! my country! sacred objects, sentiments dear to my heart, accept my] last sacrifice. My life was devoted to you, and you will render my death easy and glorious.
>
> Just Heaven! enlighten this unfortunate people for whom I desired liberty. Liberty! it is for noble minds, who despise death, and who know how, upon occasion, to give it to themselves. It is not for weak beings, who enter into a composition with guilt, and cover selfishness and cowardice with the name of prudence. It is not for corrupt wretches, who rise from the bed of debauchery, or from the mire of indigence, to feast their eyes upon the blood that streams from the scaffold. It is the portion of a people who delight in humanity, practice justice, despise their flatterers, and respect the truth. While you are not such a people, O my fellow-citizens! you will talk in vain of liberty. Instead of liberty you will have licentiousness, to which you will all fall victims in your turn. You will ask for bread; dead bodies will be given you, and you at last will bow down your own necks to the yoke[8]

Madame Roland's widely circulated '*Apostrophe to Liberty*' has an air of disappointment about it. The people were just not up to it. It is the portion of the people who delight in humanity, practise justice ... respect the truth' that really deserve it. But that elitist view must have been challenged by the horrible scenes of violence following the attack on the Bastille, by the crowd violence of October 1789, and by the peasant attacks on landlords in the Great Fear. And the violent language of revolutionary oratory was well established before this golden couple turned up in Paris in 1791. Was it really likely that their vision could be achieved and that the flood of well-crafted enlightened reformist prose would prevail over the raw emotions and extreme language that had become common currency by 1792? Or was Madame Roland in the grip of a delusion that she and her allies were so clever, so able to produce good arguments, and powerful phrases that they could drive events that were obviously getting out of control? Is that why she stayed in Paris when it was so unsafe that she slept with two pistols under her pillow? Was her execution a way of making a sort of debating point that a woman could meet her death bravely knowing that she was in the right?

Charlotte Corday

It might seem unacceptable to categorise Charlotte Corday as deluded as she became a post-revolutionary heroine. Her assassination on 13 July 1793 of the radical Jacobin journalist Marat in his bath has been seen as one of history's great acts of courage. She was seen as 'the angel of assassination' by the nineteenth-century historian Jules Michelet, and inspired acts of violence in the wartime French Resistance. Dissenting voices in the US were raised after Lincoln's assassination in 1865 when political murder was seen in a less heroic light, but her reputation stands on something she probably never said 'I have killed one man to save thousands'. She did write in a last letter to her father 'I have avenged many innocent lives; I have prevented many other disasters'.

She was the daughter of a minor aristocrat from Normandy whose modest house in the village of Ecorches was far from the grand chateau usually associated with nobility. He sent Marie Anne Charlotte de Corday d'Armont to an abbey in Caen when his wife died, and there she read widely – not only Enlightenment writers but works from the Ancient World, especially Plutarch's 'Lives' of noble Romans, which she took with her to Paris when she went to kill Marat. She was impressed with the virtues she read about of Republican Rome, and when she went to live with a cousin, she met Girondin sympathisers, but the Revolutionary events which unfolded from 1789 had little direct impact on her life. Her sympathies were with the revolution, but she was shocked by the rising tide of popular violence, especially the September Massacres, and blamed the influence of radical Jacobins, especially Marat and his radical journal *L'Ami du Peuple.* Marat was an outspoken enthusiast for Republican purity and violence, but quite why she singled him out is obscure. Perhaps this intellectual young woman was shocked at the abuse of the printed word; perhaps Marat was just a high-profile target.

She took the trouble to write an explanation and justification for posterity in an 'Address to Frenchmen who love law and peace'.

Her original idea was to kill Marat in the Convention, but she was not up to date enough with her information to know that a painful skin disease prevented him from attending to pour forth his murderous denunciations. He was reliant on baths to ease pain and discomfort, and after failing to be admitted to see him on 13 July 1793, she returned with tantalising news of a Girondin conspiracy which excited Marat with the prospect of more traitors to be killed. Instead, he himself was killed by Corday's kitchen knife. Almost killed herself by an angry crowd, she was taken for interrogation. Condemnation was inevitable, but she did an odd thing. She asked for a sketch to be made of her. One of the officers was a skilled artist and obliged. It was important for her reputation that she left behind not only justifications but an accurate likeness for posterity. She was executed on 17 July 1793 and in an unsavoury scene, one Legros who picked up her head and slapped it was imprisoned for improper behaviour. The Revolutionaries seemed to offer her a sort of respect. Indeed, she gave them far more than she had taken. Marat became a revolutionary martyr. The painting by the famous artist David of him lying dead in his bath was one of the most famous images of the revolution. It had an almost religious significance with Marat becoming a sort of secular Christ-like figure quite at odds with his real-life personality. The Terror received justification as now the revolution did really seem to be in danger – and from a provincial aristocrat and a Girondin. This was a wonderful opportunity for the Jacobins to identify their political enemies with counter-revolution. The tempo of repression was increased. Far from saving thousands, she increased the peril for all those suspected of counter-revolution and elevated a sickly journalist to a revolutionary saint. The execution of Madame Roland was probably a result. Far from promoting the rights of women, Corday's act increased suspicion of any political activity by women. It confirmed all sorts of prejudices – that women were treacherous, too easily moved by their emotions, irrational. Marat had trusted her to come to his intimate space, naked and suffering and she had struck him while pretending to be a supporter. She had become a symbol of female hysteria, not a heroine.

This is not the way that posterity generally has seen it. She became the subject of plays, films, even an opera and modern video games. But it does seem she was in the grip of a delusion. Marat's death would not stop the radical revolution or the violence in the capital or the divisions in the provinces. It could not possibly stop civil war whose causes were far deeper than the influence of Marat. The most likely result was a that division, popular violence, and revolutionary terror would increase. There was no follow-up plan, no organisation and perhaps a degree of vanity about the enterprise. It was really a delusion to think that a revolution which had let violence get out of control could be moderated by an act of violence. Charlotte Corday's act has to be seen as part of a cycle of violence, not something that might have prevented it. The delusion was that violence could bring about the rule of law and internal peace. It had dogged the whole progress of the Revolution, as noble ideals and political theories were proposed and the raw violence that the revolution had brought about was ignored or justified in elaborate terms of virtue. Robespierre's speeches abound in this talk of 'virtue' and 'purity'. Charlotte inhabited a similar moral world – an act of violence would somehow purify the revolution. Marat would be a sacrifice in the name of law and peace. She had entered into the delusions of her enemies.

Thérouanne de Méricourt

The final category is the view that women displayed characteristics of derangement or uncontrollable hysteria. The most famous representative of this group is Théroigne de Méricourt. Few women of the Revolution have featured as a character in a popular video game or been portrayed by Sara Bernard or written about by Baudelaire.

The historian Linda Kelly portrays her vividly on 10 August 1792 in the disturbances which ended the monarchy. At the Feuillants monastery where suspects were imprisoned, she urged the crowd to murder dressed in red with a plumed tricolour hat. She tried to kill a royalist journalist Seulier herself and exulted in his decapitation. 'Already showing signs of the insanity to which, she would later succumb'.

In his widely read study of the Revolution, '*Citizens*'[3], Simon Schama ends with an account of her final years of madness as though a warning that participation in revolution leads women to mental disorder. The portrait of the young girl and the older woman might be an indication of the dreadful plight of activists.

Much of what is generally believed about her derives from misogynist pamphlets. According to these, Théroigne had been active since 1789. She had been a prominent figure in the events of 5 October 1789 along with the infamous 'fishwives' who had armed themselves and taken the lead on a march from Paris to Versailles, resulting in horrific scenes. She was not only a deranged inciter to violence, but she was also phenomenally promiscuous and slept with dozens of Assembly members, shamelessly dressing as a man.

The Role of Women in the Revolution

Reality shows a more complex picture. Anne-Josephe Terwagne was an Austrian subject born in 1767 in modern-day Luxembourg then part of the Austrian Netherlands. From a reasonably well-to-do farming family, she received a convent education; but her early life after her mother's death was hard. After working as a cow herd and seamstress she was lucky enough to be taken up by a wealthy family as a governess, travelled aboard and hoped to become an opera singer. A relationship with a rich Englishman and then an elderly French marquis allowed her to settle comfortably in Rome. It seems she was a successful courtesan. Her story until 1789 was colourful but not untypical of her time. However, what seems strange is her fascination with the developing events of the revolution in France. She had lived in Paris from 1784 to 1787, and her protector and patron the Marquis de Persan had been a member of the *Parlement de Paris*, but why she went to live in the capital and followed the debates in the National Assembly so attentively is not clear and seems out of character with her previous life. She lodged at Versailles to be near the Assembly and then, after 5 October when the king and the Assembly were forced to move into the city, she followed. Deeply interested in these events, there is no evidence she took part or led them and no evidence she was present at other revolutionary milestones such as the storming of the Bastille. Her next step, the forming of a political club in January 1790 and her confidence in speaking in public in the Cordeliers Club and on the steps of the Assembly may be seen as a result of the effects of the huge wave of political awareness in the capital, but might be seen as a form of exhibitionism, as she wore riding clothes and a plumed hat which drew attention to herself. She became the target of ridicule and hatred in the pamphlets of the royalists and became known as Théroigne de Mericourt. Her money was running out and she was under pressure from abuse, so she left for home in 1790 but her notoriety led to her arrest by the Austrian authorities who ruled Belgium, and she suffered a period of imprisonment and brutal treatment before being released and returning to Paris as a heroine of the Revolution in January 1792 as a result of her imprisonment.

Her speeches and writing now became more outspoken as she demanded equality for women and called for an armed force of women to defend the revolution. She spoke in the radical Jacobin Club and took a leading part in the events of 10 August which saw the overthrow of the monarchy. Her role in inciting the massacre of royalist suspects is documented, though there is no evidence she actually tried to kill the royalist journalist Seulier who had written unfavourably about her. This accusation of personal violence seems to be part of a myth.

Though she pressed for women's rights, she was drawn politically not to the Jacobins but to the more moderate Girondins and was caught up in the political infighting among the revolutionaries. On 15 May 1793, she was attacked by a group of Jacobin women and badly beaten. This second bout of violence pushed her over the edge and on 20 September 1793, she was declared insane and spent the rest of her life until her death in 1817 in an asylum.

The poet Baudelaire in his 1857 poem summed up the success of royalist propaganda.

> See Théroigne, by blood and fire enraged,
> Hounding a shoeless rabble to the fray,
> Who plays herself on a flaming stage,
> As she climbs, sword in hand, the royal stairway.

Anne-Josephe did not climb the royal stairway in Versailles in October 1789, and most of her life was not spent hounding shoeless rabble. She suffered as a child from abusive behaviour by family members who treated her as a servant. She was reliant on older lovers. She suffered from lies by royalist pamphleteers and abuse from captors as a political prisoner. It was not revolutionary enthusiasm that lay behind mental illness, but dreadful experiences in her life, culminating in a savage beating at the hands of women whose cause she promoted. What was remarkable about her was her interest in political discourse and writings and speeches which promoted the cause of women, but this is not what has caught the interest of posterity. The image is of a deranged revolutionary harridan – but with elements of victim and of being delusional. To see her as typical of the experience of women in the Revolution would be to over-emphasize her role.

Olympe de Gouges

The other major female radical who emerged from the Revolution is Olympe de Gouges a prolific producer of pamphlets and writings promoting reform and best known for what has become a seminal text of revolutionary feminism, 'The Declaration of the Rights of Women', this energetic woman has been seen as a beacon of progress. Less problematic as an iconic feminist, her writings have become the focus of considerable historical research.

Marie Gouze was her real name, and she was the daughter of a butcher who had married into a well-to-do family of drapers in the town of Montaubon, north of Toulouse in southwest France. Her paternity was uncertain, with rumours certainly encouraged by herself later on in life, that she was the illegitimate child of a radical literary aristocrat. Her education was neglected, and it has been suggested that she could barely read and write. She was married off at seventeen to a local businessman but the marriage failed. When he died, she began a liaison with another wealthy businessman who set her up in Paris where she reinvented herself as a fashionable hostess using her mother's name Olympe and adding, perhaps as a nod to her supposed father an aristocratic 'de'. Gouze was changed to Gouges. She mixed in quite elevated circles, friendly with the radical Duc of Orléans who was possibly her lover, the liberal aristocrat Condorcet and the doyenne of the salons Madame de Montesan. There was plenty of discussion of political ideas and reform, of poetry and plays and Olympe became a renown and controversial playwright. Her attack on slavery in the play *'The Enslavement of the Blacks'* of 1785 was notorious. As well as political discussions in the drawing room, she took part in meetings of the political clubs, such as the Society of the Friends of the Revolution. When the Revolution broke out in 1789, it was a natural progression to start producing a mass of pamphlets demanding all sorts of changes. This body of work, probably dictated, established her as a major political theorist. Ideas flowed out on houses of refuge for abused women and their children; relief for the unemployed; equal rights for women in divorce and inheritance; an end to the stigma around illegitimacy; the opening of the professions to those with talent. She embraced the new dawn, signing herself 'citoyenne' (citizeness), but was concerned about the rising tide of violence, but not enough to stop advocating change. Her most famous and enduring polemic came with the 'Declaration of the Rights of Women' a parody of the 'Declaration of the Rights of Man'. This is her main claim to significance. The following gives some idea of the tone and the appeal for new rights and new attitudes.

> Woman, wake up; the tocsin of reason is being heard throughout the whole universe; discover your rights.
>
> Oh, women, women! When will you cease to be blind? What advantage have you received from the Revolution? A more pronounced scorn, a more marked disdain
>
> Deploy all the energy of your character, and you will soon see these haughty men, not grovelling at your feet as servile adorers, but proud to share with you the treasures of the Supreme Being. Regardless of what barriers confront you, it is in your power to free yourselves; you have only to want to...
>
> Marriage is the tomb of trust and love.[9]

It is not surprising; given the tone and confidence of this sort of writing that she has been seen as a forerunner of later feminism or has excited interest for her views which went way beyond the conventions of her time.

Politically, like Manon Roland, Charlotte Corday and Théroigne, she was drawn to the Girondins and became increasingly concerned about violence, terror and the power of the Jacobins. Dangerously for a high-profile intellectual and publicist, she advocated mercy for the king and offered to defend him. The greater radicalism shown by the king's death in 1793 and the strain of internal and external war made dissent difficult. Her pamphlet 'The Three Urns' argued that France should have a choice between the centralised Revolutionary Republic developed to fight the wars with the monarchs of Europe and to defeat the internal enemies of the Revolution and two other forms of government. One was a decentralised Federalist state and the other a return to Constitutional Monarchy. The pamphlet was couched in strange terms and may well have been a sign of instability and lack of judgement, given the likely consequences of even considering a return to monarchy. Going for broke, she wrote an insulting and critical letter to Robespierre. In the heated atmosphere of Paris in 1793, with fears of invasion and betrayal and a developed theory of revolutionary justice, this opposition was highly dangerous. Arrested and interrogated, Olympe de Gouges was denied defence representation, and her claims that she was pregnant were not convincingly investigated. Famously, she had claimed that 'if a woman has the right to mount the scaffold, she must equally possess the right to mount the speaker's platform.' She exercised both rights and was guillotined on 3 November 1793.

A scholarly industry has emerged to analyse her publications and she has gained an almost saintly reputation. Her latest biographer Michel Faucheux[10] argued that she should be buried in the Patheon as one of the greatest French people. But the contemporary revolutionary newssheet *La Feuille du Salut Publique* offered a different view that she was 'born with an exalted imagination and mistook delirium for the inspiration of nature'. A study by a French military psychiatrist in 1904, using original sources, concluded that she had a hereditary predisposition to mental illness. Her early life and the effects of chronic gynaecological problems led her to a form of paranoia. The evidence he produced based on material in the national archives showed a father prone to violent outbursts, an unhappy marriage which she left, reliance on older partners and a tendency to irrational rages. The archives of the *Comédie Française* revealed furious outbursts and accusations about the production of her dramas. Contemporary memoirs show her belief in the reincarnation of people as animals and her conversations with a menagerie of dogs, cats, rabbits, and parrots. The pamphlet which brought her downfall is used to illustrate a disturbed mental state. Suicidal in its political content, suggesting the possibility of both a federalist decentralised regime and a constitutional monarchy, it was inscribed as being the work of 'an airborne traveller'. She had written 'I call myself Toxicodendron. I am from the land of the mad. I arrived from Monomolopa' and claimed that the work had been dictated by God. During her interrogation, she claimed to be pregnant and railed against Robespierre, which however justified, was tantamount to condemning herself to death. The flood of pamphlets, which she probably dictated as her education had been so patchy that she may not have been able to read or write fluently was seen as a sign of a loss of contact with reality rather than a flood of inspiration. The letter to Robespierre was so insolent and provocative that it showed a death wish. What characterised her activity was a defiance which is, today, seen as heroic. The Declaration of the Rights of Women was a polemic satire, adapting the words of the Declaration of the Rights of Man, directed at hypocrisy rather than a call to arms composed by herself. What emerges is a restless, reckless and provocative person who had created an image for herself which she developed regardless of dangers and the limited appeal that her ideas had for contemporaries, as opposed to future generations.

Beyond Biographies

The focus on women's role in the Revolution through accounts of these individuals has its limitations. They might be seen to sum up aspects of the period or have ideas ahead of their time and had vivid and tragic life stories. However, it is something of a distortion to see women only through these 'famous figures'.

One element that emerges from looking at the biographies is the growth in political consciousness. Madame Roland's eager devouring of literary and political writings of the Enlightenment and her interest in Greek and Roman authors, shared with M. Roland from their early acquaintance is mirrored in Charlotte Corday's readings on Ancient Rome and the political lessons drawn from them. The spirit of enquiry that led Olympe de Gouges and Théroigne to take such an interest in political discussion was part of their time and has been fascinatingly explored by historians looking at the publication of women's demands during the period of national discussion prior to the meeting of the Estates General in 1789. Though only a few women took part in voting for the delegates to this body, and no woman was elected as a deputy, nevertheless there is evidence that they considered what demands they wanted to put forward and went so far as having some of these sets of demands printed – an expensive business. How great the participation was is difficult to assess and much depends on the survival of the pamphlets. We cannot know what discussions went on in households, but it seems reasonable to see the sort of political interest and awareness of the individuals so often studied as the tip of an iceberg. The huge political interest in meetings held to draw up lists of grievances for the Estates General to address gave rise to pamphlets and demands either on behalf of women or by women themselves. They demonstrate that women had moved from the purely domestic sphere into the public sphere, making public demands and taking a stance on public issues. This is the context in which individual pioneers and also groups of women who acted as participants in the Revolution operated. The newspaper *The Women's Journal* founded by Madame de Beaumer in 1759 wrote scathingly to male critics in an editorial in 1762 'Mind your own business and let us write in a manner worthy of our gender…to uphold its honour and its rights'.

The pamphlets which reflect that attitude survive include publications from both Paris and the provinces. The tone of the demands of 1789 may be gathered from this, compiled by an anonymous woman from Normandy known as Madame B…B… It is titled *Cahier of Grievances and Demands of Women* and was written before the calling of the Estates General but published in the summer of 1789.

> The role of women has been to work, obey and shut up. But today, enlightenment and reason have shown the absurdity of this. Women are obliged just as men to pay taxes and it is entirely just that they should bring their grievances to the king. It may be argued that women are represented by men, but a man cannot represent a woman. Representatives should have the same interests as those represented. Women should be represented by women.[10]

This anonymous pamphleteer from provincial France offers a view of an awareness of women's rights beyond the more famous individuals usually considered and may show a much more widespread change in attitudes than standard accounts consider.

The pamphlets are not all so strident or overtly political. Many deal with the need to educate boys and girls equally. Some, however, offer political solutions – that single people and couples without children pay a special levy to educate poor children. Also, that family life should be strengthened if women were given instruction in religion and morality. The role of the state in education and family life is a radical concept. There were also demands that the independent role of women in economic activity should be strengthened, by protecting a monopoly in key trades like embroidery and fashion and to be protected from malpractice such as adulterated soap. The demands, too, include social modernisation by requests that dowries be abolished. The demands often are accompanied by requests for stricter morality and distinguishing respectable women who deserve rights from sex workers who should wear special marks on their clothes to set them apart. This was to counter prejudices that demanding rights and greater equality put women into a category similar to prostitutes. Given the resort to accusations of immoral behaviour made against unpopular women from Marie Antoinette, on one hand, to Théroigne on the other, this was not an unreasonable concern. There is evidence of much greater participation in the general public sphere, both before 1789 but particularly in the turbulent months of public debate prior to the evolutionary events of 1789 which involved collective meetings, discussions, and demands and is a different aspect than the individual heroic figures who often dominate the narrative.

A pamphlet *'Request of women for their admission to the Estates General'* had a distinctly political tone:

> You have met, gentlemen, to renew France, A gap of 175 years prevents this assembly being exactly the same as the last Estates general. Since 1614 the kingdom has changed. Some provinces have ceased to be part of France; many others have been conquered or reunited to the Crown. The number of administrative districts has greatly increased, The Third Estate has become the most important ...[10]

This language is far from the family-orientated pamphlets produced by some women and enters directly into the world of politics.

A Key Event – the October Days

While women were part of the revolutionary activities both in Paris and in France as a whole in 1789 – the storming of the Bastille (though their names do not appear in the roll of honour of the attackers) and the attacks in the countryside known as 'The Great Fear', they have become famous or notorious for the so-called October Days. In standard accounts, this is their moment, the time when they took the Revolution forward.

On 5 October 1789 was the event which more than any other showed the direct participation of women in the development of the Revolution. High prices and the reports of the king carousing with loyal army officers and trampling underfoot the revolutionary symbol of the hat with a cockade led to a march on Versailles from the centre of Paris in which women were prominent. Accompanied by the National Guard the crowds entered the Palace of Versailles, killed two of the royal guards, and terrorised the royal family. They forced the king and his family to live in semi-captivity in the centre of Paris and, perhaps more significantly, the Assembly, too, moved to Paris, where it was more under the influence of the crowds than at Versailles. The weakening of the monarchy and the power of popular action took the revolution to a different level and women played a key part.

Most accounts talk of the 'Fishwives' of the Paris markets being the key component. Did concern for their families and for the high price of bread take these women into the public sphere and did they by this action come to personify the popular force of the Revolution even briefly? It certainly suited the pamphleteers of the day to show them as revolutionary leaders. And for the enemies of the revolution, it was even more suitable to have 'fishwives' getting out of control and dominating the action. They could symbolise both revolutionary fervour and anarchy and hysteria when traditional disciplines broke down. But whatever view was taken, this was more of a collective action and there is no evidence it was led by Théroigne. The leadership of 'The Queen of Les Halles', the so-called 'Reine Audu', actually a fruit seller called Louise Leduc, is not well documented, though she was imprisoned in the aftermath and became part of the myth.

The term 'fishwife' has the image of rough and foul-mouthed women in English, but the *Poissardes* of the markets – the '*dames de la Halle*' were a high-status corporation of women traders they had special privileges, like congratulating the king on special events. They had gone to Versailles in a special delegation on 7 August 1789 to congratulate Louis XVI on accepting a new constitution. Many of the trades pursued by women were organised, corporate and worked hard to defend their privileges. There had been discussions about how to deal with the bread shortages in the weeks prior to October, and there was evidence of interest in religious and political matters way before the events of October 1789.

Evidence for the dominance of a politically conscious group of market women from the fish market can be found in the journals of a Paris bookseller called Hardy who noted acts of disobedience and unrest from 1787 among this group, refusing to shout '*Vive le Roi*' at a royal visit, having to be forced to present bouquets, being involved in demands to take part in elections in Paris in April 1789 and perhaps more significantly taking part in processions in August and September with the National Guard and led by drummers to state their role as defenders of the city of Paris in some of the endless processions and ceremonial events that took placed in 1789. This might explain their role

The Role of Women in the Revolution

on 5 October, their procession with the National Guard and their sense of purpose in representing the city in a demand for bread and supporting taking the king back to look after the city. The group confidence, sense of mission and cohesion are notable, but the actual situation was more complex as other evidence shows. To see this as a 'riot' led by spontaneous action by out-of-control women is quite wrong, but it is common to see this in general surveys of the Revolution.

After the event, a commission of the Assembly held an enquiry and as modern research showed in a study of 1789[11] the story is rather more complex than of furious fishwives leading a murderous assault. Madelaine Glan who was a cleaning woman, not a fishwife had been forced to join a crowd going to Versailles to ask for bread on Monday 5 October 1789. She spoke of a known prostitute with a rusty sword who spoke of killing the Queen who was silenced by the women around her. When the women got into the National Assembly, some demanded bread and meat should have a low fixed price, but Madeleine disagreed asking only that there be regular supplies. Like many of those interviewed a week later, she denied any violent behaviour. Another deposition from Jeanne Deliassment who was a seamstress said that she was forced to go by an angry crowd of women carrying weapons but that they were disarmed on the way. She denied entering the Palace. An unmarried lacemaker called Marie Rose Barre also told of being forced by a crowd of a hundred women to go to Versailles. She found herself part of a delegation talking to the king and asked for bread supplies for Paris to be guaranteed. The king expressed concern and promised to try and ensure deliveries. The women shouted *'Vive le Roi'*!

If the testimony is to be believed, not all the women were fishwives, not all took part in violence and there was a rational request made for food supplies to reach Paris. The march to Versailles was undertaken by women from many districts and trades and there was a conscious aim of a permanent solution to the shortage of bread. Too much credence has probably been given to male witnesses. A leading member of the National Guard, well known for taking part in the storming of the Bastille, Stanislas-Marie Maillard also testified. On 5 October he was sent to the City Hall (Hotel de Ville) where a large crowd of women were occupying the building, complaining of food shortages. A crowd of men then entered and took weapons from the City Hall. To defuse the situation, Maillard said that he offered to accompany the women to the National Assembly. He said he persuaded those women who were armed to lay down their weapons in the Champs d'Elyseé. He persuaded them to go peacefully through the village of Chaillot. They stopped coaches but did not assault their occupants and threatened a horseman not wearing the revolutionary cockade in his hat but did not assault him. They entered Versailles crying '*Vive Le Roi*'. A soldier thought to have fired on the women was surrounded and abused but got away. Another National Guardsman Fournier testified that he had had to persuade some of the women at the Hotel de Ville 'with the name and outward appearance of *poissardes*' to go to Versailles but deploying some of the bad language that they used and understood. 'The King is going to f... you over!' And that the only way was to get the king back to Paris – this led to 50,000 moving to Versailles. That these men could in a few minutes organise large numbers of women – though not surely 50,000 – with a strong corporate identity and experience of acting together and political awareness to undertake a 12-mile walk by a bit of bad language seems questionable.

The complexities of this event are glossed over in most general accounts but what seems likely is that there was a mixture of women caught up in the need to be able to secure vital supplies of bread, not all of whom participated in violence but were able to express legitimate concerns and whose participation was to some extent hijacked by more violent elements.

The Expansion of Political Discourse

From the discontent of market women to the elevated discussions of the salons, there was an increase in the public role of women. The political activities of individuals can be charted but the first major Republican political club of 1793 represents more than the individual initiative of pioneers of feminism. The Society of Republican Women, founded by radical activists, was highly influential but in a negative way. The leaders came from a lower middle-class background shared by the sans-culottes whom they championed. Ann Félicité Colombe ran a printing press which published Marat's radical *Ami du People*. Pauline Leon's parents were chocolate makers. Claire Lacomb (sometimes Lacombe) was a professional actress. In February 1793 they had asked the Jacobins for the use of their meeting hall for a woman's meeting place. Initially refused the group did finally have access to the meeting room and registered officially as a club in May 1793. They demanded that women have equal rights in defending the Republic. Leon had been demanding a female military force since 1791, and these demands were the basis of the aims of the club – the right to be fanatical supporters of the Revolution. They moved away from the Jacobins to the more extreme enrage movement. They adopted the Red Cap of Liberty as a sort of uniform and debated revolutionary survival. Membership has been estimated at between 200 and 300, remarkable for the time.

Unfortunately, though their rules survive, an account by an observer of one of their meetings by a writer called Pierre Roussel is unreliable and may have been made up. In his account of 1802, he describes a sixty-seven-strong meeting listening to a woman called Monique give a historical survey of women warriors and a speech by Olympe de Gouges calling for a new religion of dedicated sans-culottes and saying that 'men are our slaves'. The artisans fell foul of the market women who objected to their ideas of enforcing revolutionary dress on women. These women protested to the Commune who were responsible for licensing clubs and in November the society was made illegal. When the members protested, they were met with a diatribe from a hostile Commune official, Anaxagorus Chaumette, who accused them of impudence and wanting to become men. Sadly, this rant has cemented his place in history. The reaction against women participating in politics saw the execution of Olympe de Gouges and Manon Roland and the prosecution of the leaders of the society.

When women were accused of inciting attempted coups in 1795 because of outbreaks of protests against further food shortages and soaring prices, the government, now called the Directory, introduced legal restrictions. Women were not permitted to attend the meetings of the Assembly and not permitted to meet in public in groups of more than five. The reaction against women's rights was confirmed during the rule of Napoleon and the legal code of 1804 enshrined male supremacy in law. Women's rights in nineteenth-century France were slow to progress, and French women did not gain the right to vote until 1946.

The Civil War

Women were victims of the repression that they wished to impose on others and it is somewhat ironic that the idea of women taking up arms for their beliefs was not a feature of the Revolution, whose armed forces were male, but of the counter-revolution that emerged in the provinces as a result of resentment to the centralising measures of the Republic to fight a total war and of the persecution of non-juror priests. The measures of terror undertaken against the provinces saw women as victims but the extremity of the Republican response to opposition led to female participation in opposition to policies which took on some of the aspects of genocide. It may be here that women had some of their most significant influence on the revolution. The impression of devout Catholic women asserting their opposition to a godless revolution by kneeling at the altar is not that offered by a number of memoirs of women in provinces which opposed the Revolution in a bitter civil war from 1793 to 1795. Unusually, there were printed accounts of ten women who were part of the counter-revolution in the remote region of La Vendée. Some were regional aristocrats, some the wives of leaders of the insurrection. But others were peasant women: Renée Bordereau, known as the 'Vendean Joan of Arc' fought in the rebel army dressed as a man, The one-eyed Francoise Despres was a messenger and troop leader. Louise Barbier was an innkeeper's daughter. These memoirs from across the social spectrum reveal how much women were affected by the revolution and how they took on active roles. Not all were fighters. Viscountess Turpin de Crisse tried to negotiate a peace between the Vendee military chiefs and the Republicans. Madame de La Rochejaquelin was married to a rebel general and was seen in 1793 as an inspiration and a legend. When he was killed, she was heavily pregnant and had to escape Republican forces and attached herself to a guerrilla force. Suffering hardship and the death of her children she survived until the amnesty of 1795 and married the brother of the leader of the rebel army. Her memoirs became famous, but the memories of Renée Bordereau were much more obscure. She wrote that the killing of her father and other relatives drove her to revenge, describing atrocities and killing Republican troops who had bayonetted a baby. One claim is that she killed two Republican soldiers, one with a pistol and another with a sabre in a fury. Another cross-dressing woman solider Jeanne Robbin did not survive the war and was killed at Thouars in a major battle in November 1793.

The war bitterly divided provincial France. While some women suffered from repression, dislocation and war, others took a very different view. There were special ceremonies for crowds of women dressed in white to take the oath of loyalty to the Republic and thousands took part in special processions in Tours and Bordeaux in 1791. This sort of female demonstration would have been unthinkable in other countries at the time and seems redolent of the much later suffragette processions, though the political context is very different. Provincial sources reveal passions on a grand scale and passionate involvement in political life. This goes far beyond a few individuals in Paris and indicates a far greater involvement in the Revolution than textbooks and general histories suggest.

There is evidence of growing political awareness and participation of women in the public sphere in the eighteenth century and of considerable hope for change once the Revolution got underway. These were bitterly opposed not just by royalists but by male revolutionaries. This often resulted in repression and a distorted view of developments. The reaction against women continued into the rule of Napoleon and he could be said to have consolidated it. The symbols of the Revolution were often in female form – liberty was personified by a woman and 'Marianne' with her revolutionary cockade became the Britannia equivalent. But though happy to use the female form, French rulers denied women in person political equality and representation.

Notes

1. Eric Hazan, *A People's History of the French Revolution* (Paris, 2012; Verso, 2014)
2. John Roberts, *A Short Guide to The French Revolution* (OUP, 1981).
3. Simon Schama, *Citizens* (Penguin, 2004).
4. Mlle de Echerolles, *Memoirs* (New York, 1904).
5. Olympe de Gouge, letter, quoted in Linda Kelley, *Women of the French Revolution*, 1970
6. John Fisher, *The Elysian Fields* (Cox and Wyman, 1966).
7. Linda Kelly, *Women of the French Revolution* (Hamish Hamilton, 1969).
8. John Abbott, *Madame Roland* (NY, Harper, 1904).
9. Michel Faucheux, *Olympe de Gouges* (Folio 2018)
10. French Revolution Pamphlets, 1761–1807, Special Collections Spotlight, Collection Essays, Robert D. Farber University Archives and Special Collections, Brandeis University.

Chapter Seven

Slavery, Racism and Empire

The slave revolt in the French colony of Saint-Domingue in the West Indies in 1791 was one of the most important events in the era of the French Revolution. One historian, David Brian Davis, described it as being 'like Hiroshima' in its impact on the whole issue of the emancipation of slaves. It led to the only black independent state which had resulted from Africans breaking free of colonialism with the establishment of Haiti in 1804. Frederick Douglass, the nineteenth-century civil rights campaigner in the US, an ex-slave himself said in 1893 that 'Until Haiti spoke, the church was silent and the pulpit dumb' on the issue of slavery. It established a precedent for the ending of colonialism and led to famous black leaders especially Toussaint Louverture leading armies, negotiating with Western powers and achieving a reputation as a forerunner of Fidel Castro in the region. It contributed to the ending of the slave trade in 1807 and it shook assumptions about race not only in the West Indies but in Europe and the US.

Unsurprisingly, it is the subject of a considerable amount of academic interest, especially in the US and is much studied in American schools and colleges. Toussaint Louverture is known to British school children, too, at Key Stage 3 History, now in a way that would have been unthinkable a generation ago. A West Indian Marxist historian broke new ground in his famous study of the Haitian Revolution, *'The Black Jacobins'* in 1938. But the work of CLR James was pigeonholed in Caribbean history rather than leading to the events in Saint-Domingue becoming an integral part of the study of the French Revolution. Those Year 9 students who go on to A-Level History and study the French Revolution will not find Haiti or Toussaint often in the syllabuses, whereas in many US colleges, the Haitian Revolution and its leaders are seen as on a par in significance with the developments in France.

So in one sense, the Haitian Revolution is a neglected aspect of the era of the Revolution and yet in another sense, there are prevailing myths about it and its place in Revolutionary History. In his overall survey of American *Revolutions*[1] Alan Taylor writes 'In 1791, the French Revolution inspired a massive slave revolt'. This followed the classic association of French

Revolutionary ideas with the slave revolt by CLR James categorising the rebels as 'Black Jacobins'. Much of the writing about the revolt centres on the study of its leader Toussaint. The latest biography[2] takes up an epithet from a French general of 'Black Spartacus' and deals with his 'epic life'. But the assumption that the Haitian Revolution was part of the same process as the Revolution of 1789 and that it was dependent on 'epic' individuals may be challenged.

Broadly speaking, the accepted narrative is that the events of France in 1789 divided the white colonists and eventually inspired a slave revolt. The revolt saw the rise of some exceptional leaders and against the odds the French as well as other colonial powers hostile to the revolt, notably Britain and Spain, were unable to overcome the revolt. Though Toussaint was captured and sent off to imprisonment and death in France, even Napoleon's armies riven with disease could not reassert control and re-establish slavery so that Haiti became and remained independent, isolated and facing hostile colonial neighbours. The slaves were emancipated; black leaders were able to establish and defend a new state which anticipated the much later decolonisation and slave emancipations in the Americas. Given these dramatic and significant changes, it seems odd that they do not figure more in the standard histories of the French Revolution. However, it is worth examining whether the broad narrative does not perpetuate some myths.

Saint-Domingue before the Revolution

The French had established an extensive colonial empire in the seventeenth century, but the richest element was the island of Saint-Domingue, the northern part of the Spanish island of Hispaniola, because of its sugar plantations. France played a leading role in the slave trade. Until 1642 French ships took or bought slaves from foreign ships and carried them to French colonies, but slave trading as such was legalised by Louis XIII in 1642 and the crown paid a subsidy for each slave brought to a French colony in 1672. Ships from seventeen French ports, but mainly Nantes carried out over 3,000 shipments and in the eighteenth century transported between 450,000 and 600,000 Africans to the Americas. In all, it has been estimated that between 1625 and 1848 over 2 million people were transported. The profits from sugar, coffee, cotton, tobacco, and indigo were such that there was considerable pressure for a workforce in the Caribbean possessions of the European powers. The French became the leading exporters of sugar, coffee and cotton, and the West Indian possessions were of vital economic importance. The French American and Indian empire, lost to the British by 1763 was not based primarily on cultivation of valuable products but on trading arrangements and settlements. In common with the British, Spanish, Dutch and Portuguese, the French colonists regarded slavery as a form of property.

There were regulations for slavery dating from 1685 issued by Louis XIV but drawn up by his finance minister, Colbert. These referred to 'the Islands of French America' and were based on reports to the government and the interests of the church. Jews were to be expelled and slaves to be baptised and instructed in the Catholic faith. No other religion was to be practised. Only Catholics should have authority over slaves. Slaves should not work on Sundays or religious holidays. The practice of fathering children by slave concubines was made illegal, but if free Catholic men married the mother of their children, then she and the children should be free. Slaves were to be punished for carrying weapons. Gatherings of slaves from different masters were forbidden and repeat offences could be punished by death. Slaves were not to sell sugar or other produce. Slaves too old or sick to work should be cared for. They had no legal rights. Slaves striking their masters should be executed and slaves would be branded and have their ears cut off if they tried to escape. If reoffending, their hamstrings should be cut; the third offence would lead to death. Whipping was allowed by masters, but not mutilation. Slave husbands and wives with prepubescent children should not be separated and sold separately. Freed slaves should enjoy the status of other subjects in France as well as the islands.

In the Age of Enlightenment, the *Code Noir* came to be seen as unacceptable by some. The famous French writer Voltaire wrote against it and there were impassioned opponents, especially as it became clear that even the limited protections it offered were not observed in practice. However, as with debates in post-independence America, there was tension between ideals of liberty and notions of property; also, the economic importance of the trade in colonial products was huge. The general view was that the trade depended on plentiful and cheap labour. Even the American colonists had embedded slavery in the United States constitution of 1787. The Declaration of Independence had claimed that 'All men are created equal and endowed by their creator with Inalienable rights'. But 'men' for all except a minority, meant 'white men' (not women) and excluded slaves. There was a belief that black slaves were racially so different that they did not all within the category 'men'. Though this gave rise to difficulties when some had been freed. There was also the problem of people of mixed race – how much 'white blood' was needed before they were considered as part of mankind and not as equivalent to working animals?

There were all sorts of arguments advanced against slavery, but the pressure to avoid these moral dilemmas and merely maintain the institution because of its importance in economic terms was considerable. Other nations had not responded to liberal arguments faced with the need for cheap labour and the profits from agricultural produce grown on slave plantations.

One of the most pressing arguments was the danger of slave revolts. This was made by a liberal mixed-race planter from Saint-Domingue, Vincent Ogé, to a congress of plantation owners meeting in Paris in 1789:

> Freedom, the greatest, the first of goods, is it made for all men? I believe so. Should it be given to all men? I believe so! We will see blood flowing, our lands invaded, the objects of our industry ravaged, our homes burnt. We will see our neighbours, our friends, our wives, our children with their throats cut and their bodies mutilated; the slave will raise the standard of revolt.

This was all too prescient, for Saint-Domingue experienced a revolt in 1791 that had violent consequences and led to the loss of the colony and to the first successful slave revolution in European colonies. It was so significant because this small part of an island was the jewel in the crown of the French overseas empire. To describe the development of the colony is to plunge into a Hellish world made all the worse by the disgusting practices of French rule taking place in what all visitors to this part of the world will see as a tropical paradise. But what went on in Saint-Domingue was very far from that.

If it is true, as the novelist LP Hartley, said that the past is a foreign country, then the development of white exploitation in the West Indies really does take us well into the interior of an alien and utterly indefensible world. The powerhouse of French colonial trade was an area approximately the size of modern-day Belgium. It was the western part of an island which is now divided between the states of Haiti and the Dominican Republic. Columbus first brought it to the notice of Europe, and Spanish rule was devastating for the initially welcoming original inhabitants. For France, all overseas territories were to be for the benefit of the mother country. The colony of Saint-Domingue turned out to be even more beneficial than other islands in the Caribbean as it was so suitable for two massively profitable crops – sugar on the plains and coffee on the hills. Developed by private enterprise, the island turned into a relentless capitalist enterprise where profit was all. Both crops were labour-intensive – especially sugar. The original inhabitants and French settlers and workers could not provide this, so the only available source of labour was slaves. Trading with West Africa gave a ready supply for the slave ships operating from the ports of Europe and colonial America. Despite the moral qualms of some, the eighteenth century was not very troubled by what the modern world sees as an obvious moral concern. Indifference was common and there were even unlikely justifications on various grounds. These included religious salvation for 'heathen' Africans and paternalistic claims that slavery was good for the slaves and that their owners gave them better lives than those lived by exploited peasants and workers in France. All of these nonsensical defences were also to be part of the justification for slavery in America.

The hideous process began in the slave pens in the African ports, overcrowded and squalid. Dehumanisation was developed during the voyage on the slave ships. Crowded into unsanitary holds, chained, beaten, abused, sometimes killed or jettisoned like cargo in storms, these poor people endured unimaginable suffering and there was a high death rate. Cleaned up at the end of the voyage, they were taken to auction pens, examined like animals for their state of health, sold and branded. The idea that they endured passively is wrong. There was often resistance before and during the voyage, but by the time they arrived, the traumatic experience had taken its toll. Initially, there was an acclimatisation period for the captives to get used to the different climate, but as the pressure for more and more cultivation and profit grew after the 1760s and there was a greater importation of Africans, the new arrivals were often put to work quickly.

By 1760 there were 200,000 slaves in Saint-Domingue but by 1789 because of an astonishing increase, there were over 450,000. Such were the skills in handling arrivals that small numbers of masters were able to control and exploit large numbers of captives. There were 30,000 whites on the island in 1789, with six men to every white woman. Unarmed and disoriented people were at the mercy of well-organised and experienced oppressors.

A picture of slave-owning society might emerge of a sort of *'Gone with the Wind'* society with elegant mansions, a developed aristocratic culture, a bygone elegance and a docile slave population, some of whom were family servants. Whether this was ever really true in pre-Civil War America is doubtful, but it was certainly not the case in Saint-Domingue. Though the capital Cap Français was quite a developed urban area about the size of colonial Boston with theatres, cafes and some fine living, this was not typical of the island as a whole. Affable slaves and elegant plantation houses were not the norm. Sugar required military discipline and constant labour – digging irrigation trenches, planting, tending, harvesting, grinding the cane, and packaging. There was no streamlined mechanical process; the hot and often dry soil had to be broken by sheer hard labour in sweltering conditions. Without incentives of rewards or loyalty to the owners, work rate in a long day was enforced by punishments. There were even handbooks to guide the wielders of whips and scourges. Fear that slaves would flee or turn on their tormentors was such that the cruellest possible sanctions were used against any insubordination or perceived laziness or even worse, threats of revolt or revenge.

Often stories of torture and mutilation were exaggerated, but this does not seem to have been the case. Loss of ears, whippings followed by application of salt or boiled sugar, castration, and hamstringing are well documented. For more serious offences death by all sorts of horrible means went unpunished – even burning alive and burying victims up to the neck and then pouring hot sweet syrup over their heads for insects to devour. Both sexes were tormented and there was even an instance of digging a hole to allow pregnant women to be tied face down to be spreadeagled and whipped. Paternalistic owners were often simply not present because of absentee ownership, and managers and overseers often had little sympathy for their charges.

There was a very high concentration of labour with a 600-acre plantation often having over 400 slaves and this was made worse by the increase in importance in the increase in importation in the twenty years before 1789. The huge profits from sugar encouraged a careless attitude towards labour as a resource. If people were worked to death and profits were made, then more labour could be imported to replace them. This was better economically than looking after workers and adopting a shorter working day which might mean less sugar produced. There was no economic, as opposed to moral, incentive to take care of slaves. Even without exploitation, there was a high death rate. Ironically, the climate proved more deadly for whites than for Africans – though in absolute terms thousands more Africans died, their death rate was 40 per 1,000 while for whites it was 250 per 1,000. This was not a place to spend more time in than absolutely necessary for a profit to be made and taken back to France. The pervasive presence of death often encouraged brutal behaviour and rampant sexual activity as a distraction, even among those who were supposedly more cultured and 'well born' and mixed-race offspring abounded.

However, it would be too simple to see society on the island as simply mass slaves and rich planters. There was a complex mix of administrators from France; the *Grands Blancs* – the larger planters; the poorer white settlers; the mixed-race 'mulattos', divided legally into different categories depending on how much 'white blood' they had. Not all non-whites were slaves, there were

30,000 freedmen and women, mostly of mixed race but with some blacks. These sometimes became slave owners themselves after being freed, and there were bands of runaways who evaded capture in the mountains and forests and threatened the planters. However, the bulk of the people were the enslaved workers. A minority enjoyed special treatment as household servants or specialised workers, but the majority laboured long hours in cruel conditions and suffered punishment and indignity.

The divisions in this strange society increased in the period before 1789 with efforts by the whites to curtail the rights of the substantial mulatto population, who included wealthy planters and to discriminate on racial grounds by reducing their rights. There was a gap between the royal officials and other members of the white community. Conscientious officials were often prevented from taking action against abuses of the legal code by pressure from planters who were seen as vital in France's trade and profit. The wealth flowing into French ports from slave trading and the products of slave labour was huge and, in practice, the planters had free rein. But with the coming of the Revolution in France, and with the greater interest in Enlightenment ideas, more liberal members of the island elite were calling for reform.

Despite persistent repression and attempts to restrict all persons of colour, there were various forms of resistance. A constant fear among the white population was poisoning and deliberate harm by slaves. Incidents of poisoning and sabotage persisted despite punishments and brutal interrogations. Then there was flight –which even had a name – 'Maronnage' and this type of advertisement was common in the island's press.

Then there was the activity of the uncontrolled groups of runaways. Sometimes sporadic violence was undertaken, but there was a much more organised and sustained campaign organised by a strong leader, the legendary Makandal. The increase in imported slaves in the 1780s brought more African religious practice into the island and an extension of African religious practices known as *vodou*, encouraging a desire for freedom and a separate identity – also shown by the growth of a distinct French-speaking element who did not look at Africa as 'home' – sometimes called Creolisation. Into this mixture came the Revolutionary developments in France.

The Impact of the French Revolution

Pre-Revolutionary France was proud of its boast that no slavery existed on French soil. There were legal cases where slaves who had been brought into France had successfully claimed freedom in French courts. However, this was reversed in the 1780s as a threat to property. There was some concern about the reports of abuse of slaves in its colonies. Enlightenment writers like the Encyclopaedist Diderot condemned the institution and in 1788 The Society of Friends of Black People was formed with the aim of ending the slave trade and gradually abolishing slavery itself – though not immediately and not without compensation. This society included some eminent figures – the reforming Marquis de Condorcet; the hero of the American Revolution, the Marquis de Lafayette and the Comte de Mirabeau, a leading figure in the Estates General. The famous female campaigner Olympe de Gouges wrote a play about the plight of blacks. However, the enlightened middle classes who led the Revolution had rather lukewarm attitudes to change. Only forty-nine of the hundreds of *cahiers* mention slavery. Some 150 members of the Estates General-owned colonial property. Concern about financial matters meant that disruption of the trade and the income from France's richest colonial possession was not welcome. The revolutionary assembly was slow to accede to demands for non-white free persons to be given rights and did not abolish slavery until 1794. When news of the slave revolt of 1791 was announced, the immediate reaction was to send forces to gain control of France's colonial 'jewel in the crown'. Olympe de Gouges's play closed after three nights because it caused riots. In the end, France was the only colonial power actually to reimpose slavery in its colonies in 1803.

So, if the ideals of liberty in France itself did not extend to slaves in its rich colonies, did the Revolution have an impact on the actual colonies? The substantial planters and merchants – the so-called *Grands Blancs* saw the call for liberty in terms of ending restrictions that all imports and exports had to be carried in French ships. They craved even more slaves to be carried in by ships of other nations and they sought freedom to trade independently of royal control. They also desired to be free of restrictions by the crown and its representatives on the treatment of slaves. The Revolution for them, once the news of events in Paris had reached them six months later, meant a colonial assembly and control of the island's affairs by white elites. This was not very different from the American Revolution in the hostility to taxation and trade controls by the royal government of George III and a desire to expand to dispossess and massacre the native Americans in the cause of liberty while affirming the institution of slavery in the Constitution of 1787. There was more awareness of some of the more radical ideas of the Revolution by the poorer whites, but they were intent on preventing any rights being gained by the free non-whites. Well-educated and prosperous free non-whites ('mulattos' and blacks) had visited Paris to plead for equality. This did not extend to emancipating the slaves on whose labour they depended. But racial hatreds were strong in the colony. an attempted uprising led by the free non-white Vincent Ogé and an ex- soldier Julien Raimonde in October 1790 to demand enforcement of the equal rights granted by the French Assembly led to horrific repression. Ogé and Raimonde were broken on the wheel in Cap Français – that is, tied to a wheel while their limbs were broken by an iron bar. They were then beheaded. Strict property qualifications were set for participating in the island's local Assembly leaving the non-white free population embittered. Any whites of liberal sympathies who recommended rights for free blacks or any change in slavery were liable to persecution and attack.

Thus, while Republican ideas spread on the island and there was support for local independence from 'despotism', the bulk of the inhabitants were not to be included in any change. Given that Revolutionary ideas were held by their owners and tormentors, it was natural for blacks to be more inclined to royalism. There were rumours that Louis XVI was in favour of emancipation and that the king's government wanted better conditions. Though it has been claimed that some slaves had knowledge of French pamphlets on the Rights of Man, it seems that the main influence of the Revolution on the revolt that took place in August 1791 was that it divided and distracted the whites of the island and that the repression of the Ogé revolt had undermined the common interest of white and free non-white property owners in maintaining slavery.

The trend among historians now is to see the events of August 1791 as an African rebellion not to see the slaves as 'Black Jacobins'. The massive importations of slaves from West Africa which continued through the Revolutionary period after 1789 meant that there was a lot less assimilation than in other colonies where the rate of imported labour was much less. Many of the slaves had military experience in West Africa and there was a high incidence of desertion, especially in the northern province. Opposition predated the Revolution as in the case of Makandal. Evidence is inconclusive about whether he organised guerrilla-type raids on plantations or just pursued lower-level conspiracies involving poisoning, but he seems to have maintained a network of opposition before being caught and burnt to death in 1758. Poisoning was common enough to be a major source of anxiety for the white planters and showed the existence of herbal and medical knowledge from Africa.

The social hierarchies of the African homelands were maintained and there was a slave elite. The leaders of the 1791 revolt were not escaped slaves, but rather people of authority on plantations such as coachmen who enjoyed more freedom of movement than field hands. They had held meetings with conspirators from all parts of Saint-Domingue prior to what is always seen as a key meeting on 14 August 1791. This was held at an isolated wooded place called Bois Caiman and the leaders were slaves called Boukman, Biassou and Jean François.

It is here that some problems arise. The evidence for this meeting and what happened comes from a History of the Revolution of Saint-Domingue by a colonist called Antoine Dalmas who left the island to live in the US and whose account was not finally published until 1874. He tells his readers that the specifics of the plan of revolt were decided at this meeting 'where the negros gathered in great numbers'. An oath was taken and 'a black pig surrounded by objects they believe have magical powers was offered as a sacrifice to the all-powerful spirit of the black race'.

Though sometimes described as a Vodou (older books use the term Voodoo) rite, this is doubtful, as pig sacrifice was not part of African religious ceremonies. However, it was, if the account is accepted, an African ceremony more than anything derived from the French Revolution. On 22 August 1791 planned raids on plantations took place.

The accepted view is that there was a great deal of violence unleashed, but again this is dependent on white sources such as contemporary newspaper accounts and histories written some years after the event. 'The news from Saint-Domingue is horrifying,' reported the Paris-based *Le Courrier Extraordinaire* on October 30, and told its readers that 200 plantations had been set on fire and 300 whites massacred. Historical narratives tended to characterize the revolution in much the same way. The two-volume '*Saint-Domingue, a History of its Revolutions*' anonymously published around 1804, spoke of 'General revolt of the negroes. Massacre of the whites'. Images of violence continued to be common in reports and histories such as this one from an 1805 book '*An Historical Account of the Black Empire of Hayti*', by Marcus Rainsford – an army officer who had been stationed in Saint-Domingue during the British occupation of the island. The account by a Jamaican planter called Brian Edwards horrified readers with accounts of a carpenter sawn in half and a Madame de Sejourne raped on the corpse of her husband, her baby ripped from her womb and her husband's head sewn inside her. However, like the accounts of tortures inflicted on slaves, these horrific stories come from restricted sources and there is an absence of written material from slaves and rebels. What is notable though in the attacks is the lack of reference to Republican sentiment. One of the leaders told his followers to act in the name of the king. The leaders were sometimes referred to as 'kings'.

The scale of the rising – perhaps 200 plantations burnt and rebel forces of 100,000 being formed within weeks was remarkable as was the speed of events. However, not all parts of the island revolted in the same way, and not all slaves joined. There is evidence of loyalty. There was also some inconsistency in actions and aims. Edwards' account states that the Baillon family were spared death and destruction because of previous good treatment of their workers. A local official called Gros wrote an account of being captured by a body of rebels led by a leader called Jannot. The whites saw a savage beating of some captives and were told that two of them would be killed every day to prolong the pleasure of Jannot. But the group were saved by the arrival of another black leader Jean François who rescued them from being burnt to death. Also, although the rebels fought against French rule, not all of them supported emancipation.

In the West, the rebellion took a different turn with some poor whites joining with slaves and free non-whites. This resulted in free communities which took the form of African peasant egalitarianism, rather than anything on the French Revolutionary agenda. When the French Republic finally sent forces to restore order, the rebels allied with Spanish authorities in Santo Domingo rather than accept French Republican rule.

The particular nature of the development of Saint-Domingue in comparison with other French West Indian islands, Martinique and Guadeloupe or the Spanish possessions had led to the view that this was essentially an African revolt, organised with a large amount of collective action by elite African leaders. Among these could well have been Toussaint Breda, later Louverture, but he was not at the forefront and was not as has been claimed, comparable to Fidel Castro as the leader of a Caribbean Revolution.

Toussaint Louverture

As the revolt grew, Toussaint Breda emerged as a major leader and, eventually, the dominant influence, eventually becoming the virtual dictator before falling foul of another self-made military leader who took political control of a revolution – Napoleon Bonaparte. Though famous and now the subject of much historical attention, he remains a somewhat elusive figure, and there is no certainty even about what he looked like. Despite various depictions of him appearing, there is no contemporary likeness available, and he remains a difficult subject for biographers, as the historian Sudhir Hazareesingh has shown. He did not know the exact date of his birth, and legends that he was the son of a West African king have no foundation in African records. His early life runs contrary to the general picture of life in Saint-Domingue, possibly because a lot derives from evidence from a Creole lawyer Moreau de St Méry who was born in Martinique but moved to Paris.

Toussaint did not experience the cruelties suffered by some, but was given a trusted position on the planation owned by a Paris-based aristocrat but run by a humane and intelligent agent. Possibly because of his status as the son of a high official, well known for his medicinal skills, Toussaint, who was named Breda after the plantation on which he worked, became an elite slave, a coachman and agent. He was freed and went on to own slaves of his own who worked on his property. He elected to remain at the Breda plantation as his family remained slaves. This complex web of relationships makes it difficult to offer a simple picture of the colony as simply a brutal slave colony. Breda was of course not the only non-white to own slaves as there were many non-white slaveowners dependent on imports of more and more forced labour. Toussaint Breda remained in touch with his African roots through African medical knowledge and some *Vodou* traditions but was attracted to Catholicism. The French Catholic priests on the island were often hostile to slavery and worked with slaves. He may, too, have been influenced by Enlightenment ideas at least about the rights of man as his constant aim, in contrast with some other black leaders, to free the slaves.

It has been suggested that he was influenced by the example of Makandal but without any convincing evidence, and how far he was involved in the planning of the rebellion of August 1791 is not really known. As the rebellion spread, his influence as part of the black elite, grew. But his participation did not grow out of personal hardship or any belief in creating a black republic or instating the changes taking place in France. No evidence places him at the key meeting of Bois Caiman.

The revolt had not led to the rebels gaining total control of the colony but it did result in a great deal of damage. The new National Guard formed by the colonial assembly could not control the rising. Negotiations failed, and destruction and bloodshed continued into 1792. Initially the revolt had been confined to the north, but it spread west and south. The Assembly in Paris conceded equal rights to free blacks and mulattos in April 1792, but slavery remained. In September 1792 three commissioners and 6000 troops arrived on the island. The campaign offered the first real challenge to the slave forces. It also offered Toussaint the chance to develop his military leadership. Military failure by the French was compounded by disease. Around 3,000 of the troops sent from France died within two months.

The fighting developed into an international struggle. Spain hoped to regain the whole island which had been lost to France in the previous century, while Britain saw an opportunity to weaken Revolutionary France and improve its chances of winning the war against it. Britain was fearful that slave revolt would spread to its own West Indies colonies, especially Jamaica, and was eager to grab the rich French colony. The British landed in support of the white planters who opposed the French Republic's policy of granting rights to free blacks. The slave rebels forged an alliance with the slave-holding Spanish government in Santo Domingo against Republican France. The French Republican commissioners Sonthonax and Polveral offered freedom to all those blacks who fought for the Republic, but the slave leaders distrusted any offers even initially the belated ending of slavery by the Jacobin-led Republic in 1794.

These complex events took the Haitian revolution away from a simple revolt against reactionary French planters influenced by ideas of liberty from France. The slave leaders which now included Toussaint preferred to work with the Spanish royal government which maintained a slave system over two-thirds of the island and who ruled over the slave colony of Cuba. Toussaint did not even have the support of all of his fellow leaders for abolition. The Republican French leaders faced war with British troops and reactionary French landowners who opposed Revolutionary policy and Spanish forces aided by black slave rebel armies. This was not like the colonial wars of liberation in the twentieth century or the struggles of Castro and his revolutionaries against a reactionary dictatorship backed by the US. One of the major leaders of the black forces had been a slaveowner and others rejected emancipation to preserve their alliance with the Spanish. Even when French leaders accepted emancipation, the slave leaders did not immediately join forces with the French Republican army, whose watchwords were liberty, fraternity and equality, but stayed with an alliance with Spanish leaders who had tyrannised and enslaved native peoples of the New World and vigorously supported slavery.

The Progress of the Revolt

The revolt led to some key changes. The fighting allowed black leaders to control most of northwest Saint-Domingue. In desperation, the commissioner of Revolutionary France announced an end to slavery in August 1793, but this was not confirmed by the government in France until the spring of 1794.

In this bizarre mixture of violence, a notable feature was the lack of unity within different groups. The European colonists were divided; the colonial powers France, Britain and Spain were at war; the black revolutionaries were also divided. Toussaint's brother was killed when he was ambushed by a rival leader.

Toussaint emerged as a key figure – a popular and energetic commander and organiser, he changed his name to 'Toussaint Louverture' in August 1793 – for reasons which remain obscure. He took a key decision in May 1794 influenced by personal contacts with the French representative Laveaux and switched sides to lead 4,000 men in driving out the Spanish from the west of SaintDomingue. Oddly, some of his fellow leaders still favoured alliance with reactionary Spain and Toussaint s army had to defeat his rival Jean François in July 1794 by force.

The wealth of the island led to a British invasion in September 1794 which the Toussaint-Laveaux alliance could not prevent, but in 1795 there was a major victory when Spain ceded Hispaniola to France, and Toussaint was made a brigadier general, a high- ranking solider of the Republic.

By the summer of 1796, Toussaint was the dominant force, promoted to be a full general and controlled the north of the island. But developments still defied stereotyping. He proved more conservative than the French Revolutionary commissioner Sonthonax in wanting to restore the property of white planters and trying to get black workers back on the plantations by paid labour rather than land redistribution. Unlike Sonthonax his priority was to maintain the island's economy not to spread the ideas of the French Revolution. His energies were also directed at expelling the British whom he defeated in 1797.

By this time, the revolutionary impetus in France was dying down. Toussaint was becoming the dominant force as Commander-in-Chief and was losing interest in working with the French. He forced Sonthonax out in August 1797 and he himself negotiated a British withdrawal in 1798.

The rise of a black leader was a genuinely revolutionary development, even if his policies were not always revolutionary. By October 1798, he was negotiating a return to trade with the United States. The former slave was taking a major diplomatic role with powers that were major uses of slave labour and still conducting a slave trade. There were shades of George Orwell's *Animal Farm* in this and in the policy of ordering slaves to return to the plantations for obligatory waged labour. The priority had been freedom, but not social and economic equality. In order to survive, the new Saint-Domingue had to maintain its economy. The links with revolutionary France were less important than new links with racialist and imperial powers.

This divided black islanders and a pro-French mixed-race general, Rigaud, led opposition to the commander-in-chief until his forces were defeated in the summer of 1798 and he fled to France in 1800. Faced with opposition, the rule of Toussaint came to be more repressive. There were arrests for criticism of his rule and his own nephew was executed on his orders for leading a revolt against him.

The *de facto* rule of the well-born African military dictator came to resemble that of Napoleon in France. There was social and political control, prestige projects such as the building of a new city named after him. The basis of his authority was military success. There was territorial expansion when Toussaint invaded and occupied Spanish Santo Domingo. There was a new constitution in May 1801, which rather like Bonaparte's, established overall power in the hands of a military leader.

The colonial world was at something of a turning point. In France, a successful military leader Napoleon Bonaparte had taken power beginning with a coup in 1799 and leading to the establishing of a lifelong position of power as Consul for Life in 1802 and Emperor 1804. Like Toussaint, he came from an elite family from overseas (Corsica) and, like Toussaint, had risen through military and diplomatic ability. Like Toussaint, he had an interest in nation-building and, while admiring principles of liberty and equality, put order and authority first.

Bonaparte could have recognised Toussaint's authority, maintained control of a wealthy colony, and laid the basis of a military alliance which would have led to French dominance of the Caribbean and huge influence in the Americas. Toussaint could have had the chance to develop his benevolent dictatorship and offer an example of colonial development without slavery. Racism was not endemic in France itself and in a fascinating study '*The Black Count*', the historian Tom Reiss charts the career of the black republican general Thomas-Alexandre Dumas, father of the famous novelist who led the Black Legion, volunteers from France's free black population given equal rights by the Assembly in April 1792.

His story is revealing about attitudes to race. The son of an aristocratic planter in Saint-Domingue and an African slave he was educated in France, accepted at military academy and made his way through the ranks of the army to be a leading commander in Bonaparte's Italian campaign in 1795. A dashing cavalry commander, he accompanied Bonaparte in his invasion of Egypt in 1798 but the two men clashed over strategy. Dumas left Egypt and was captured and imprisoned in Naples.

So the idea of working with a black commander and of black soldiers fighting for France was not new or outrageous. But this was not to be. Bonaparte put authority before vision. Early on he declared that colonies were to be ruled by special laws. When it was clear that the US and Britain would not prevent France from re-establishing direct control in 1801, even though it was in their political and economic interests to ally with Toussaint, the die was cast for more colonial repression. A belief in a 'natural order' and authority was too strong. Once again, the concept of 'property' – even human property – came before 'liberty' and 'equality'.

In 1802 a French expeditionary force of 21,000 men arrived and French forces in total came to amount to over 40,000. In a brief period where France was not engaged in warfare with the other European powers, Napoleon saw an opportunity for swift victory, possibly thinking of his highly successful campaign against non-Europeans in Egypt in 1798. The expedition was led by his brother-in-law, the veteran general Leclerc, with secret instructions to overthrow Toussaint's regime by any means.

The heaviest fighting in the whole revolt took place and Toussaint showed considerable military skill. It would not be accurate to see this as 'a slave revolt' but more a war to maintain a sort of multi-racial home rule as Toussaint's forces and supporters did contain whites and people of mixed race. Strikingly, women fought against the French. Toussaint Loverture was able to employ cavalry and also had the support of black troops who deserted from the French forces. Once again, the idea of a sort of slave revolt would not be entirely accurate.

The result of a prolonged conflict was that Leclerc's forces backed by naval power controlled coastal regions while Toussaint held the interior. Both sides sought a truce. Toussaint probably rightly thought that disease which had taken a considerable toll on French forces would ultimately force a French withdrawal. His island was facing economic ruin because of the fighting and his own side was divided, with some desertion and some disagreement about whether to pursue total independence. But strangely he seems not to have been able to make the break with France. His strong relationship first with his former owner and then with the fatherly French commander Laveaux and his fears of an independent Saint-Domingue being prey to foreign powers led him into negotiations with the French and a truce was arranged. The French on their part were conscious of losses and the difficulty of defeating Toussaint's forces and the opportunities that a ceasefire might offer.

This proved to be the case. Toussaint's second-in-command Dessalines worked against him and offered false evidence that Toussaint was not observing the terms of the ceasefire. Leclerc, knowing that Bonaparte had secretly ordered an overthrow of the Toussaint regime, ordered his forces to provoke incidents. In order to overcome problems and maintain the truce, Toussaint met a French delegation without taking his usual precautions of a heavily-armed escort. He was captured and hurriedly put on a ship together with his family to France. To break him, he was imprisoned in a cold fortress in the Jura mountains, and his pleas for clemency were ignored by Bonaparte.

The command of the interior passed to one of the more controversial leaders Jean Jacques Dessalines. Toussaint had held to a belief that white participation was vital to maintain Saint-Domingue and had restricted brutality during his campaigns. He was also willing to negotiate with colonial powers and had never advocated independence. Dessalines, born in 1758, had endured a harsher existence as a slave than Toussaint. Like him, he showed remarkable military ability but with a ruthlessness that earned him the nickname 'The Tiger'. He thought the future lay in complete independence and was more violent in his treatment of whites than Toussaint.

Dessalines's more uncompromising attitude was matched by the French commander who succeeded Leclerc. Rochambeau took the view that a final solution to the issue of control was to embark on a virtual genocide.

Leclerc had written to Bonaparte that he needed 'to destroy all the negroes of the mountains, men and women, and keep only the children below twelve years old, to destroy half the blacks living on the plains and not to leave on the colony a single man of colour who has worn an epaulette' (ie been an officer in a rebel army)[3] and his successor put these ideas into practice by a relentless campaign of shooting, burning, drowning and killing with dogs.

The brutalities of this war of independence make sickening reading. A 100-year-old relative of Toussaint was drowned and there were massacres by French troops which met with reprisals. Dessalines provided as hard to defeat as Toussaint, and yellow fever took its toll leading to a French withdrawal in 1803, as Bonaparte prepared for a large-scale war in Europe.

It was thought that Dessalines aimed to solve the long-term issue of control by a genocide of whites. However, his main concern was the portion of the French forces which had stayed behind and offered an ongoing threat. Though there were massacres, the historian Julia Gaffield[4] has shown that they were restricted to armed opponents and their supporters and those who had taken part in the massacres of blacks. Not all whites were killed or driven out, and examination of census returns shows a continuing white presence.

Dessalines had taken on the power given to the overall commander in the Constitution of 1801 and after the French withdrawal faced internal opposition. Formal independence was not declared until December 1894. While many history books talk of the 'Republic of Haiti' of 1804, this refers only to a breakaway regime established in the south. Dessalines in the North declared himself king and subsequently emperor during a civil war which was ended when he was overthrown by his former military allies, and his body dragged through the streets before being dismembered.

The Legacy and Importance of the Revolt

The war was massively costly in terms of black lives as well as for the French forces, and also in respect of the destruction of economic potential. The French reintroduced slavery in neighbouring Guadeloupe but could not secure the reimposition of French colonial rule in Saint-Domingue. It was not just the climate and yellow fever that thwarted Napoleon but the skills of black leaders.

The tragedy was that the major architect of independence did not live to see it. He did not leave a legacy of Republicanism and may well be seen as more of an African ruler than a standard bearer for the French Revolution. His successors were not democrats, but rather kings and, like him, they did not revel in Republican purity, but rather negotiated with white colonial powers and were recognised by them. But this was at a price. Post-revolutionary France with its restored monarchy drove a hard bargain to finally recognised Haitian independence in 1825 and imposed a considerable financial indemnity to compensate for the loss of land. Though reduced in 1830 it was a burden for the new regime in Haiti well into the twentieth century. Incredibly, repayments ended only in 1947. By 1900 80 per cent of the revenues of Haiti were going to loan repayments to foreigners.

Comparison with later freedom fighters and revolutionaries are misplaced, as the new Haiti (named after the original inhabitants' name for the island, not after any African connection) did not lead to campaigns for freedom or revolutionary or egalitarian internal policies in Haiti. Haiti did not manage to maintain its independence completely, as it was occupied by the US from 1915 to 1934 after the president ordered the killing of 167 political prisoners and was killed by a mob who dragged him from hiding in the French embassy. The legacy of the early dictators was carried on by the infamous Duvalier family who imposed a brutal and corrupt rule between 1957 and 1986 after a period of economic decline and instability.

The only successful slave revolt did not lead to the colonial powers or the US drawing the conclusion that slavery should be abolished. Slavery ended in France's empire only in 1848. It continued in the US until the Civil War (1861–5). It was ended in the British Empire in 1833. In Brazil, it went on until 1888. Peru re-established slavery after independence from Spain. It lasted in Puerto Rico until 1874 and in Cuba until 1886. While it is true that the US and Great Britain ended the slave trade in 1807 and 1809, this was partly because of analyses of the Saint-Domingue revolt being led by recent arrivals rather than admiration for the abilities of former slaves to run their own affairs. The example of the revolt tended to harden white attitudes in Spanish and Portuguese America, while the alarm created by white exiles who fled to the US and Cuba reinforced racial fears. Toussaint's labour policies were redolent of reactionary post-emancipation policies, and equality did not follow even when there was an end to slavery.

However, the fact remains that the revolt did show the ability of oppressed people in colonies to act in a concerted way and to achieve success against colonial forces and should be seen as a major world development which emerged from the French Revolution, even if rather indirectly. The leaders have been compared to later figures – Toussaint to Castro, Dessalines even to Malcolm X, but this is doubtful for a number of reasons. It is unhistorical to see the complex and dramatic events in Saint-Domingue through a European prism.

The French Revolution obviously facilitated the revolt, but its roots may lie much more in the African experience. When doubtful about ending the conflict with Leclerc, Toussaint consulted a vodou soothsayer. The bulk of black troops for all their European insignia and uniform were relatively recent arrivals into the Caribbean. Political models for all the European vocabulary were often taken from Africa. Dessalines's proclamation in 1804 has been compared to the US Declaration of Independence of 1776.

> Vow before me to live free and independent and to prefer death to anything that will try to place you back in chains. Swear, finally, to pursue forever the traitors and enemies of your independence.

The philosophical content of the US Declaration of Independence with its reference to fundamental rights did not actually guide policy; and Dessalines's decision to make himself a hereditary ruler, first king, then Emperor was not part of the French Revolutionary experience.

The importance given to the revolt in the history of anti-colonialism seems somewhat strained. The fears it generated led to stronger control of slaves in North and South America. The world was not universally amazed at black rulers, given that European control of West Africa lay well into the future and independent African states were not a novelty. The ending of the slave trade was a recognition by Britain and the US of the African nature of the events in Saint-Domingue as it was seen as dangerous to introduce more Africans into the farms and plantations and better to focus on controlling existing slaves.

The Real Story of the French Revolution

Toussaint's most recent biographer[2] considers the development of the representation of this leader in pictures and statues. He has come to personify the Haitian Revolution even though he never supported independence The problem is that the participants in the so-called 'Haitian Revolution' did not behave in the way that the post-colonial world, conscious of the Civil Rights movement and of concerns about racism and equality, might have hoped they would. Toussaint, compared to Castro or even Martin Luther King, had been a slave owner. Dessalines, compared with Malcolm X even though the latter was never an armed fighter, never ordered massacres and made himself king. The radical French revolutionaries of 1789 who spoke so movingly about the rights of man were often investors in slave plantations and rejected even the mild requests from mixed-race educated Saint-Domingue liberals for political representations. Radical Jacobins were more concerned with maintaining French control than 'the sovereign people' if they were not white. Bonaparte who spoke of combining liberty with order reimposed slavery and his representatives engaged in destructive genocidal repression. Progressive historians have sometimes seen developments in Saint-Domingue as an extension of European history rather than looking at events from the perspective of the participants. But in a sense, there is little point in trying to separate reality and legend. The reality is that the myths of the Haitian Revolution and its most famous leader are one of the most important and influential legacies of the Revolutionary period.

Notes
1. Alan Taylor, *American Revolutions* (Norton, NY, 2017).
2. Sudhir Hazareesingh, *Black Spartacus* (Alan Lane, 2020).
3. Sudhir Hazareesingh, *Black Spartacus*, quoted p. 325
4. Julia Gaffield, *The Haitian Declaration of Independence* (University of Virginia, 2016).

Chapter Eight

The End of the Revolution? The Legacy

Much of the Revolutionary imagery went back to the ancient world and the obvious parallel was with the ancient Roman Republic. However, this ended in dictatorship and Empire and the successful soldier Julius Caesar established the rule of one man. Historical parallels closer to the time suggested that revolutions lead to dictatorships. The English Civil War resulted in the rule of the successful soldier Oliver Cromwell who very nearly ended as a monarch, though he turned down the offer of a crown. The disturbances in France of the mid-seventeenth century called the *'Frondes'* ended not with more representative government but with the absolutist rule of Louis XIV. This possibility was recognised at the time; however, there is the historical phenomenon, and indeed the common human failing, of the belief that 'this time it will be different' which prevents any serious ability to learn from the past. A resort to war in 1792 would lead to militarisation and to offer an opportunity for a successful military leader to use prestige and the loyalty of his troops to establish a dictatorship. High levels of violence and disorder could not be a permanent state. The disruption to economic and social life might be tolerated in a time of emergency, but a state, at the mercy of a radicalised underclass and offering constant insecurity, was bound to result in a desire for order – and discipline and order are most obviously delivered by a successful general.

The challenge of war swung the balance more towards mobilising popular support and even accepting horrors such as the September massacres. However, even radicalised middle-class leaders had their limits. After the end of Robespierre's influence in July 1794 – the so-called coup of Thermidor – the sans-culottes lost influence. The new regime dealt harshly with popular risings in 1795 and after 1799 there was a decisive shift to 'stability' and more conservative authoritarian rule when Napoleon Bonaparte took power.

The successful general first of all became First Consul of the Republic, then in 1802 Consul for Life and then in 1804 Emperor with a view to passing on his title to his heirs. When he abdicated in 1814 after his military luck had run out, France turned back to the Bourbon monarchy albeit with a veneer of constitutional rule. The Revolutionary Republic was relatively short-lived.

Napoleon portrayed himself as 'the heir of the Revolution', confusing the issue. Had the Revolution been brought to an end, or did it develop in a new form? This has become a well-developed historical debate and much depends on how 'the Revolution' is defined. Almost every subsequent revolutionary movement has claimed affinity with the French model. Reactionary and conservative movements have generally claimed to be finally shutting down the pernicious effects of the Revolution. The Revolution became a sort of grab bag for both revolutionaries and their opponents to pick out whatever element seems useful. Thus, Trotsky, the Russian Revolutionary leader, found the Terror the most useful element. When confronted by a multitude of enemies after the seizure of power in 1917 by a group which represented a small proportion of Russians, his savage repression was justified as 'Revolutionary Terror' in the spirit of Robespierre.

* * *

However, when Mikhail Gorbachev in the 1980s wanted to undo the dictatorship that Trotsky had done so much to establish and introduce more openness, he too went back to the French Revolution arguing that 'Glasnost' had its origins in the days of 1789– not the Terror which opened up free debate and political discourse.

Thus, the French Revolution can serve all sorts of purposes, making it difficult to assess its wider impact. In France, it clearly changed society with an end to the status of the privileged class and a wider spread of rural landownership. The property-owning peasantry was not created but certainly expanded by the sale of church and noble lands. The middle classes got access to careers in church and state. The sans-culottes and the French urban workers and poor, as usual, got little but a brief period of influence and the opportunity to die for the Revolution on the battlefield. More broadly, it has been claimed to have brought about a new sense of nationalism in Europe, to have encouraged democracy, spread liberalism, advanced the cult of the individual, had a profound effect on the arts and sciences, and brought about a new awareness of human rights. In the short term, the revolution gave rise to one of the most important figures in European history – Napoleon.

Napoleon

When the Bastille fell, the stones were removed, and a great empty space remained. There was no certainty what should replace it. How should such a

The End of the Revolution? The Legacy

momentous and historic site be memorialised? In the end, a gigantic elephant on a plinth was erected. It decayed and gradually sank into the mud between 1814 and 1846. In a sense, the rule of Napoleon was typified by this elephant. After the tumultuous and fiercely idealistic revolution came a grandiose and meaningless emblem which represented little of its aspirations and dreams and crumbled into decay. The beneficiary of the terrible years of frustrated hopes and poisoned idealism was an Italian adventurer whose personal ambition and self-regard were on an elephantine scale. His rise was made possible by the Revolution, and he used its vocabulary and pretended to honour its values, but his period of rule was dominated by a desire for domination which had little aim beyond the adventure itself. The myths surrounding him were carefully created and sustained. He produced his own version of reality in military bulletins, created an image of a saviour, surrounded himself with symbols and eventually wrote his own legend in exile. The Revolution ended in fiction and delusion. But also in bloodshed on a scale that eclipsed the years of Terror, and repression that was organised on a scale beyond the resources of the old regime and the Revolution. For all their faults, the Revolutionary leaders were men of vision and careless of their own needs. Robespierre lived simply and never sought the trappings of power. For all their brutality, the revolutionaries fought to preserve what they perceived as virtuous. However, the end result was the rise of a leader unmotivated by any clear ideal, mostly uninterested in the welfare of his people, with no clear vision of what a France or a French Empire might be in peace and even in military terms no real originality of thought. The horrendous death toll of years of futile warfare ought to make Napoleon a figure of disgust, but a look at street names and souvenir shops shows that that is not the case. Robespierre has disappeared from view. His bust is hidden away in his birthplace in Arras. He and his fellows are part of a dark past not to be memorialised in statues, stamps, plaster busts, postcards, mugs, or dedicated museums. Napoleon, on the other hand, remained a figure who could comfortably sit in homes and be remembered on street signs. Images were widespread in his lifetime and continued to be part of the commercial souvenir market. There is a Sherlock Holmes story from the 1890s involving multiple plaster busts of Napoleon. Museum shops and battlefield visitor centres do a good trade in memorabilia. There is a tourist route from the South of France to Paris in which visitors can retrace the progress of the return of the great man from exile on Elba to Paris in the so-called Hundred Days in 1815. Paris stations bear the names of some of his most bloodthirsty battles. The Arc de Triomphe commemorates his victories which cost so many lives and resulted in so little positive good for anyone.

Napoleon's rise began as a result of some enlightened policies of *ancien régime* France. His father was a lawyer and minor aristocrat in Corsica, the Mediterranean island bought by France from Genoa in 1769. Much as Britain ruled its Indian empire by alliance with the elites, so France gained collaboration by concessions to lands it conquered and Napoleone Buonaparte, born in 1769, was given an education in Paris and attended the prestigious St Cyr military academy. Slight of build, sallow and uncommunicative and with a derided Italian accent the young Napoleone had a restricted social life among the well-born French cadets, and devoted himself to reading classics, history and mathematics. The lonely self-taught regional outsider was commissioned as a lieutenant in the unfashionable artillery. Napoleon Bonaparte, as he had become known, went off to garrison duties in provincial Auxerre and might well have disappeared from history had it not been for the upheavals of 1789. Typical of a self-educated ambitious middle-class technician, Bonaparte welcomed the revolution and got leave to go back home to Corsica, where he attempted to spread it. Local politics was a dangerous business and old family feuds fuelled more than just political disagreements. Napoleon and his family had to escape Godfather-type killings and fled to France. There Napoleon moved in Jacobin circles and was close to Robespierre's brother Augustin. The outbreak of war in 1792 offered opportunities and Napoleon found himself in the right place at the right time. The British capture of the big naval base at Toulon on the Mediterranean in 1793 had been a major trigger of terror and paranoia in the capital. As an artillery officer, Napoleon played a major part in the city's recapture by an enterprising siting of cannon on the high ground. This brought him to the attention of the revolutionary rulers, but this nearly ended in disaster with Robespierre's fall and Napoleon was under arrest for a period in 1794.

His rise to national eminence is a remarkable story and a product of war and revolution. The revolution had created huge opportunities as the old military command structure was thrown into disarray and there was a demand for talented younger officers, committed to the Republic. It also created a new ruling elite and Napoleon was able to make contacts with the post-Robespierre rulers, the so-called Directors, especially Paul Barras whose former mistress Napoleon married. The fading and very sexually experienced Josephine de Beauharnais was the widow of an aristocratic colonial planter. With poor teeth and limited resources, Josephine found a protector in Barras, but both needed her to find a husband. The rather gauche young provincial

The End of the Revolution? The Legacy

artillery officer was a man on his way up and he was captivated by Josephine's social and sexual skills. Barras and his fellow Directors had faced popular unrest in Paris from both the sans-culottes and the royalists and needed military backing. The royalists were more formidable in 1795 than the sans-culottes whose two ill-planned risings had been suppressed. Bonaparte helped to see off the better-armed royalist crowds with his artillery. This rising took its name from the month Véndemiare in the Revolutionary calendar. Undeterred by slaughter in the Paris streets, which he rather inaccurately called 'the whiff of grapeshot', Napoleon became a very useful military support for the Directory.

As the end of Robespierre had not ended the wars with the other European powers, there was plenty of opportunity for military leadership on a wide front from the Netherlands to Northern Italy. From a rather narrow base. the French army of Italy faced the armies of the Italian kingdom of Piedmont and more significantly the forces of the Austrian Empire well established in Lombardy.

It was his command of the army of Italy that enabled Bonaparte to establish the reputation that eventually took him to power. The myth goes something like this. The young officer took over a demoralised and neglected army and persuaded sceptical older officers to follow him. He issued a rousing call to arms and pursued revolutionary tactics of rapid movement and dividing his enemies. In a whirlwind campaign, he, first of all, knocked the ill-led forces of Piedmont out of the war and then amazed the Austrians with the rapidity and brilliance of his manoeuvres. Unlike his aristocratic opponents, he fought alongside his men. Not a remote and out-of-touch leader, he became '*le petit caporal*' sharing the dangers in the manner of a non-commissioned officer, not a general. He stormed a bridge at Lodi and loaded guns himself. Napoleon went on to take Venice, ending the ancient Republic and fulfilling a long-held French dream of dominating Northern Italy. From Milan Napoleon became a state maker, bringing in the progressive ideas of the Revolution. Victories led the Austrians to negotiate with Napoleon in the famous Peace of Campo Formio in 1797 making France the ruler of Northern Italy. Military genius, innovator, revolutionary general, statesman, diplomat, and the heir of the Revolution, Napoleon came home in triumph. But adventure called. In 1798 he took an expedition to Egypt with a view to conquering the middle east and cutting off the trade routes of the hated English, whose subsidies and powerful navy kept opposition to the Republic going among European states. This was Revolutionary and Enlightened warfare – scholars went with the troops to discover more about ancient Egypt. The daring and scale of this campaign caught the imagination of France, fed by bulletins from the great commander. Large-scale battles, one of which was fought at the site of the great pyramids, confirmed the genius of the general who used new techniques of warfare to destroy the Egyptian armies. Not even disaster could damage Bonaparte's reputation. His ships were sunk at anchor by another genius – the British admiral Horatio Nelson, stranding the French army. Plague struck, but even this became a means of showing Bonaparte's compassion and bravery as he embraced plague victims. Prisoners were slaughtered, but this violence, which exceeded anything done at the September Massacres to unarmed and helpless victims, was not held against him. The fact that he abandoned his men to a lingering defeat and often horrific reprisals as British-armed and -supplied local forces took their revenge was as nothing. His arrival in France was greeted with almost hysterical acclaim.

By 1799, France, it seems, needed a strong man to restore order. The Directory, it seems, was faced with opposition from both left and right and was seen as corrupt and divided. A faction led by the veteran revolutionary Sieyès needed support for a coup which would strengthen the central government. Who better than General Bonaparte to support this move so necessary to win the war and maintain the Republic? Just as with his 'whiff of grapeshot', Bonaparte offered military support. He entered the assembly – the Council of 500 as it was known, and supported by his troops brought it to an end. He then became First Consul together with two others – using the terminology of the Roman Republic as a sign of national renewal. He stated that he was saving the Revolution and offering France the vital element of order needed. Of hugely greater ability than his fellow consuls, he dominated the new regime and took the Revolution in a new and more purposeful direction, ending the war with military victory and introducing major new domestic reforms. These brought greater unity, completing the work of the revolution in many aspects. He took the title Consul for Life in 1802 but in order for his achievements to be maintained he decided to become Emperor in 1804 – but a Revolutionary Emperor who kept the key elements of the Revolution but brought about a new stability at home and respect abroad.

The rest of the story is one of overreach. He fought one of the greatest campaigns in military history in 1805–7 defeating three major military powers, Prussia, Austria and Russia. He dreamt of dividing the world between Russia and France when he met the Russian Tsar at Tilsit in 1807. With only Britain against him, unassailable because of the naval power which defended the British Isles against him, he was master of a great European empire. However, there were signs of weakening military strength as other nations caught

The End of the Revolution? The Legacy

up with his tactics. Battles against Austria in 1809 were less decisive. His attempt to defeat Britain through an ambitious economic blockade cutting Europe off from British goods provided ineffective and unpopular. Relations with Russia cooled, and Napoleon became embroiled in a war in Spain which drained resources in vicious guerrilla fighting and allowed Britain to engage with French forces and for a determined British general, the Duke of Wellington, to show that France could be weakened. The fatal decision was to invade Russia in 1812 with a huge army made up of conscripts and volunteers from all over his European empire. But no army was a match for the Russian winter. After a costly and indecisive battle at Borodino, the giant but poorly supplied French force took Moscow only to find that Tsar Alexander I would not admit defeat. Fires destroyed the city and Napoleon led a slow and painful retreat. The mind-boggling casualty list reached over 450,000 – dwarfing the casualties of the Terror and any campaign of the Revolutionary wars. Given the relatively small population of Europe in 1812, this was a colossal amount of death, all of it utterly pointless and wasteful. It makes statues and memorabilia of Napoleon highly questionable morally. But still the war continued with new cannon fodder being brought up for campaigns in Germany in 1813. However brilliant the leadership was, sheer weight of numbers forced a retreat to France where Napoleon's luck ran out and his generals and administrators had had enough. He abdicated in 1814 and was exiled to the small island of Elba where he ruled as Emperor. A dangerous piece of whimsy on behalf of the victor powers as before the great peace conference in Vienna was over, Napoleon was back. He gained support on a progress from the South of France to Paris, declares a new and more liberal constitution and took an army into Belgium. His genius and his luck deserted him and in a grim encounter with Wellington's hastily assembled army, he managed to destroy the cream of his forces in unimaginative frontal assaults until the arrival of Prussian forces drove him from the battlefield of Waterloo. This time there was no joking. No whimsical installation of a mini-empire on a Mediterranean island. He endured cruel captivity on the barren Atlantic Island of St Helena, rewriting the truth of his career until his death in 1821.

It is difficult to know where to start to penetrate this breathless narrative, much of it generated by Bonaparte himself in the bulletins he offered and by his own account of his life. The post-Robespierre period has not seemed to be very successful and Napoleon's military skills, analysed by generations of military historians, have seemed to be self-evident. Warning bells start to ring, however, with the story of Bonaparte's appeal to the army of Italy. This often appears as a typical product of the Revolution – the young idealistic general taking his revolutionary army into his confidence in a way that the old aristocratic officers would never have done.

> Soldiers, you are naked and ill-fed! Government owes you much and can give you nothing. The patience and courage you have shown in the midst of these rocks are admirable; but they gain you no renown; no glory results to you from your endurance. It is my design to lead you into the most fertile plains of the world. Rich provinces and great cities will be in your power; there you will find honour, glory, and wealth. Soldiers of Italy! will you be wanting in courage or perseverance?[1]

In fact, though often attributed to the great man in 1796 it was never delivered and concocted after 1815 as part of fictitious and self-justifying reminiscence by the defeated Emperor. As the army was not naked or a decrepit and weak force of sans-culottes but a battle-hardened force of 41,000 men, the soldiers might have been rather surprised. Though in theory outnumbered by 25,000 troops of the King of Piedmont and 38,000 men of the Austrian empire, the enemy forces were separate and not under a unified command. The dazzling campaign owed a lot to elements outside the young general's control. The Piedmontese had been contemplating a separate peace and while the rapid approach of Bonaparte's men contributed to this decision, there was only an indecisive battle at Ceva, not a spectacular equivalent to the destruction of non-European forces lacking modern arms and equipment as in Egypt. Austria was distracted by having to fight France in other areas, and the war was not the sweeping success for Bonaparte that his own accounts made out. The famous incidents in which he led an assault on the bridge at Lodi took place when Austrian forces were already withdrawing. In another heroic and legendary assault at Arcola, the general fell into the river. What characterised the campaign was an agility on his part when he met unexpected attacks and a determination to succeed at all costs. But by 1797 he still faced heavy resistance from substantial Austrian forces and his policy of 'living off the land' to be able to move swiftly without heavy baggage trains had led to bitter hatred and resistance among the peasants of Northern Italy. His armies depended on long and insecure lines of communication with the homeland and food and supplies were uncertain. He was lucky that Austria was prepared to bring the war to an end. But the peace of Campo Formio was proclaimed as a triumph and the campaign had become a popular success, fuelled by well-crafted and heroic bulletins.

The Egyptian campaign of 1798 offered the chance for easy victories. Bonaparte was well aware of innovations proposed by eighteenth-century

The End of the Revolution? The Legacy

military theorists – well-placed light artillery and effective deployment of troops in squares. Against the much less sophisticated tactics of the enemy forces in Egypt, French firepower was devastating at the so-called Battle of the Pyramids on 21 July 1798. Thrilled by the accounts of victory, the French public seemed less concerned with some basic mistakes. The great man had not secured his fleet properly when anchored in the Nile at Aboukir Bay, and it was sunk by a rapid attack by British ships under Horatio Nelson, leaving the French stranded. Also as in many colonial wars, disease was a major and unforeseen problem with plague decimating the French forces. There was limited medical provision or arrangements for dealing with prisoners so sick Frenchmen died in hastily prepared hospitals exhausted by burning heat, and healthy Egyptian prisoners were slaughtered on the seashore because there was no alternative plan to deal with them. The objectives of the expedition remained obscure. As in Italy, Bonaparte revelled in state building, but a model middle eastern Empire crumbled as Britain supplied his enemies by sea and interrupted supplies. An advance into the area now part of Israel collapsed when French forces could not take the key city of Acre. But by that time Bonaparte was back in France, using the remaining ship to abandon his men and return as a hero.

In developing the myth of the national saviour, Bonaparte was clear that he had saved France from a corrupt, divided inefficient regime that had succeeded the Robespierre terror. In November 1799 after a coup which brought him to power, he addressed the people of France.

> I left you peace. I find war! I left you conquests, I find our enemies at our borders! I left you the millions of Italy. I find misery and extortionate laws! Where are the brave hundred thousand soldiers, my companions in glory?

This sort of nonsensical proclamation is typical of the self-styled 'man of destiny'. He had not left peace. He had brought the war with Austria to an end temporarily, but the general European war continued. The enemies were not suddenly at France's borders and to suggest that the rulers of the Republic had brought 'misery and extortionate laws' was an exaggeration. The Directors had dealt with internal unrest quite effectively. The 'conquests' in Egypt were not secure and he had suffered a considerable defeat at the hands of the British navy. The Directors who ran France had been successful in reforming the taxation system and controlling inflation. Bonaparte had never commanded forces of a hundred thousand, brave or otherwise.

The Real Story of the French Revolution

The problem was that as with 1793–4, the dangers from war had increased with a renewed coalition of European powers financed by Britain. The Directors feared that war would bring about old divisions and had increased reliance on censorship and repression. By November 1799 some of the rulers had decided that there needed to be a stronger government and 'a sword' was needed to bring about a new constitution.

The actual circumstances of this coup were closer to face than to the decisive actions of a revolutionary man of action. The assembly – the so-called Council of Five Hundred – moved away from the centre of Paris to the suburb of St Cloud. Fearing a coup, some of the deputies determined to resist being disbanded. Bonaparte strode in and was shouted down. Flustered, he shouted abuse and was hurried out. Helped by his brother Lucien and a small force of troops who entered the assembly and forced protesting deputies to flee, Bonaparte recovered his dignity and got on his horse – then fell off. There was little popular support for the Assembly or the Directors, so a new government was quickly established with Bonaparte as the first of three 'consuls' of the Republic.

The Revolution's fascination with the Republic of Ancient Rome was reflected in this somewhat archaic arrangement. Given Bonaparte's huge and inflated reputation and his support among sections of the army and the need for military success, it was not likely that his fellow consuls would be a bar to increasing dictatorial power. It was not very clear quite what the new consul stood for and he was lucky in that he achieved military victory in Italy at the Battle of Marengo in Northern Italy on 14 June 1800. All generals need luck, but this was an especially fortunate encounter. Bonaparte had been defeated and the Austrians were recovering when another French force which the Council had sent away suddenly appeared and Bonaparte saw his opportunity for a renewed assault. The commander of this force had shown remarkable initiative and saved the day. He was killed in the battle. To get to Italy, Bonaparte had crossed the Alps on a mule with his men. But a later heroic painting showed him on a mighty stallion. That sums up the gap between image and reality.

The Revolution succumbed to an opportunist who left an indelible impact on France and Europe denied to the far more idealistic and inspired leaders thrown up by the tumultuous events of 1789 to 1799. In a relatively brief period of peace the Consul – who became First Consul and then Consul for Life – threw his energies into a remarkable series of internal changes which had some revolutionary elements but were a long way from the ideals of the Revolution. Catholicism was restored as the religion of France but closely controlled by the Napoleonic state. The agreement with the Papacy of 1801 was a masterstroke in ending the conflicts over religion and restoring the traditional relationship between church and state with the church leaders becoming virtual agents of the Consul. The property lost by the church and taken by new owners in sales by the Republic was not restored and there was religious toleration. Bonaparte was indifferent to religious feeling, as to all other ideals, revolutionary or otherwise. Education reform resulted in closely controlled state schools and the centralised curriculum remained a feature of French life. The lycées were less a fulfilment of Jacobin dreams of a widespread popular education to instil ideals of Revolutionary virtue than a basis for recruitment of elites versed in technical knowledge to become administrators and military leaders. There was little provision for girls' education and limited national provision. Little sense of idealism ran through the changes. The Bank of France was designed to secure sound national finance to finance war on the model of the successful British Bank of England. The establishment of a national code of laws which had long been worked on by various legal bodies during the Revolution was quickly brought to a conclusion with the famous *Code Napoléon* of 1804. Largely technical in nature, it established the right of property owners to pass on their property to other members of the family than just the eldest son; property rights to lands bought from former nobles and the church were protected. The authority of male heads of household over wives and children was strengthened and married women lost the right to own property. Unfaithful wives and disobedient children could face imprisonment. Property was all important and in an unusual instance of this retrograde development, slavery in French colonies was reimposed. Though uniform laws had been a hope in 1789 it is difficult to see these developments as a natural development of revolutionary idealism. The downgrading of the rights of women after all the hopes of female pioneers of liberty seems cruel. The reimposition of slavery seems to reverse the ideals of the Rights of Man. The control of workers was increased by the extension of the '*livret*', a compulsory work report book, recording good behaviour which was necessary for future employment.

More powerful central government had been a feature of the Revolution as part of a national effort to defend the Revolution. It was institutionalised by Bonaparte in the form of eighty-three prefects with considerable powers over the departments appointed by the Consul. The central government also appointed mayors of larger cities and nominated regional and municipal councils. The possible control by elected assemblies was reduced by having an appointed Senate as an upper house and having a complex system of elected assemblies. The Tribunate could propose and discuss laws but did not vote on them. The Legislature could vote but could not discuss. Though this system has its defenders, it is difficult to see it as having any meaningful democratic content. Voting was complex – 6 million eligible male voters chose a list of 60,000 who then chose 6000 who made up the Notables who voted for assemblies with little actual power. The Notables were made up only of those who paid most taxes – landowners, merchants, and professionals. From their ranks, the Council of State appointed by Bonaparte chose the sixty senators – wealthy men over forty years old. The Notables chose the 100 members of the Tribunate and the 300 members of the Legislative Body.

The 'active citizens' of the Revolution were far more numerous than the 'notables'. The days of the political clubs, of the frantic debates of the Sections, the talk of rights of men and women, the belief in the wisdom and goodness of the people seemed a distant memory by the time Bonaparte made himself Emperor in 1804. The authority of the regime rested to an extent on consultation as there were elaborate exercises in consultation with the plebiscites. These referenda, as they would be now known, asked the people if they agreed with the increase in power of the great man and the results were a foregone conclusion. The increase in police powers, censorship, spies and informers and the resort to repression and illegal acts has led some historians to see Napoleonic France as a 'police state'. However, this term has more application to later dictatorships with greater means of policing and control than was available to Bonaparte. Newspapers were controlled, opposition suppressed, police powers increased and former implementors of terror like Fouché employed as policing ministers. However, difficulties in communication, remote regional communities, relatively small numbers of gendarmes and record keepers put a merciful limit on control. After 1804 the emperor Napoleon could be away from France on campaign for long periods without facing rebellion. Even in the face of terrible losses and defeats later in his reign, there was limited opposition in France. Even following his abdication in 1814, after horrendous losses in an invasion of Russia and powerful international opposition resulting in the invasion of France, he was still able to come back in 1815 and gain enough support for a renewed major military campaign.

The key to understanding why this was may well lie in Napoleon's coronation in 1804. It was Revolutionary in that the Imperial crown was not inherited but gained by strenuous personal effort. If the Revolution had ended privilege and opened the way for the individual, then why could enterprise and individual merit not be worthy of the highest prize? The Revolution had provided all sorts of public ceremonies and here was one that was even grander than the various planting of liberty trees or celebrations of the Supreme Being. It was pure theatre. Bonaparte took the crown from the Pope, no less, and put it on his own head. He swore in his Coronation Oath 'to govern only in the interest, the wellbeing and the glory of the French people'. Elites and property owners were secure. The eccentricities and wild enthusiasm of 1792–4 were over. No more rampaging sans-culottes or foul-mouthed rants from *enragés*. But no more aristocratic and clerical privileges. No more threats of invasion, but rather glory and prestige. There were worthwhile public works – roads and canals. There was financial stability. Concerns about inflation and deficits had disappeared. Provincial France was largely left alone without Godless revolutionary fanatics appearing with armies of Parisian riff-raff. A lot of the ambitions of the *Cahiers* of 1789 had been met – uniform administration, common law codes, financial stability, an end to abuses such as *lettres de cachet*. An end to monarchy had never been on the agenda and in place of a shambling and indecisive Louis XVI there emerged a talented, confident and military-minded ruler who consciously made a link, with his famous bee symbol which appeared on his official robes, to the ancient Merovingian warrior kings of France.

If the Revolution is seen in terms of the self-satisfied elites of 1789, then it indeed was fulfilled by Napoleon and so he could ride off in ever more costly and pointless European military campaigns confident of his support at home. If the Revolution is seen in terms of the wider aspirations of the sans-culottes in their committees and clubs; of the pioneers of women's rights; of the seekers after Revolutionary virtue and a new beginning for mankind or the desperate desire of the rebels of Saint-Domingue for freedom. then Napoleon was a destroyer, not a saviour. His later claim that his conquests in Europe had given birth to a new sense of nationalism have little foundation except for a common hatred of French rule.

The Wider Legacy

The revolutionary tradition did not die in France, but the passions of the 1790s were rarely revived for long. The restored Bourbon monarchy was ended by a revolution in 1830 but only to replace one branch of the royal family with another – the Orléanist Louis Philippe. He was overthrown by another revolution in 1848 and a brief republic was ended in 1851 when Napoleon's nephew Louis went from being president to Emperor as Napoleon III in 1851. This second empire did not end with revolution but with military defeat in 1870 and was replaced by a conservative Third Republic.

The Real Story of the French Revolution

A brief resurgence of violent popular revolution came in 1870 with the Paris Commune formed by radicals to fight the Prussians. It ended by being crushed by the forces of conservatism and the regular French army with a mass of executions. There was to be no repeat of 1793. The Third Republic had little time for radical revolution. Like the Second Empire, it was ended by military defeat in 1940. Post-war France had two Republics, but neither sought to return to the example of the first revolutionary republic.

It could be said that the Revolution had established ideas of liberty and democracy which permeated not only French politics, but also the politics of the world. Ideas expressed during the Revolution were an inspiration for many. Radicals in Britain were moved to correspond with French radical activists. There were liberal sympathisers in many countries who took the Revolution as an example – sometimes suffering extreme repression. Some see a direct line between ideas for change expressed during the revolution and later campaigns for change: for example, about women's rights, about the Rights of Man, about opposition to slavery, about the rights of all the people to have a political voice. The excesses of the Revolution and the counter-revolution however may have had a much greater influence. The execution of Louis XVI and the executions of the Terror put back the cause of change and reform more than the lofty ideas of the radicals promoted it. Frustratingly for liberal reformers, popular sentiment was not always with the revolution. The Church and King mobs in Britain were fiercely xenophobic and persecuted radicals with the connivance of the British establishment. Struggling farm workers who had tried to form a union were equated with bloody revolution and transported to Australia in the 1830s. Magistrates in Manchester, faced with quite staid and responsible demonstrations by working people for political representation in 1819, were seen as the equivalent of rabid sans-culottes and violently suppressed in the infamous Peterloo Massacre. Liberal nobles who had sympathised with some of the ideals of the Revolution were subjected to cruel indignities by the royalist rabble of Naples – the *lazzaroni* – while Admiral Lord Nelson, accompanied by his beloved Emma, Lady Hamilton looked approvingly on, hanging one such 'revolutionary' from the yardarm of his flagship. After 1815, Germany was subject to harsh censorship and suppression of any movements for liberalism or nationalism by the Austrian premier Count Metternich. Nicholas I of Russia (1825–56) was ardent in his persecution of any demand for change. In the later eighteenth century, there had been a willingness for reform among the 'enlightened despots' in Prussia, Spain, Russia and Austria. The association of reform with extreme revolutionary violence ushered in a period of opposition to change and repression which was arguably the most important political consequences. Against this horror of revolution, progressive forces made little headway. The widespread revolutions of 1848 succumbed to fears among middle-class revolutionaries that the lower orders might again be running amok with heads on poles, and the divisions and hesitancies opened the way for rulers to deploy military force to restore order. The Europe of 1889, now ruling over great empires of subjected peoples, was probably further away from liberty and equality than the Europe of 1789. The largest European country Russia was an autocracy with no national parliament and harsh repression of any radical activity. Even when countries had parliaments, the franchise was restricted. In Britain, only one person in 7 voted by 1914, and the masses had little representation in government. Women had no political rights in Europe. In France, they did not vote until 1946. Franchise was limited in Italy where a Piedmontese elite dominated the other regions and had waged a bloody civil war against the south in the 1860s. Desire for empire displayed a racialism that was all-pervasive and resulted in massive inequalities, keeping the rest of the world as subjects of Europe and liable to violence and ill-treatment. The horrific behaviour of Leopold of Belgium to his African subjects was seen as extreme, but the colonial repression by all the 'white' powers, including the USA was much greater than the repression exercised by absolute monarchs in Europe before 1789. No European monarch cut off the hands of supposedly lazy or rebellious workers in the way that the Belgians did in the Congo. The repression of the Boxer Rebellion in China in 1900 by international forces exceeded anything in eighteenth-century France. The class divisions between colonisers and colonised were greater than any inequality between the orders in the old regime. The French Revolution did not usher in a century of progress.

Opposition movements may have been inspired by the Revolution in a general sense but the great figures like Danton, Robespierre, St Just were not obvious role models. For Karl Marx, the great revolutionary socialist theorist, the main object of historical interest was the Paris Commune of 1870 not the sans-culottes of 1793. These small masters were not really the revolutionary workers that Marx and his communist followers saw as the harbingers of revolution. The emergence of the British labour movement from the Chartists of the 1830s, who campaigned for working-class political rights to the socialists and the labour activists that established the Labour Party by 1903 did not look to French Revolutionary models. The French radicals did view the Revolutionaries sympathetically, but the shadow of the terror was considerable. Modern scientific socialism did not involve bizarre ceremonies, incomprehensible talk of 'virtue' or frenzied bouts of guillotining and heads on pikes. When it came to campaigns for women's rights there was limited knowledge and interest in figures like Olympe de Gouges. The English writer Mary Wollstonecraft was more influential and US female suffrage leaders made little or no reference to the French feminist pioneers. When there was anti-slavery agitation, it was not to Toussaint Louverture that campaigners turned as a model. The Haitian Revolution's main effect had been to strengthen resistance to change and a means to discredit campaigns to abolish slavery. Events in Haiti made change harder and offered limited inspiration until much later. In the twentieth century, the French Revolution was more notable for its negative impact. The theorists of fascism made it clear that they were reversing the radicalism of the Revolution, though in fact with the emphasis on political terror, with abstract ideas coming before humanitarian concerns and with a willingness to dispose of political rivals in the name of political idealism, it is the Nazis who might be seen as the real heirs of the first French Republic.

'The Nation in Arms'

The long series of wars brought about by the Revolution are often seen to usher in the 'total war' which characterised the great world wars of the twentieth century. Before 1789 warfare was a limited phenomenon in which professional armies were led by aristocratic officers who had more in common with their fellow leaders in opposing armies than their own men. There was little ideological conflict as armies fought formal battles to gain sufficient advantage for favourable peace treaties to be made which involved generally minor exchanges of territory or colonies. Except if they happened to be in a war zone, civilians' lives were little affected. After the Revolution, it is claimed, warfare came to be between whole peoples with mass conscription, control of all resources and repression of any sign of dissent. Governments took unprecedented control over civilian life to fight wars which would result not merely in some civilised diplomatic discussion but in massive change. Total war in the sense of a lack of distinction between military and civilian participation was certainly a feature of both World Wars and is a characteristic of modern warfare. And it certainly seems that mobilisation of the whole nation was an aim of the Revolution. A much-reproduced statement of the Convention in August 1793 seems to show a massive change.

> Every Frenchman is permanently requisitioned for the needs of the armies. The young men will go to the front.; the married men will forge

arms and carry food; the women will make tents and clothing and work in hospitals; the children will turn old linen into bandages; the old men will be carried into squares and rouse the courage of the combatants and to teach hatred of kings.[3]

A levy on men between eighteen and twenty-five drawn mainly from the countryside, not primarily from the Sections of Paris did produce a remarkably large army of between 750,000 and 1 million by 1794. However, the officers were predominantly recruited from France's pre-war armed forces. Nearly 90 per cent of generals had been in the army before 1789. Also, conscription in itself was nothing new. Most European armies called up royal subjects. The percentage of Frenchmen serving in the War of the Spanish Succession in the early years of the eighteenth century was about the same – 2.5 per cent – as the proportion fighting for the Republic in 1793–4. In total, the Revolutionary armies were bigger but in actual campaigns until the later years of Napoleon, the size of forces was about the same as in most eighteenth-century battles. An important battle at Fleurus in 1794 which decisively halted invasion by foreign armies was won with 70,000 troops not hundreds of thousands of frenzied sans-culottes in arms. What was new was the greater commitment of the Revolutionary armies and the trust that commanders could put in them to operate in smaller units, allowing greater flexibility in tactics and the use of massed columns to attack. However, key elements to success included the use of artillery integrated into the battle lines which was part of the military theory of the old regime and had little to do with the Revolution except for allowing more imaginative commanders like Bonaparte to emerge regardless of strict rules of seniority or aristocratic preferment.

In the emergency period 1792–3, where internal opposition and foreign threats really did present an existential threat, there was a change in the sheer size and nature of French forces and something like total warfare in as much as the Republic could actually enforce it. However, this could not be sustained. By 1797 army size had fallen to below 400,000. The desertion rate had risen to 8 per cent and the numbers being recruited were below some years of the *ancien régime*. Political control over generals which had resulted in sixty-seven being executed for supposed treason or incompetence in 1794 alone was ended in 1796. French forces returned to being professionally led by trained military personnel not controlled by political fanatics. It is true that Napoleon went on to raise very large forces – 630,000 men were taken into Russia in 1812, but two-thirds were recruited from outside France. There was a return to the international make up of armies of the *ancien régime* and the only ideological element, if indeed it was, was loyalty to the emperor. The fervid enthusiasm for liberty and equality did not drive Napoleon's veterans but rather traditional loyalty to comrades, regiments and leaders. Also, idealism, total commitment by civilian populations and total lack of restraint in support of a cause were just as much features of warfare by the opponents of the Revolution. Total warfare was pursued by the guerrillas of Spain in their intense opposition to French occupation between 1808 and 1813 and by the internal forces of counter-revolution, especially the so-called Chouan rebels of the protracted civil war in the west of France which lasted from 1794 to 1800.

Obviously, elements of the total wars of later European history were present in the Revolution but not throughout the whole Revolutionary period. The millions of men supported by total mobilisation of highly industrialised and technologically advanced nation-states were on a totally different scale. Total war was prolonged and made possible by developments which were not present in the 1790s. Mass urban populations could be enlisted and persuaded by modern propaganda techniques which relied on mass communications and literacy. Modern transport could carry huge numbers of men to the battlefields and supply them. Modern factories could produce horrifically efficient means of mass slaughter. Entire civilian populations could be mobilised by modern methods of administration and resources could be controlled by rationing and requisitioning of resources. The gap between all the 1790s was greater than the gap between the attempts at 'total war' of the Revolution and the warfare of the ancient regime.

The Nation and Nationalism

The regional diversity of France before 1789 meant that the main unifying factor was not language or a common sense of what it meant to be 'French' but simply being subject to the French crown. The Revolution exposed the gap between the government in Paris and the sense of provincial identity. For all the talk of 'the nation' and 'the people', when the Revolution threatened local loyalties to the church, imposed taxes and demanded men for its armies then the loss of the common bond of monarchy led to provincial revolts and the danger of 'France' disintegrating. The fall of the more extreme Revolutionaries and the establishment of a more conservative Republic and then a military dictatorship maintained an uneasy unity. But how much was changed as a result of the Revolution is open to question. A wave of legislation, new departments with uniform local government and eventually uniform laws,

The End of the Revolution? The Legacy

changes to education, conscription and a massive national effort to defend France by creating 'a nation in arms' suggests that the divisions of the old regime were swept away. However, there was a considerable gap between passing legislation and actually enforcing it. There was a great deal of continuity between pre- and post-revolutionary France simply because the Revolution did not promote fundamental economic change, so the majority of France remained rural.

Key characteristics of a fragmented inward-looking rural country, whose inhabitants had fallen under French control at different periods, remained well into the nineteenth century. Its pre-industrial characteristics of isolated and individual rural communities dominated by local customs and ideas of justice continued. Awareness of national issues and knowledge of the national language were not as widespread as might have been expected, given the seemingly momentous changes since 1789. A valuable piece of evidence is a survey of 1863 which revealed that many or most of the communes (local districts) in fifty-three out of eighty-nine departments were said to be non-French speaking. It has been estimated that by 1880 only 20 per cent of the population used standard French comfortably. That would mean that officials and public servants like doctors and priests communicated with the people in many parishes only with difficulty. A linguistic map shows that in all the departments of the Midi (South) French was either spoken by under half of the population or that there were substantial areas where it was not used. In the North, there were twelve departments where patois or regional dialect was widely used. In Brittany and in East and Northeast France there were areas where 'normal' French was hardly spoken.

This was by no means unusual before forces of unification which were not directly linked to the Revolution made their impact. Broadly, these were railways and improved means of transport, conscription on a large scale, newspapers combined with greater literacy, free and compulsory education. Italy, despite the greater unification brought by Napoleon, remained deeply divided well into the nineteenth century and in some areas beyond. Germany even after a greater degree of unity under French control and then unification in 1871 had regional differences in religion, language, culture and political experience.

In France, the existence of large areas of barren land and the remoteness of many communities together with strong and somewhat secretive local cultures and traditions meant that many areas were not permanently affected by the Revolution. Civil war had a huge impact, but traditional ways of life remained, as did local prejudices and superstitions that were little affected by theories of the Enlightenment. A third of the population continued to live in isolated farms or hamlets of fewer than thirty-five people. Smaller communities were often virtually self-governing as they had been for centuries before 1789. In 1835 there was a *cause celèbre* when a woman was burnt as a witch in a place called Beaumont en Cambrésis. This was not in some remote Pyrenean village but in an industrial department in Northern France. It probably was the tip of a very large iceberg of rural 'justice' and superstition. Local saints and religious beliefs dominated and the strange pagan decorations at the church at Rennes le Château in Languedoc which has captivated some modern authors weaving fantasies about Templars, Holy Grail and dark secrets were probably not untypical of the survival of older pre-Christian traditions.

After 1870 the Third Republic pushed hard to enthuse France in regaining the lost provinces of Alsace and Lorraine annexed to the new German Empire after the war of 1870–1. These areas were a symbol of national humiliation which had to be revenged, of suffering French citizens who needed to be rescued or the mission of a united nation. Yet in 1914 half of all recruits to a massive army built up in the cause of a national renewal had little knowledge that Alsace and Lorraine had been lost. The Revolution had not brought about by 1815 a modern unified nation-state for all the rhetoric and the modernising aspirations of the middle-class elites. Napoleon's claim that his rule had given birth to European nationalism had little substance except possibly to unite disparate elements in European states under his control against him.

Cultural Life

In late eighteenth-century Europe, there was a move away from the dominance of personal and institutional patronage in the arts. The notion that creative artists should be free to develop their inspiration and not be bound by commissions was gaining ground. It seems depressing to us that Haydn should have been tied to producing works for Count Esterházy in a Hungarian backwater and should have had to plea for leave to go home by writing his 'Farewell' symphony in which the members of the orchestra gradually leave the stage. That the aristocratic Prince Bishop Colloredo of Salzburg should have had his servants kick out Mozart as an insubordinate servant has blackened that prelate's reputation. The aristocratic commissions of painters like David painted before 1789 seem so much more restrictive than the grand canvases he produced in the heat of revolutionary enthusiasm which led him to sit in the Convention and vote for the death of the king. Thus, it might be expected that the end of aristocracy and monarchy might have had a galvanising effect on the arts and allowed for new freedoms. However, there is limited evidence of this. The great works of the Revolutionary period continued to be produced for specific commissions. The ability of composers to rely on income from royalties or from performances was too limited to allow for a distinct and independent profession to emerge. Composers were not necessarily revolutionary. Mozart might have made fun of a noble in 'The Marriage of Figaro' but was not noticeably moved by anything that was happening in France and continued to aim to please the Imperial court in Vienna with his opera of 1791 'The Clemency of Titus' in a way reminiscent of the operatic grovelling of composers who honoured Louis XIV and Louis XV in order to enjoy royal patronage.

Beethoven continued a string of 'rescue operas' where noble and virtuous high-born liberals are rescued from the villainous clutches of tyrants in the one opera with a revolutionary theme that has passed into general repertoire. Set in Spain, but often now staged at the time of the Revolution, it involved the heroine Leonora pretending to be a prison guard to rescue her husband Florestan from the hands of the villain Pizzaro who wants to kill him before the prison is inspected by an authority figure. As the Revolution was responsible for thousands of imprisonments and deaths, it is difficult to see this as extolling events in France. However, it did reflect a belief in freedom, and in 1804 Beethoven famously ripped out a dedication of his Third symphony to Napoleon when he heard that he had become Emperor and changed it to just 'a hero' – hence 'Eroica'. However, as the hero had already effectively become a sort of repressive military dictator as Consul for Life, it does not say a lot for Beethoven's sympathies with the ideals of freedom, and the great composer relied heavily on aristocratic patronage, hobnobbing with princes and dedicating his work to them. Haydn may have got fed up with Count Esterházy and did take advantage of concerts open to the public rather than just being performed, as was the Beethoven's Eroica symphony, in a private lordly grand hall. However, there was little sign of revolutionary influence. His most experimental works, much darker and more passionate than those of his maturity were written before 1789 in the midst of what has been called the 'Sturm und Drang' period of European culture in the 1770s.

There is relatively little 'storm and stress' in the work of composers of the actual revolution. These compositions have largely disappeared from view and were generally the work of professional musicians who were glad to get commissions from the Revolutionary authorities as private patronage from the church or the nobility dried up. It is possible that the occasional works of Méhul, Spontini, Grétry and Gossec have their admirers and some of their simplistic efforts have been recorded. Rather like Soviet symphonists who pleased Stalin with banal and over-orchestrated folk-based melodies in the general style of Tchaikovsky to show their willingness to write music accessible to the workers, these minor masters simplified their already not very complex compositions to show their admiration for 'the sovereign people'. Those curious as to what 'Revolutionary' music might sound like should listen to Francois-Joseph Gossec's *'Le Triomphe de la République'*[3] which was performed at the Paris Opera in January 1793. No recording of *'L'Offrande à la Liberté'* exists. This cantata apparently includes a representation of the famous tocsin which summoned the sans-culottes to protests, demonstrations and slaughter as well as cannon, anticipating Tchaikovsky's populist 1812 Overture. Very few occasional pierces had artistic merit. Even Beethoven's 'Wellington's Victory' could not rise above banality. Gossec offered the small change of eighteenth-century choral and operatic writing with hymn-like choruses and some revolutionary songs. Those who can listen for more than ten minutes are remarkably tolerant or have a taste for historical curiosities. In terms of innovation, it is difficult to see any lasting impact technically. Later composers did not depend on patronage and the rise of popular concerts, more accessible opera going, and better-organised royalties allowed composers to become distinct from working musicians. However, this built on pre-Revolutionary trends which were accelerated by the decline of noble and ecclesiastical patronage. This did not entirely die, though. Wagner depended heavily on the support of the King of Bavaria at one stage of his career and Tchaikovsky was financially supported by the rich and aristocratic Madame von Meck, but it was a feature of what has been called 'the bourgeois century' that middle-class ticket purchase and support for the arts became dominant and in that sense a revolution which so boosted the status and material wealth of the middle class may well have contributed to change, but indirectly.

The public festivals of the Revolution did create a demand for art, music and design, and Napoleon sponsored public buildings, but, as with music, the long-term effects of this were not very significant. The dominant artist of the Revolution was Jacques-Louis David who was heavily influenced by a revival of interest in the classical world which predated 1789. Huge canvases linked classical events with contemporary developments, and it was his famous depiction of the murdered Marat in his bath which was probably the single most influential Revolutionary picture. The diseased and malignant radical journalist was glorified in a brilliant picture which elevated him to the status of a classical martyr. The more grandiose pictures continued into the rule of Napoleon and established mythical representations of events such as Napoleon's crossing the Alps in 1800. But David returned to portraiture in later years – though of middle-class subjects rather than the more aristocratic sitters of his early career. The taste for large-scale historical depictions cast in heroic mode did continue into the nineteenth century. The long-term impact of the Revolution on the development of art is harder to establish. Public art was already a phenomenon before 1789 and it might have been accelerated, but the actual manifestations of art and design during the Revolution varied in quality and were often a 'dead end' as far as future influence was concerned.

In literature, the dominant element was theatre. The festivals of the Revolution were a form of public theatre, and it has been observed that an element of theatricality ran through the main events and developments. Gestures, images, representations of reality rath reality itself were common. Oratory was often on a high level of abstraction rather than concerned with the reality of government as though the speakers in the various Assemblies were addressing a theatre audience. So, theatres took up revolutionary themes to match. Such works were essentially part of their time and were heavily influenced in language by classical productions before 1789. Oddly, the legislators of the Revolution distrusted actors who suffered restricted voting rights. As with composers and many of the artists of the Revolution, playwrights of the Revolutionary period offered little that has engaged the interest of posterity. Great and intense events perhaps were so inherently theatrical and dramatic that attempts to reflect them on stage were doomed to offer only anti-climax.

* * *

Most of the history of the French Revolution was really centred on events in Paris. With a population of under 550,000, it covered less than 13 square miles. More people lived there than in the next six largest cities. Visitors found no suburbs to offer a smooth transition from city to countryside. Instead, there was a sudden feeling of entering a sparsely populated 'frontier' area on leaving the city. So much of the dramatic history of the Revolution was confined to a relatively small area relatively self-contained and untypical of the rest of France. And much of the history of the period is about myth and misunderstanding. In the Paris 'bubble' it was easy for rhetoric and rumour to become reality. The causes of the Revolution were analysed at the time by talk of 'despotism' but compared with the later exercise of power by the Revolutionary Committees and Napoleon this was a very limited despotism and Louis XVI had few features of a despot. Then there was a 'crisis' of monarchy and an insoluble 'deficit' but again compared to periods of real crisis and financial ruin, this was more a matter of perception than reality.

Delusions continued to dominate the events of 1789 as the king and his ministers seemed to think that to raise expectations of massive change by elections and statements of grievances in an unprecedented public consultation could be met simply by having a traditional assembly along the lines of 1614 and having no real plan. Rumours and fears of a royal backlash triggered the attack on the Bastille and utterly unfounded fears of noble attacks triggered the widespread peasant unrest of 'the Great Fear' of the summer of 1789. Delusion of a more profound kind led the comfortable middle-class reformers of the Estates General to think that stability could be ensured even if there had been sickening crowd violence and a constitutional monarchy had no precedent in the past or equivalent in contemporary Europe. Again, delusion was evident in the belief by a middle-class rationalist elite that the religion of the majority of the French people could be interfered with without consequence and a war would somehow solve problems. Of all the delusions, the move to war had the greatest unforeseen consequences for all concerned. It led to a rapid uptick in violence and the influence of a politicised minority of Parisian sans-culottes and to a republic. The first republic was seen by Adolphe Thiers, the conservative statesman of the next century, as being characterised by 'blood and imbecility'. Eccentric experiments such as renaming the months and ceremonies dedicated to 'the Supreme Being' were accompanied by the Terror both in Paris and more extensively in the rebellious provinces. Even the supporters of severe measures to win the war and save the Republic were surprised to find themselves victims when they dared to suggest that the terror might be reduced. Violent advocates of terror and the rights of the common people met a similar fate. And the most dominant influence in the defence of a virtuous Republic, Robespierre was also guillotined. The hopes of most of the major players in this Parisian drama turned out to be illusory.

The men of 1789 found that a programme for a modernised monarchy led to a Republic over which the lower elements of society who were utterly unrepresented in the Estates General had unexpected and baleful influence. The sans-culottes who formed the democratic clubs and committees of the little self-governing republics of the Paris Sections found themselves sidelined and then suppressed. Their brief period of influence did not lead to a democracy but paved the way instead for a military dictatorship. Though the rule of a successful general – even one whose successes were partly more myth than reality – was predicted by some but not foreseen by those politicians who brought Napoleon to power. The delusion that a successful and ambitious general who was not even French could bring stability was shattered by relentless warfare which brought more casualties than any previous warfare and certainly than any revolutionary terror. More people died in pursuit of establishing an utterly unsustainable and unrealistic European Empire than in the pursuit of the ideals of 'Liberty, Equality and Fraternity' and in furthering the Rights of Man. But it was Napoleon who won the battle of history with the idealists being hidden from sight or ridiculed. Eager to avoid this period of delusion and disastrous unexpected consequences being seen as too negative, it has been comforting for many historians and public figures to extend the myths of the period to supposed significant and beneficial long-term results. Whatever its cost in reality, it has been seen as sending 'lances into the future', paving the way or setting precedents for all sorts of worthy or at least important developments. Human rights, the development of national awareness, movements against colonial oppression, democracy, liberal capitalism, the freedom of artists, modern warfare, and significant political ideologies have all been linked to the Revolution. Studies have gone beyond France to show the international influence of the Revolution. However, *'post hoc'* is not necessarily *'propter hoc'*. Because important things happened after the Revolutionary period, it does not follow that they were caused by that period.

The Revolutionaries often looked at the Classical world for precedents and justifications, though not always looking at the right part. Thus, the vitality and patriotism of the Roman Republic were rather more attractive than the arrival of dictators and then corrupt and over-ambitious emperors. In the same way, the ideals of 1789 proved more attractive than the violence of 1793–4 or the arrival of Bonaparte in 1799 and his self-elevation to Emperor in 1804. The idea of female emancipation was more attractive than the repression of female rights and the fates of some of the leading feminists. 'Liberty, Equality and Fraternity' were more inspiring than the all-important fourth element 'property'. The democracy of the Sections was more appealing than the paranoia and unthinking violence. France seems happy to retain the Marseillaise as its national anthem and have a holiday and celebrations on 14 July because for all its faults, myths, and delusions, the Revolution was a uniquely vivid and passionate period of the history of France and the wider world.

Notes

1. Napoleon Bonaparte, *Correspondence de Napoléon Ier, Vol. 1* (Paris: Henri Plon, 1858).
2. Geoffrey Best (ed), *The Permanent Revolution* (Fontana, 1988), quoted p. 56
3. Chandos Records, CHAN 0727 (2006).

Bibliography

A full bibliography of this topic would be the equivalent of a book, given the huge amount of writing, so this list is restricted to some of the works used and referred to.

John Abbott, *Madame Roland* (Harper, New York, 1904).
David Andress, *French Society in Revolution 1789–1799* (Manchester UP, 1999).
Nigel Aston, *The French Revolution 1789–1804, Authority, Liberty and the Search for Stability* (Palgrave, 2004).
Harold Behr, *The French Revolution* (Sussex Academic Press, 2015).
Geoffrey Best (ed), *The Permanent Revolution, The French Revolution and its Legacy* (Fontana, 1988).
Olivier Blanc, *Last Letters, Prisons and Prisoners of the French Revolution* (Deutsch, 1987).
Francois Claud-Amour Bouille, *Memoires de la Revolution Francais* (1797).
Edmund Burke, *Reflections on the Revolution in France* (1790) (Penguin Edition, 1968).
Jeanne Louise Henriette Campan, *The Private Life of Marie Antoinette* (The History Press, 2008).
William S. Childe-Pemberton, *The Baroness de Bode, 1775–1803* (Longmans, 1900).
Charles Dickens, *A Tale of Two Cities* (London, 1856).
William Doyle, *Origins of the French Revolution* (OUP, 1980).
Mlle des Echerolles, *Memoirs* (John Lane, NY, 1904).
Michel Faucheux, *Olympe de Gouges* (Folio, 2018).
John Fisher, *The Elysian Fields* (Cox and Wyman, 1966).
Anatole France, *The Gods Will Have Blood*, (1912) (Penguin edition, 2017).
François Furet, *Revolutionary France* (Blackwell, 1992).
Julia Gaffield, *The Haitian Declaration of Independence* (University of Virginia, 2016).
Jacques Godechot, *France and the Atlantic Revolution of the Eighteenth Century, 1770–1799* (The Free Press, 1965).
Eric Hazan, *A People's History of the French Revolution* (Verso, 2014).
Sudhir Hazareesingh, *Black Spartacus: The Epic Life of Toussaint Louverture* (Allen Lane, 2020).
Memoires de Hua, *Député de l'Assemblée Legislative*, published by his grandson, 1871.
C.L.R. James, *The Black Jacobins* (1938, Penguin, 2001).
Alison Johnson, *Louis XVI and the French Revolution* (McFarland, 2013).
Colin Jones, *The Fall of Robespierre* (OUP, 2021).
Linda Kelly, *Women of the French Revolution* (Hamilton, 1987).
Emmet Kennedy, *A Cultural History of the French Revolution* (Yale, 1989).
Stanley Loomis, *Paris in the Terror* (Cape, 1965).
Latude and Linguet, *Memoirs of the Bastille* (Routledge, 1927).
G. Lenotre, *Les Massacres de Septembre* (Texto, 2017).

G. Lenotre, *The Tribunal of the Terror* (London, 1909).
Darline Gay Levy, Harriet Applewhite and Mary Durham, *Women in Revolutionary Paris, 1789–1795*.
Gwynn Lewis, *Life in Revolutionary France* (Batsford, 1972).
Hilary Mantel, *A Place of Greater Safety* (Penguin, 1992).
John Markoff, 'Violence, Emancipation and Democracy' in *The French Revolution, rewriting Histories* ed Gary Kates (Routledge, 1998, p. 183).
Laura Mason and Tracey Rizzio, *The French Revolution, A Documentary Collection* (New York, 1999).
Christopher Prendergast, *The Fourteenth of July* (Profile Books, 2008).
Tom Rees, *The Black Count* (Vintage, 2013).
Edward Rigby, *Letters from France, 1789*, reprinted (Hansebooks, 2020).
Graham Robb, *The Discovery of France* (Picador, 2007).
J.M. Roberts, *The French Revolution* (OUP, 1978).
R.B. Rose, *The Making of the Sans-Culottes* (Manchester UP, 1983).
Simon Schama, *Citizens, A Chronicle of the French Revolution*, Viking, 1989
Ruth Scurr, *Fatal Purity, Robespierre and the French Revolution* (Chatto and Windus, 2006).
Peter Taafe, *The Masses Arise – The Great French Revolution 1789–1815* (Socialist Publications, 2009).
Timothy Tackett, *When the King Took Flight* (Harvard, 2003).
Alan Taylor, *American Revolutions* (Norton, NY, 2017).
Peter Vansittart, *Voices of the Revolution* (Collins, 1989).
Netta Webster, *The French Revolution* (Constable, 1926).
Mike Wells, *The French Revolution and Napoleon, 1774–1815*, Hodder Educational, 2018
Gwyn A Williams, *Artisans and Sans-Culottes* (Arnold, 1968).
Marilyn Yalom, *Blood Sisters, The French Revolution in Women's Memory* (Pandora, 1995).
Arthur Young, *Travels in France* (1792).